IPSec

The New Security Standard for the Internet, Intranets, and Virtual Private Networks

Second Edition

Naganand Doraswamy
Dan Harkins

PRENTICE
HALL
PTR

Prentice Hall PTR, Upper Saddle River, NJ 07458
www.phptr.com

Library of Congress Cataloging-in-Publication Date

Doraswamy, Naganand.

    IPSec: the new security standard for the Internet, intranets,
and virtual private networks, Second Edition / Naganand Doraswamy, Dan Harkins.

    p. cm. -- (Prentice-Hall PTR Web infrastructure series)

    Includes bibliographical references and index.

    ISBN 0-13-046189-X

    1. IPSec (Computer network protocol) 2. Internet (Computer
networks) -- Security measures. 3. Intranets (Computer networks) --
Security measures. 4. Extranets (Computer networks) -- Security measures.
I. Harkins, Dan. II. Title. III. Series.

    TK5105.567 .D67 2002

    005.8 -- dc21

                                          02-23833

                                             CIP

Editorial/Production Supervision: *Mary Sudul*
Page Layout: *FASTpages*
Acquisitions Editor: *Mary Franz*
Editorial Assistant: *Noreen Regina*
Manufacturing manager: *Alexis Heydt-Long*
Art Director: *Gail Cocker-Bogusz*
Series Design: *Meg VanArsdale*
Cover Design: *Anthony Gemmellaro*
Cover Design Direction: *Jerry Votta*

© 2003 by Prentice Hall PTR
Prentice-Hall, Inc.
Upper Saddle River, NJ 07458

Prentice Hall books are widely used by corporations and government agencies for training,
marketing, and resale.

The publisher offers discounts on this book when ordered in bulk quantities. For more information,
contact Corporate Sales Department, phone: 800-382-3419; fax: 201-236-7141; email: corpsales@prenhall.com
Or write Corporate Sales Department, Prentice Hall PTR, One Lake Street, Upper Saddle River, NJ 07458.

Product and company names mentioned herein are the trademarks or registered trademarks
of their respective owners.

Printed in the United States of America

10 9 8 7 6 5 4 3 2

ISBN 0-13-046189-X

Pearson Education LTD.
Pearson Education Australia PTY, Limited
Pearson Education Singapore, Pte. Ltd.
Pearson Education North Asia Ltd.
Pearson Education Canada, Ltd.
Pearson Educación de Mexico, S.A. de C.V.
Pearson Education — Japan
Pearson Education Malaysia, Pte. Ltd.

To Amma, Appa, Roopa, Ananth, and Anu.
Naganand

To Marina, the giant on whose shoulders I stand.
Dan

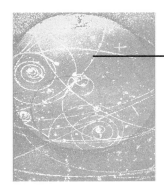

Table of Contents

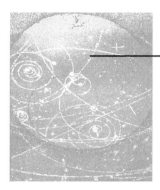

Preface

The Internet connects millions of people around the world and allows for immediate communication and access to a seemingly limitless amount of information. Data, video, and voice, almost every single type of communication, travels across the Internet. Some of this communication is private.

The language of the Internet is IP, the Internet Protocol. Everything can, and does, travel over IP. One thing IP does not provide, though, is security. IP packets can be forged, modified, and inspected en route. IPSec is a suite of protocols that seamlessly integrate security into IP and provide data source authentication, data integrity, confidentiality, and protection against replay attacks.

With IPSec, the power of the Internet can be exploited to its fullest potential.

- Communication is the lifeblood of business. Without a guarantee that a customer's order is authentic, it is difficult to bill for a service. Without a guarantee that confidential information will remain confidential, it is impossible for businesses to grow and partnerships to be formed.

- Unless there is a guarantee that records and information can remain confidential, the health care industry cannot utilize the Internet to expand its services and cut its costs.

- Personal services, such as home banking, securities trading, and insurance can be greatly simplified and expanded if these transactions can be done securely.

The growth of the Internet is truly dependent on security, and the only technique for Internet security that works with all forms of Internet traffic is IPSec. IPSec runs over the current version of IP, IPv4, and also the next generation of IP, IPv6. In addition, IPSec can protect any protocol that runs on top of IP such as TCP, UDP, and ICMP. IPSec is truly the most extensible and complete network security solution.

IPSec enables end-to-end security so that every single piece of information sent to or from a computer can be secured. It can also be deployed inside a network to form Virtual Private Networks (VPNs) where two distinct and disparate networks become one by connecting them with a tunnel secured by IPSec.

This book discusses the architecture, design, implementation, and use of IPSec. Each of the protocols in the suite commonly referred to as "IPSec" (the Authentication Header, Encapsulating Security Payload, and Internet Key Exchange) is examined in detail. Common deployments of IPSec are discussed and future work on problem areas is identified.

This book is intended for an audience with an interest in network security as well as those who will be implementing secure solutions using IPSec, including building VPNs and e-commerce, and providing end-to-end security. Cryptography and networking basics are discussed in early chapters for those who are neither cryptography nor networking professionals.

Organization

This book is split into three parts: overview, detailed analysis, and implementation and deployment issues.

Part One is composed of the first three chapters. Chapter 1 discusses the basic cryptographic building blocks upon which IPSec is built. Symmetric and public-key cryptography and their use for both encryption and authentication are explained. Chapter 2 discusses the basics of TCP/IP and the advantages and disadvantages of implementing security at various layers in the TCP/IP protocol stack. Chapter 3 is an overview of IPSec. The IPSec architecture is discussed and each of the protocols—AH, ESP, and IKE—and their interrelationship is touched upon.

Part Two consists of Chapters 4 through 7. Chapter 4 is a detailed discussion of the IPSec architecture. The basic concepts of IPSec, the different modes, selectors, Security Associations, and security policy, are discussed. Chapters 5 and 6 discuss in detail the two protocols used to protect IP, the Encapsulating Security Payload and the Authentication Header, respectively. Construction and placement of protocol headers are discussed as are input and output processing rules. Chapter 7 is an indepth discussion of the Internet Key Exchange. The different phases of negotiation, the different exchanges, the various authentication methods, and all the negotiable options are explained.

Part Three is made up of Chapters 8 through 12. Chapter 8 is a discussion of policy and its implication on IPSec. An architecture to support IPSec policy and a policy module is presented. Chapter 9 presents the issues surrounding the implementation of IPSec in a TCP/IP stack, in a platform-independent manner. Chapter 10 discusses different IPSec deployments: end-to-end security, VPNs, and the "road warrior" situation. Chapter 11 discusses how IPSec is deployed to protect a network. Chapter 12 discusses future work items for the IPSec community. These include integrating network layer compression with IPSec, extending IPSec to multicast traffic, issues associated with key recovery, IPSec interaction with the Layer Two Tunneling Protocol (L2TP), and public-key infrastructures.

Acknowledgments

We would like to thank our editor, Mary Franz, for helping us through the entire process and for giving us this opportunity.

We would like to thank our reviewers: Scott Kelly, Andrew Krywaniuk, and Tim Jenkins. Their comments and suggestions have made this book more readable and complete.

IPSec is the result of the IPSec Working Group of the IETF and we would therefore like to thank Ran Atkinson, Ashar Aziz, Steve Bellovin, Matt Blaze, John Ioannidis, Phil Karn, Steve Kent, Hugo Krawczyk, Hilarie Orman, and Bill Simpson, whose contributions to the development of these protocols have been invaluable.

Network Diagram Key

In the network diagram figures, a *dotted line* indicates a logical connection (i.e., the two devices are not physically attached), a *solid line* indicates a physical connection (i.e., there is a physical link between the two devices and they are directly attached, and a *pipe* indicates a secure connection between two devices.

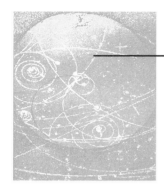

CHAPTER

1

Cryptographic History and Techniques

Since the beginning of time people have kept secrets. Probably from the beginning of your memory you have done the same. It's a natural human desire. People have always had, and always will have, some secrets that they either want to keep to themselves or share with only a privileged few. The easiest secret to keep is one that you will tell to no one. The more people you wish to share a secret with, and the more public the forum in which you will communicate your secret, the harder it is to keep your secret a secret.

Secrets in History

In antiquity it was easier to keep a secret because the ability to read was a privilege known to a select few. The number of people who could read a written secret was very limited. Merely by restricting access to the written word, a secret could be retained. The security of such a scheme is obviously limited.

As the ability to read became more prevalent the need to keep secrets from those with the ability to read became more necessary. This need manifested itself most notably in war. While those doing the actual fighting were most likely illiterate, the ones who waged the war were not and each side, no doubt, employed soldiers who could read and speak the language of their enemies. Military communications in the battlefield were probably the genesis of cryptography.

Early attempts at cryptography were simplistic. It is rumored that Caesar used a rudimentary cipher to obfuscate his messages. Those with whom he wished to share a secret were told how to reconstruct the original message. This cipher, *The Caesar Cipher*, was a simple substitution cipher: Every letter in the alphabet was replaced by the letter three places away modulus the length of the alphabet. In other words, the letter A became D, B became E, X became A, Y became B, Z became C, etc. It's a simple cipher to decode but *li brx grq'w nqrz krz lw'v qrw reylrxv!*—in other words, if you don't know how it's not obvious! Another variant of this is the ROT-13 cipher. Each letter is rotated 13 places.

Simple substitution ciphers are not very good since each occurrence of a letter is replaced by the same letter. Analysis of a language will result in the probability of letters following other letters—notice the occurrence of the letter *r* in the above "ciphertext." It's probably a vowel—and this information can be used to determine the substitution offset.

Confidentiality was not the only concern in antiquity. Authentication was another. When few could write, a signature would probably suffice. As the knowledge of reading and writing became more prevalent, wax seals bearing the unique mark of the "signer" were used to authenticate letters, documents, and edicts. The rise of industry brought the capability to make such a seal to more people and the seal ceased being unique. In effect, it became trivial to forge a seal.

Jumping to modern times, ciphers, and their cryptanalysis, have a very notable place in history. Prior to the United States' involvement in World War II, the United States Army was able to crack a code used by the Japanese government. This capability allowed the United States to be forewarned about the attack on Pearl Harbor. This knowledge was not put to good use, though, and the United States suffered great losses as a result of this "surprise" attack. During the same war the German government used an encryption device called Enigma to encipher its communications. This device used a set of rotors (Enigma machines had 5 but only 3 were used for any given communication) that contained the letters of the alphabet and could be independently set. Each letter of input text was transformed into a seemingly random character of output. Seemingly random, because the permutations of transposition were astronomical. The cracking of the Enigma machine was an incredible feat started by the Polish and finished by the British and the story behind the cryptanalysis of Enigma is large enough to be its own book. In fact, several books have been written on the subject.

Communication technology has grown steadily from the days of Caesar to modern times. From papyrus paper to telegram, telex, telephone, FAX, and e-mail, the ability to communicate has been made easier and more ubiquitous. At the same time, the ability to keep such communications secret has remained something of a black art known only to a few—generally governments and military organizations.

The security of each method of communication is dependent on the medium over which the communication is made. The more open the medium the greater the possibility of the message falling into the hands of those for whom it was not intended. Modern day methods of communication are open and public. A telephone call or FAX transmission goes across a shared, public, circuit-switched phone network. An e-mail is transmitted across a shared, public, packet-switched network. An entity in the network between communications endpoints could easily intercept the message. Retention of a secret transmitted using modern methods of communication requires some sort of cryptographic technique to prevent any of these eavesdroppers from learning the secret.

At its base modern cryptography relies on a secret known by the intended recipient(s) of the message. Typically the method of encipherment, the algorithm, is known but the "key" to unlock the secret is not. There are certain cryptosystems that are based upon a secret algorithm—so-called "security through obscurity"—but typically people are reluctant to use an algorithm which is not open to public scrutiny (the debate over the Clipper Chip is a prime example of this).

The problem, then, is to ensure the secrecy of the key—that it is obtainable only by those to whom it should be known. Modern cryptography provides for this.

Rise of the Internet

The popularity of the Internet has given rise to many claims on it. Everybody from browser companies to workstation vendors to router vendors lays claim to being the genesis of or the backbone of the Internet. Most agree, though, that the modern Internet was born in the late '60s under the name ARPANET. The ARPANET was a research tool for those doing work for the United States government under the direction of the Advanced Research Projects Agency (ARPA). The original contract was awarded to BBN of Cambridge, Massachusetts.

ARPANET traffic consisted of communications between universities and military and government laboratories. Researchers at disparate locations were able to exchange files and electronic messages with each other via ARPANET. As the network grew it split into two: MILNET, which was used for military use, and ARPANET (it retained the name), which continued to be used for experimental research. In the early '80s, a standard for ARPANET communications protocols, actually a suite of protocols, was specified. This was termed the TCP/IP protocol suite which eventually became just TCP/IP. It is the base of almost all network traffic today.

In 1987 the National Science Foundation (NSF) funded a network to connect the six supercomputer centers that were spread out nationwide. This network, called NSFnet, spanned the United States from San Diego, California on the west coast to Princeton, New Jersey on the east coast. The original NSFnet was over 56K leased lines, fast in those days but slow by today's standards, so NSF also solicited proposals to build a new high-speed network. The winning proposal was submitted by MCI, IBM, and MERIT (an organization which came out of a network at the University of Michigan), and the backbone of what we call the Internet was built.

Over the course of the '90s, the backbone of this network grew by the addition of different long-haul carriers providing leased line connections and local Internet Service Providers (ISPs) providing local access and short-haul connections. Today, through mutually beneficial service agreements, networks are connected with each side agreeing to carry the other's traffic on the condition that its traffic is also carried. This has created a worldwide network in which, for the price of the initial connection, access is provided to a virtually unlimited amount of resources spanning the entire globe.

Internet Security

The Internet is an ethereal thing. It can appear quite different when looked at for different purposes. For the purposes of secret-sharing, imagine the Internet as a huge town hall which is packed with people. Attempting to communicate a secret in such an environment is difficult, and the chance of others overhearing a conversation between two people increases as the distance between those two people increases. Since the Internet is truly global, no secret of any value can be communicated on it without the help of cryptography.

As the Internet grows (almost exponentially in recent years), its utility increases. Messages can be sent cheaply and reliably and communication is the lifeblood of business. For a company to engage in electronic commerce—the sale of goods and services over the Internet—security is a must. Sensitive information such as credit card numbers must be protected and a business must be able to authenticate each and every sale. In addition, businesses can use the Internet to inexpensively connect disparate offices. Interoffice electronic mail and even phone calls can be routed over the Internet. Because sensitive corporate information would most likely be transmitted over these links, the need for security should be obvious.

But, Internet security concerns are not solely business'. Each and every person has a need and a right to privacy, and when someone goes on-line, the expectation of privacy does not disappear. As consumer electronics become more and more Internet-aware, the need for security grows. When our phones and VCRs become accessible over the Internet, we won't want pranksters or hackers to steal our phone line or randomly turn our VCRs on and off.

Privacy is not just confidentiality, though; it also includes anonymity. People must be comfortable in cyberspace and an often ignored component of that is the ability for an individual to remain anonymous. What we read, where we go, to whom we talk, for whom we vote, and what we buy is not information that most people traditionally publicize, and if people are required to disclose information in cyberspace that they would not normally disclose in real life, they will be reluctant to engage in Internet activity.

Thankfully, cryptography can address these concerns.

Cryptographic Building Blocks

Every system that is established can be hacked or attacked. Each different hack or attack represents a distinct threat against the system. For every threat a threat analysis is done to determine the viability of that threat and what damage can be done if that threat is acted upon. Depending on the threat analysis countermeasures are taken such that the cost of launching the attack is greater than the expected gain from the attack.

Cryptographic tools represent such countermeasures. There is no single cryptographic tool. There are various techniques for encrypting messages, for securely exchanging keys, for maintaining the integrity of messages, and for guaranteeing authenticity of a message. These tools can be thought of as building blocks to construct protection against attack.

A single cryptographic building block solves a particular problem— how to authenticate bulk data, how to establish a shared secret—and they can be combined to build a cryptosystem to protect against threats. The cryptosystem must be stronger than the threat against it.

Generally, the strength of a cryptosystem is measured in its complexity. If 2^{32} separate operations are required to break a cryptosystem then the complexity of a particular system is 2^{32}. That's a lot of operations, but if each operation can be performed by a modern computer in hundredths or thousandths of a second, the system might not be strong enough to protect against the threat. Because of this the term *computationally secure* is used to express the security of a modern cryptosystem.

When building a cryptosystem it is necessary to ensure that the component building blocks are used properly and together maintain the necessary strength. For instance, if the strength of the building block used to establish a shared secret is 2^{90} but the strength of the building block used to encrypt the data is only 2^{40} the cryptosystem would be 2^{40}, and that is not computationally secure using modern computers.

One-Way Functions and Trap Doors

A good portion of public key cryptography relies upon a foundation of one-way functions and trapdoors. A one-way function is something that is easy to compute in one direction but difficult, bordering on impossible, to compute in the other direction. A trapdoor is a way to sneak back, in effect a way to cheat and return using a secret passage.

For a one-way function to be useful in cryptography it must exhibit its one way-ness with *any* input. For example, in a finite field it is easy to compute the product of numbers but difficult to factor that product.

Another example is the Discrete Logarithm Problem: with a large prime, p, and a generator, g, for a particular value y, find x where

$$g^x = y \bmod p$$

Modular exponentiation is easy, but doing a discrete logarithm to recover the exponent is hard. For any class of numbers—odd numbers, palidrome numbers, numbers divisible by 47—the problem of solving the discrete logarithm is still very hard.

There are no mathematical proofs of one-way functions but certain functions seem to have the properties that a one-way function would have and are generally referred to as such. There may be ways to factor numbers that are just as fast and easy as producing the product but no one has discovered it yet. Because of that we can put our knowledge on the difficulty in factoring to good use.

Trapdoor functions are a bit harder to explain. Modern cryptographic algorithms use them but it's hard to point to a particular one and say, "that's it!" An example of a trapdoor function is a tree with many branches. To get from a leaf to the trunk is straightforward and requires no choices. To get from the trunk back out to a particular leaf requires choosing a branch, then a subbranch, then another subbranch, et cetera, and finally choosing the leaf. The trapdoor would be a description of which branch to take.

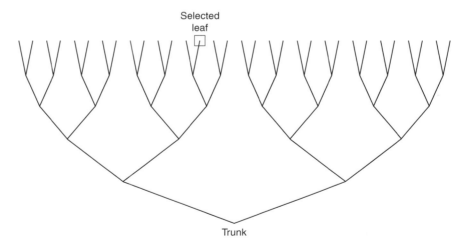

Figure 1.1   A Trap Door Function Tree

The difficulty in finding a particular leaf depends on the depth of the tree. The tree in Figure 1.1 is of depth 5 and there are therefore 2^5, or 32, leaves. The trapdoor to go from the trunk to the indicated leaf would be the "key" of LEFT-RIGHT-RIGHT-LEFT-RIGHT. It should be noted that this "trapdoor function" is wholly unsuitable for any kind of cryptographic purpose. But to illustrate the concept of a trapdoor, it is adequate.

One-Way Hash Functions

One-way hash functions are used in modern cryptosystems for authentication and integrity purposes. A one-way hash function is different than the concept of a one-way function just described. Hash functions take a variable-sized message as input, compress it, and produce a fixed-sized digest. The output of a hash function will be identical for identical input. Since the output is fixed for any length input it should be obvious that there will exist two distinct inputs, X and Y, for a hash algorithm H, such that $H(X)$ equals $H(Y)$. Such an occurrence is called a collision. One-way hash functions are designed such that finding collisions—that is, finding two random inputs that will produce identical hash digests—is difficult.

Popular hash functions in use today are: MD5 (Message Digest 5), SHA (the Secure Hash Algorithm), and RIPEMD. They all produce a different-sized digest and have different speed and collision-resistant properties, but are all used extensively today.

Use of one-way functions, which are based on a trapdoor, are much more computationally intensive than using one-way hash functions. Guaranteeing the integrity of a message using a one-way function with a trapdoor—such as a digital signature scheme—takes considerably more time than guaranteeing the integrity of the message using a hash function. There are situations, though, in which it is not possible to use a one-way hash function. In later chapters you will see how IPSec and IKE use both techniques.

Another technique used quite a bit is the simple exclusive-or (XOR) function. This is neither a one-way function, nor a trapdoor function, but is, nonetheless, a useful tool in building cryptographic systems. Remember from early math classes that the XOR of two zeros is zero, the XOR of two ones is zero and the XOR of a zero and a one (or a one and a zero) is one. XOR has a very important feature that it is commutative. Taking any data and XORing it with a key of the same size (one bit, one byte, or more) will produce an output that can be XORed with the key again to recover the original data. It is the most simplistic "encryption" algorithm. Note, however, that knowing either input and the output it is possible to deduce the other input. This is not generally a characteristic of a real encryption algorithm and illustrates the weakness of using XOR for such a purpose.

Ciphers

Data confidentiality is provided by encryption algorithms which convert a message (plaintext) into gibberish (ciphertext) and back again. Some encryption algorithms are symmetric—the ability to encrypt implies the ability to decrypt—while some are asymmetric—without the use of a trapdoor it is not possible to decrypt what has been encrypted. Asymmetric algorithms are treated not as two separate functions (one for encryption and one for decryption) but as a single algorithm. So, regardless of the "symmetry" of a particular algorithm, encryption algorithms are commutative.

$$plaintext = Decrypt(Encrypt(plaintext))$$

This should be most obvious because any algorithm that permanently scrambled its input would be secure but of little use.

Symmetric Ciphers

Symmetric ciphers use a single key to do both encryption and decryption. There are two types of symmetric ciphers, block ciphers and stream ciphers. Block ciphers, such as AES, CAST, and Blowfish, operate on data one block at a time, with the size of the block depending on the algorithm (AES has a 128-bit block size while both CAST and Blowfish have a 64-bit block size). Each block operation is treated as an atomic act. Stream ciphers, such as RC4, on the other hand operate on data one bit (or one byte) at a time. Appropriately seeded with a key, they will produce a stream of bits which can be XORed with the input. The encryptor and the decryptor must be syncronized to ensure that the same bit in the stream used to encrypt a particular bit of plaintext is also used to decrypt the corresponding bit of ciphertext. If the two ever get out of syncronization the plaintext will not be able to be recovered. It is this syncronization problem that makes stream ciphers inappropriate for use with IPSec. If a packet is dropped using a block cipher that will not affect the processing of subsequent packets, but if a packet is dropped using a stream cipher all subsequent packets will be affected until the two side re-synchronize somehow.

Both types of symmetric ciphers are ideally suited for bulk encryption. Since block ciphers are used exclusively in IPSec, the reader is referred to the literature for an in-depth description of stream ciphers.

Block ciphers process data by first dividing it up into equal sized chunks. The size of each chunk is determined by the *block size* of the cipher. Since there is no guarantee that the length of the input is a multiple of the block size of a block cipher, it may be necessary to pad the input. If the block size is 64 bits and the last block of input is only 48 bits, it may be necessary to add 16 bits of padding to the block prior to performing the encryption (or decryption) operation.

The basic way to use a block cipher is in Electronic Code Book (ECB) mode. Each block of plaintext encrypts to a block of ciphertext. This causes problems though since the same block of plaintext will encrypt, with the same key, into the same block of ciphertext. Therefore it is possible to build a code book of all possible ciphertexts (using all possible keys) for a known plaintext. If we know that an IP datagram was encrypted, we know that the first 20 bytes of ciphertext represent the IP header and that certain fields of an IP header are predictable. An attacker can use that knowledge, with a code book, to determine the key.

To foil the code book attack against a block cipher it is necessary to use the block cipher in a feedback *mode*. A feedback mode chains blocks together by feeding the results of prior operations into the current operation.

Cipher Block Chaining (CBC) (Figure 1.2) mode takes the previous block of ciphertext and XORs it with the next block of plaintext prior to encryption. There is no "previous block" for the first block so this mode is jumpstarted by XORing the first block with something called an Initialization Vector (IV). The length of the IV must be the same as the block size of the cipher to ensure the entire first block is processed. The IV must have strong pseudo-random properties to ensure that identical plaintext will not produce identical ciphertext. Decryption is the opposite of encryption: Each block is decrypted and XORed with the previous block prior to decryption. The first block is decrypted and XORed with the IV. All ciphers currently defined for use in IPSec are block ciphers operating in CBC mode.

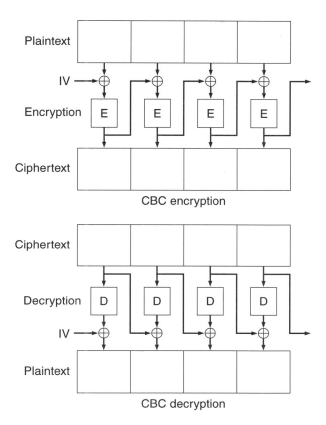

Figure 1.2   Cipher Block Chaining Mode

Other popular modes are Cipher Feedback Mode (CFB), where the previous ciphertext block is encrypted and XORed with the current plaintext block (the first block of plaintext is merely XORed with the IV), and Output Feedback Mode (OFB), which maintains a cipher state that is repeatedly encrypted and XORed with blocks of plaintext to produce ciphertext (an IV represents the initial cipher state).

Asymmetric Ciphers

Asymmetric algorithms are also known as public key algorithms. There are two keys, one public and one private. One key does the encryption, the other the decryption, and given a public key it is computationally impossible to determine the private key (as defined above, we can say that good public key algorithms are *computationally secure*). Good public key algorithms are based on one-way functions.

Public key cryptography is generally held to have been invented by Whitfield Diffie and Martin Hellman in their paper "New Directions in Cryptography," published in IEEE Transactions on Information Theory in 1976. Recently the Communications-Electronics Security Group (CESG) of the British government—the UK version of the United States' NSA— declassified some papers that showed that their cryptanalysts had actually invented the concept six years earlier. In 1970, James Ellis wrote an internal CESG report entitled "The Possibility of Secure Non-Secret Digital Encryption" which discussed an existence theorem, while Clifford Cocks and Malcolm Williamson wrote papers describing practical schemes that closely resemble the RSA and Diffie-Hellman schemes, respectively. Regardless, publication of the Diffie-Hellman paper was a seminal event whose importance is underscored by the nearly 20-year delay in release of the classified British papers. It is not beyond the realm of possibility that if "New Directions in Cryptography" had not been published, this knowledge would still be a classified secret known only to a few.

RSA   The most popular public key algorithm is RSA, named after its inventors Ron Rivest, Adi Shamir, and Leonard Adleman. The security of RSA is based on the difficulty in factoring the product of two very large prime numbers. This is a one-way function: it is easy to compute the product of two large prime numbers but extremely difficult to factor the product into the original prime numbers. One of the features of RSA is that either key can be used to encrypt data that the other key can decrypt. This means that anyone can encrypt a message in your public key that you alone can decrypt. Also, you can encrypt anything with your private key that anyone with your public key can decrypt. You're probably thinking, what's the point then? But this concept is very important in non-repudiation and digital signatures (which will be discussed shortly).

A drawback of RSA is that it is quite slow and can operate only on data up to the size of the modulus of its key. A 1024-bit RSA public key can only encrypt data that is less than or equal to that size (actually, it's 1013 bits because the definition on how to encrypt using RSA requires an encoding that consumes 11 bits). While this is a restriction similar to a symmetric block cipher, the speed of RSA makes it unsuitable for bulk data encryption. This does not mean that RSA is not useful. On the contrary, it is a de facto standard for such important techniques as key exchange and digital signature.

El-Gamal Another public key cryptosystem which is suitable for encryption is El-Gamal, named after its inventor, Taher El-Gamal. The El-Gamal cryptosystem is based on the Discrete Logarithm Problem. The main drawback of El-Gamal is that the ciphertext is twice the size of the plaintext. Given our already saturated networks, this is a large drawback. El-Gamal is quite similar to the Diffie-Hellman key exchange, which we'll discuss in detail shortly.

Authentication and Integrity

Confidentiality is necessary to keep a secret, but without authentication you have no way of knowing that the person with whom you share the secret is whom she claims to be. And with no confidence in the integrity of a received message, you don't know if it was the same message actually sent..

Authentication

Public key cryptography can be used for authentication purposes by constructing a so-called *digital signature* which has properties similar to a traditional signature. A traditional handwritten signature is difficult to forge, and is therefore difficult to repudiate. But because a handwritten signature is just more writing on a document, it is possible (although also difficult given a well-written document) for unscrupulous people to add additional text to an already signed document, giving the impression that the signer agrees to or acknowledges that text.

The Internet is a largely anonymous place and digital information can live a long time, so there are other properties we need for digital signatures in addition to those that a traditional handwritten signature affords.

A digital signature must be difficult to forge and therefore difficult to repudiate, just like a traditional signature. In addition, it must convey message integrity and must be unique. We want to prevent additional text from being added to a digitally signed file and we also want to prevent a signature from being removed from an authentic, signed document and added to other documents. These properties can all be met using public key cryptography.

It is easiest to envision digital signature as encryption and verification of a digital signature as decryption. In fact, that is the way an RSA signature works. But another public key algorithm, in fact a standard for digital signatures, aptly named the Digital Signature Standard (DSS), does not operate in that manner. The difference will be explained shortly, but for purposes of illustration it is encryption and decryption.

What the private key encrypts the public key decrypts. Provided the private key from a public/private key cryptosystem is kept secret, it can be used to construct digital signatures. By encrypting a document with a private key, anybody in possession of the corresponding public key can decrypt the document. Of course an encrypted document is hardly a signature and verification would just entail reconstruction of something that *looks* good out of the encrypted gibberish. It would also require decryption, and implicit signature verification, every time the document merely needs to be read.

A digital signature is therefore not a private-key encryption of the entire document. Digital signature techniques use one-way hash functions to reduce a document down to a digest. It is that digest that is encrypted. Remember that a hash function will produce the same digest every time it is given identical input and that the input can be of arbitrary length. Provided the hash function has strong collision-resistant properties, we can be assured that the signature is unique to the document.

The encrypted digest, the digital signature, can then be appended to an original document. Verification of the signature entails running the original document through the identical hash function to product a temporary digest and decrypting the signature to recover the original digest. If the two digests are equal, the signature is valid. This technique has all the properties we need:

1. **difficult to forge**: only the holder of the private key can generate the signature.

2. **nonrepudiable**: a signed document cannot be repudiated later due to extreme difficulty in forging.

3. **unalterable**: once signed, a document cannot be modified.

4. **nontransferable**: the signature cannot be removed and attached to another document.

It is also possible to have multiple signatures, produced from different private keys, on a single document. Each signature is generated in the same fashion by encrypting a digest of the document to be signed. These encrypted digests are merely appended, one after the other, on the end of the document.

RSA Due to its unique nature—what one key encrypts the other decrypts—RSA is well suited for digital signatures as well as for encryption. You just use a different key to do the encryption! The technique described previously is exactly what happens when using RSA with digital signatures.

There are no requirements to use any particular hash algorithm when using RSA signatures.

DSA The digital signature algorithm is similar to the El-Gamal public key scheme. Both are based on the discrete logarithm problem.

As mentioned, the Digital Signature Algorithm does not actually do encryption for signature generation and decryption for signature verification (although it does have a public and private key). Instead, the private key is used to generate two 160-bit values which represent the signature, and verification is a mathematical demonstration, using the public key, that those two values could only have been generated by the private key and the document that was signed. There is no real "decryption".

DSA requires use of SHA as a hash function for signatures. SHA is the algorithm defined in the U.S. government Federal Information Processing Standard (FIPS) for the Secure Hash Standard and was therefore selected to use for another FIPS, the Digital Signature Standard, of which DSA is the algorithm.

Message Integrity

A digital signature provides integrity on the signed document. Any modification to the document would be detected by checking the signature. One drawback of digital signatures is that they are slow and another is that the entire message must be known prior to signature generation. There is no efficient way to provide message integrity of an ongoing data stream using digital signatures.

Just as there are symmetric and asymmetric ciphers, there are symmetric and asymmetric methods of guaranteeing message integrity. Similar to symmetric ciphers, where one single key is used for both encryption and decryption, symmetric message authentication codes (MACs) use a single key for generating and verifying the authentication information. (MACs are sometimes erroneously referred to as signatures—they're not.)

Hash functions are used as MACs just as they are in digital signatures. Since the input to a hash function can be of any length, all one needs to do to generate a MAC is hash a shared secret key along with the message. The resulting digest is attached to the message, and verification of the MAC entails hashing the shared secret key with the message to produce a temporary digest and comparing that temporary digest with the digest attached to the message. This technique is referred to as *keyed hashing*. It's important to do keyed hashing because just performing a hash on some data does not really provide any authentication. Anybody could modify the data and merely run the hash algorithm over the modified data. A hash function alone is like a checksum, a keyed hash function is a MAC.

Keyed hashing can be used to provide message authentication to a stream of data by dividing the stream into easily digestible chunks and computing a MAC on each chunk. Those MACs then become part of the stream and are used to verify the integrity of the stream as it is received. Another benefit of keyed hashing is that generation of a hash digest is much faster than generation of a digital signature.

A special kind of keyed hash is called an HMAC, and was designed by Hugo Krawczyk, Ran Canetti, and Mihir Bellare. The HMAC specification is in RFC2104 and can be utilized with any existing hash function, so SHA can become HMAC-SHA and MD5 becomes HMAC-MD5. The HMAC construction is cryptographically stronger than the underlying hashing function. There has recently been a demonstrated collision attack against MD5 (where it is possible to find two different inputs which will produce the same digest), but HMAC-MD5 is not susceptible to this attack.

An HMAC is also a keyed hash but is actually a keyed hash inside a keyed hash. It uses two constant pad values—an inner pad and an outer pad—to modify the keys to the hashes. The HMAC based on hash algorithm H of message M using key K is defined as

$$HMAC\ (K,\ M) = H(K\ XOR\ opad,\ H(K\ XOR\ ipad,\ M))$$

Where the *ipad* is a 64-element array of the value 0x36 and the *opad* is a 64-element array of the value 0x5c.

All message authentication done in IPSec uses HMACs.

Key Exchanges

Symmetric ciphers and symmetric MACs both require a shared key. The security of the encryption and authentication techniques could be completely undermined by an insecure key exchange.

Diffie-Hellman

The Diffie-Hellman key exchange is the first public key cryptosystem and was the one described in the aforementioned paper "New Directions in Cryptography" by Whitfield Diffie and Martin Hellman. The Diffie-Hellman key exchange is based on the Discrete Logarithm Problem (notice how often this one-way function is used).

This key exchange is extremely important. Using the Diffie-Hellman exchange, a nonsecret, untrusted communications channel (like the Internet) can be used to securely establish a shared secret among the parties of the exchange. It is because of the Diffie-Hellman key exchange that symmetric ciphers and symmetric message integrity schemes (which both require a shared key) can be used in a scalable manner.

The usual players in describing modern cryptography are Alice and Bob and they can be used to illustrate the Diffie-Hellman exchange. All participants in a Diffie-Hellman exchange must first agree on a *group* that defines which prime, p, and generator, g, will be used. A Diffie-Hellman exchange is two-part. In the first part each side, Alice and Bob, choose a random private number (indicated by the lowercase initial of the party) and exponentiate in the group to produce a public value (uppercase initial of the party):

$$\underline{Alice} \qquad \underline{Bob}$$

$$A = g^a \bmod p \qquad B = g^b \bmod p$$

They exchange their public values, Alice gives A to Bob and Bob gives B to Alice, and they exponentiate again, using the other party's public value as the generator, to generate shared secret.

$$\underline{Alice} \qquad \underline{Bob}$$

$$B^a \bmod p = g^{ab} \bmod p = A^b \bmod p$$

Notice that A and B can be exchanged over an insecure network without lessening the security of the scheme. g and p do not even need to be kept secret. An eavesdropper (she's usually referred to as Eve) could know g and p a priori, intercept A and B over the insecure channel and still not be able to discover the secret! Once Alice and Bob share a secret they can use it to protect their communications. The Diffie-Hellman exchange allows an insecure channel to become secure. The importance of this cannot be overstated.

One drawback of the Diffie-Hellman exchange is that it is susceptible to a man-in-the-middle attack. In this attack, Mallory intercepts messages between Alice and Bob and fraudulently responds impersonating Bob to Alice and Alice to Bob. Alice thinks she's doing a Diffie-Hellman exchange with Bob but she's really doing with to Mallory. Similarly Bob thinks he's doing a Diffie-Hellman exchange with Alice but he's also doing it with Mallory. Alice can then send Bob secret information protected with the shared secret she thinks she shares with Bob. Mallory can decrypt it, copy it, and re-encrypt it with the secret that Bob has (which he thinks is shared with Alice). Neither Alice nor Bob detect anything out of the ordinary, except perhaps some delay in delivery due to Mallory's involvement.

The susceptibility to man-in-the-middle attack does not render the Diffie-Hellman exchange useless though, because the attack can be thwarted by having Alice and Bob digitally sign their public values. Mallory will not be able to fool Bob into signing her public value and will not be able to make Alice think that her signature is in fact Bob's. Keep this in mind when reading Chapter 7 on the Internet Key Exchange (IKE) Protocol.

RSA Key Exchange

With the RSA cryptosystem it is possible to encrypt with either the public or private key and what one key encrypts the other can decrypt. This capability can be put to use for doing a simplistic key exchange. If Alice wishes to use symmetric cryptography to protect her communications with Bob, she can choose a random number as the key, encrypt it in Bob's public key, and send it to him. Only Bob will be able to decrypt the key since he, alone, has possession of his private key.

An obvious problem with this approach is that anybody—such as Mallory— can encrypt anything in Bob's public key. Alice needs something to bind herself to this key. Once again, a digital signature can be used for such a binding. Alice can sign the key and encrypt both the key and her signature in Bob's public key. A drawback to this approach is that an RSA signature is the same as an RSA encryption: It can only be done on data that is less the size of the modulus and the result is the size of the modulus. If Alice's RSA private key is the same size as Bob's RSA public key, her signature will be too big to encrypt in a single operation.

Also, the benefit of a Diffie-Hellman exchange is that each side contributes to the resulting key, no one imposes the key on the other. For many applications this will be an important issue, for others not quite so much.

Crypto Concepts

Using the tools described above, it's possible to build a very complicated and very extensible system for network security. IPSec is an example. IPSec uses symmetric ciphers in CBC mode for encryption and HMACs for bulk data authentication. The Internet Key Exchange is basically an authenticated Diffie-Hellman exchange. One method of authentication is digital signatures, another involves HMACing a shared secret, a third involves public key encryption to authenticate a peer.

There are certain concepts that are important to IPSec that are not necessarily cryptographic tools.

Perfect Forward Secrecy

Symmetric keys have a much shorter lifetime than asymmetric. This is due to the complexity of the algorithms. Asymmetric algorithms are based on one-way functions, symmetric algorithms are not. While both are in the same class of complexity, asymmetric algorithms are necessarily the most difficult to solve of that class. They *may* be as difficult to solve as symmetric algorithms (it's the complexity theorists debate of whether *NP* is equal to *NP-complete*) but are believed to be more difficult. Until someone proves that these two types of algorithms are of equal complexity we continue to believe that asymmetric algorithms are more complex than symmetric ones. This is a long way of explaining that certain keys have to be thrown away, and never used again, much sooner than other keys.

When a Diffie-Hellman exchange is used to generate a symmetric key (the kind of key that must be changed more frequently), both parties contribute to the result. The key is ephemeral. If that key is thrown away and replaced by a new key, which is the result of another Diffie-Hellman exchange, the two keys will have no relationship to each other. If an attacker broke a single symmetric key, he would have access to all data that was protected by that key but not to data protected by any other key. In other words, the system that uses such ephemeral, single-use, keys has *perfect forward secrecy.*

A system would not have perfect forward secrecy if there was a single secret from which all symmetric keys were derived. In that case, breaking the root key could give an attacker all keys derived from that root and therefore all data protected by all those keys.

The important issue to keep in mind regarding perfect forward secrecy is that it is not enough to just use a different key, the keys must be unique.

Perfect forward secrecy is important for some applications but not for all. There is a definite overhead associated with doing a Diffie-Hellman exchange at each rekey interval. If the data requires such security it is an appropriate price to pay, but if it doesn't, it could be excessive. So, perfect forward secrecy may not be necessary every single time. The IPSec standard key exchange, IKE, therefore has an option for perfect forward secrecy. If the parties desire it, it is possible, but not necessary.

Denial of Service

Cryptography is not free. Doing modular exponentiation or computing the product of two very large prime numbers, even decrypting and verifying the integrity of individual packets, takes both wall clock time and CPU time. If it was possible to force a computer to do unnecessary work while trying to achieve security, it might be possible to shut down that computer. Such an attack is called a *denial of service attack*.

Denial of service attacks can be launched against cryptographic systems if the system can be induced to do unnecessary work or allocate memory unnecessarily. A denial of service attack is when the attacker can cause the attackee to do more work in response to the attack than is necessary to launch the attack.

An example of such an attack would be if Alice was willing to do a Diffie-Hellman exchange and Mallory sent thousands of bogus Diffie-Hellman public values to her, all with fake return addresses. Alice could be forced to do her part for these fake exchanges. That could be quite a bit of work! It would be almost no work for Mallory, though, because it's computationally effortless to generate a string of random bits that look like a Diffie-Hellman public value. It's much more work to actually exponentiate and generate a real one.

Another denial of service attack can be launched if Alice and Bob share symmetric keys which they use to encrypt and authenticate individual IP packets. Mallory could send thousands of packets to Bob that look like they came from Alice. Since Mallory doesn't share the key the packets would be bogus, but the only way Bob could find that out is to do the work of decrypting and verifying the integrity of the packet! It's much cheaper to generate bogus packets than it is to detect that they're bogus.

Thankfully, IPSec and IKE are constructed with partial defenses against denial of service attacks. These defenses do not defeat all denial of service attacks, but merely increase the cost and complexity to launch them.

More Information

This chapter provides a brief overview of some cryptographic concepts that will be expanded on later in this book. Cryptography is a complex art, though, and it cannot be adequately explained in a short chapter like this. There are many good books that give a solid background in cryptography that you're strongly encouraged to read. A good place to start is *Cryptography and Data Security* by Dorothy Denning, and *Applied Cryptography* by Bruce Schneier.

There are important and fascinating protocols and problems that were not covered here. For instance, the zero knowledge proof: where one party proves to another that she knows some information without actually divulging the information. Another one-way function that was not discussed is the knapsack problem. Like the discrete logarithm problem, the knapsack problem can be used to construct public key cryptosystems. Other, more complicated, key exchanges also exist, like the Encrypted Key Exchange (EKE). There are even attacks against the cryptographic tools that IPSec uses, like the Birthday Attacks against hash functions. This attack takes its name from the observation that if you are in a room with only 182 other people, the chances are even that one of those persons has the same birthday as you. If there is a room of only 23 people, the chances are even that there are two people in the room that share the same birthday. This in spite of the fact that there are 365 (sometimes 366) days in the year! The birthday paradox affects hashing algorithms because it illustrates the statistical probability of finding two random inputs that will hash to the same digest—i.e., in finding a collision. If the digest from a hash algorithm is n bits in length, finding two distinct messages that hash to the same digest would take $O(2^{n/2})$ operations.

Cryptography is probably as old as speech but it continually evolves to solve new, interesting, and critically important problems of today and tomorrow.

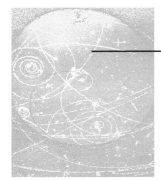

2

TCP/IP Overview

This chapter provides a very brief introduction to TCP/IP protocol for readers not familiar with the concepts of TCP/IP.[1] We then go on to discuss the advantages and disadvantages of implementing security at various layers in the stack. This is necessary to understand the reasons to implement security at various layers. This also provides the framework to discuss IP security in the following chapters.

---

1.   For a more in-depth discussion of TCP/IP protocol, we strongly recommend that readers refer to other books.

Introduction to TCP/IP

In this section, we briefly discuss the protocols used in the TCP/IP stack, the addressing architecture, the Domain Name System (DNS), and the socket interface.

In the early 1960s, DARPA (Defense Advanced Research Project Agency) funded a project that connected universities and research agencies through a network called ARPANET. In 1983, the TCP/IP protocols replaced the original ARPANET NCP (Network Control Protocols). The TCP/IP protocols running this network were open, simple, and easy to use. This network has grown considerably into what is called "Internet." The Internet is a collection of networks running TCP/IP protocol suite.

In the '80s there were other networking protocol architectures—ISOs OSI, IBMs SNA, and Digital's DECNET to name a few. However, none of these protocols were as simple and open as the TCP/IP protocol suite. This led to wide deployment, development, and support for the TCP/IP protocol suite.

The networking protocol architecture consists of various components:

- Protocol stack—This comprises various layers that communicate among themselves to efficiently transmit the packet.[2]

- Addressing—The capability to uniquely identify a destination. In order to communicate with a global entity, it is necessary to uniquely identify the entity.

- Routing—The capability to efficiently determine the path a particular packet is to traverse to reach a destination.

Protocol Stack

The TCP/IP protocol stack consists of 4 layers as shown in Figure 2.1. Each layer in the stack has well-defined functions and capabilities. Each layer exports well-defined interfaces that the layers above and below it can use to communicate with it. The layered architecture has many advantages. In addition to simplifying the design of the protocol stack, it also simplifies its usage. The design is simplified as each layer interacts only with the layer immediately above and below it. Once the service the layer provides and its interfaces are identified, each layer can be designed independently. The usage is simplified as the complexities of the networking stack are hidden from the applications using the networking stack.

---

2.   Packet is the unit of data.

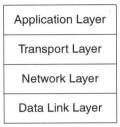

Figure 2.1   IP packets protected by IPSec in transport
mode and tunnel mode.

The functionality of each layer is described below. The protocols that implement these services are described later.

Application Layer: The application layer provides the services for an application to send and receive data over the network. It also provides services such as name resolution (refer to DNS). Applications such as World Wide Web (WWW) browsers or e-mail clients use the services provided by the application layer to communicate with its peers, WWW servers and e-mail servers respectively. The application layer also defines the interface to the transport layer. This interface is operating-system dependent. The most popular interface is the socket interface. The socket interface is provided in all flavors of the UNIX operating system and on the Microsoft platforms.

Transport Layer: The transport layer is responsible for providing services to the application layer. In the TCP/IP protocol suite the transport layer provides the following services:

1. Connection-oriented or connectionless transport: In a connection-oriented transport, once a connection is established between two applications, the connection stays until one of the applications gives up the connection voluntarily. The application specifies the destination only once, during the establishment of the connection. The best analogy for this is the telephone service. Once a call is established, it stays connected until one speaker disconnects. In connectionless transport, the application has to specify a destination for every single packet it sends.

2. Reliable or unreliable transport: In case of reliable connection, if a packet is lost in the network for some reason (network overload, or some node going down), it is retransmitted by the transport layer. The transport layer is guaranteeing the reliable

delivery of the packet to the destination. In the unreliable connection, the transport layer does not take up the responsibility of retransmission. It is up to applications to handle cases where a packet does not reach its destination because it was dropped in the network.

3. Security: This service is new compared to other services offered by the transport layer. Security services such as authenticity, integrity, and confidentiality are not widely supported. However, in the future, security will be tightly integrated with the stack and will be available widely.

An application has to choose the services it requires from the transport layer. There are advantages and disadvantages in choosing different services. In addition, there may be limitations in the combination of services one can choose. Presently, it is invalid to choose connectionless reliable transport as TCP/IP does not implement such a protocol. The discussion of these is beyond the scope of this book.

Network Layer: The network layer provides connectionless service. The network layer is responsible for routing packets. Routing can be described as the process that determines the path a packet has to traverse to reach the destination. The devices that decide how to route a packet are called "routers"[3]. In order to route the packet, the network layer needs to identify each destination unambiguously. The network layer defines an addressing mechanism. The hosts should conform to the addressing mechanisms to make use of the services offered by the network layer. This is discussed in greater detail in the addressing section (see section on Addressing below).

Data Link Layer: The data link layer is responsible for packet transmission on the physical media. The transmission is between two devices that are physically connected. Examples of data-link layers are Ethernet, Token Ring, and Asynchronous Transfer Mode (ATM).

As described above, each layer in the protocol stack is tasked with a specific function and the layering must be preserved. The application layer cannot talk to the network layer directly. It has to talk through the transport layer. Layering is also preserved between hosts as shown in Figure 2.2.

---

3. In this book we use the term "host" in the context of an end system. The host generates traffic but is not involved in any routing decisions. Routers, on the other hand, normally do not generate traffic but instead forward traffic. The term "gateways" normally refers to a router.

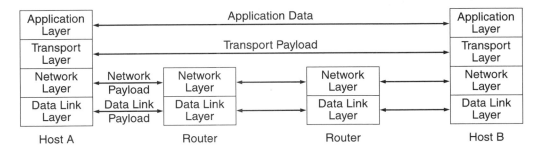

Figure 2.2   Communication between layers.

Data Flow

The data flow from source to destination is as shown in Figure 2.3.

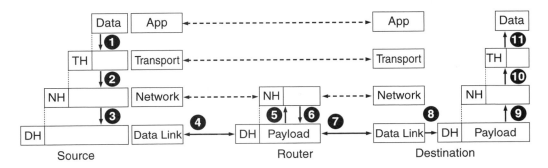

Figure 2.3   Data flow.

For the purposes of the discussion, let us assume that the transport protocol is TCP and the network protocol is IP.

1. An application on the source host sends the data that needs to be transmitted to the destination over the socket interface to the transport layer. The application identifies the destination it wishes to communicate with. The destination includes the host and an application on the host.

2. The transport layer, in this case TCP, gets this data and appends a transport header, in this case a TCP header, to the payload, the data, and sends this down to the network layer. The fields in the TCP header help in providing the services requested by the application.

3. The network layer receives the payload from the transport layer. This consists of the data and the TCP header. It appends an IP header to this payload. It then sends the payload plus IP header down to the data link layer. In addition, the network layer also identifies the neighbor the packet needs to be sent to en route to the destination.

4. The data link layer then appends a data link header to the payload from the network layer. The data link layer identifies the physical address of the next hop the packet should be sent to and sends the packet.

5. The data link layer on the next hop receives the packet, strips the data link header from the packet and sends the packet up to the network layer.

6. The network layer looks at the network header and decides the next hop the packet needs to be sent to en route to the destination and invokes the data link layer.

7. The data link layer appends the data link header to the payload and transmits the packet to the next hop.

8. Procedures 6 and 7 are repeated till the packet reaches the destination.

9. Upon reaching the destination, the data link layer strips the data link header from the packet and sends it up to the network layer.

10. The network layer then strips the network header from the packet and sends it up to the transport layer.

11. The transport layer then checks the transport header to guarantee that the application is being serviced properly, strips the transport header, identifies the application to which this packet is destined, and sends it up to the application.

12. The application on the destination receives the data that was sent to it by the application on the source.

Network Layer

In the TCP/IP protocol suite, there are two network protocols—IPv4 and IPv6. These protocols are discussed to an extent that provides good context to understand IP Security.

IPv4

IPv4 (Internet Protocol version 4) is the most prevalent network layer protocol today. It uses a simple addressing scheme and provides connectionless service. IPv4 has a very mature routing infrastructure.

Addressing

Addressing is one of the important components of a network layer protocol. IPv4 identifies each host[4] by a 32-bit address. This address is normally represented in the form A.B.C.D. This notation is commonly referred to as dotted decimal notation where each symbol is a byte (8 bits). An example of an IPv4 address is 128.127.126.125. This representation is chosen instead of a flat number space because it imparts hierarchy to addressing and also is easier to perceive.

An IP address has two parts—a network ID and a host ID. The network ID logically groups a set of IP addresses together. The grouping is required to provide efficient routing and other services, such as IP broadcast.[5] The network ID part of an IP address is obtained by logical AND of the IP address with the network mask. The network mask is always a contiguous bit of 1s. Examples of network masks are 255.255.255.0, 255.255.0.0, and 255.254.0.0. In these examples the leftmost (starting from the most significant bit) 24, 16, and 15 bits are 1's respectively. The network ID for the IP address 128.127.126.125 with the example network masks is 128.127.126, 128.127, and 128.126 respectively. This is obtained by logical AND of the network masks with the IP address as shown in Figure 2.4. An IP address is always represented along with its network mask. There are two representations: 128.127.126.125/ 255.255.255.0 or 128.127.126.125/24. Both representations have the same meaning, i.e., the network ID are 24 most-significant bits of the IP address.

Host Address					Network Mask					Subnet			
128	127	126	125	and	0x FF	0x FF	0x FF	0x 0	=	128	127	126	0
128	127	126	125	and	0x FF	0x FF	0x 00	0x 0	=	128	127	0	0
128	127	126	125	and	0x FF	0x FE	0x 0	0x 0	=	128	126	0	0

Figure 2.4   Relationship between subnets and network masks.

---

4.   A host is an entity that is involved in the communication.
5.   Broadcast is the ability to communicate with a set of hosts without duplicating the packets. In this case, the network ID part of the destination address is used to identify the destination and hence all nodes with the same network ID get the packet.

To realize the importance of network mask, let us consider an analogy of how telephone numbers are allocated and maintained. The telephone numbers in the United States have a well-known structure (xxx)-yyy-zzzz where xxx represents the area code, yyy represents the city code, and zzzz identifies the line within that city. It is important to provide the structure for the purposes of routing and telephone number allocation. Imagine what would happen if there was no such structure. How will one know if a number is already allocated or not? Moreover, if someone wants to call a number from California, how does the switch in California know how to reach all the telephones in the U.S., which is 10^{10}! IP address allocation is no different. It allows logical grouping of addresses to ease the task of address allocation, routing, and providing other services.

An organization that gets a network ID can define subnets recursively. Let us go back to the telephone address allocation. For the purpose of illustration, let us say that the top 3 digits (xxx) are allocated to a state. It is up to the state to use the lower 7 bits. The state uses 3 out of the 7 digits to identify the town. The town uses 4 digits that are left to identify the telephone of a particular house. In this case, there is a three-level address allocation—state, city, and house. Network address allocation is no different. An organization that gets a chunk of network addresses would like to allocate it to make its routing and traffic separation easy. Various departments may like to have addresses in the same range as they may want to keep some traffic local to their network. For example, if an organization receives a network ID 132.131/255.255, it can use some bits to form its own subnets. Let us say that it uses 8 of the 16 bits to form its own subnet. Then the network mask within the organization is 255.255.255.0. However, this is oblivious to the outside world. For the outside world, the network mask for the organization is still 255.255.0.0.

You may be wondering why it is necessary to define subnets. The following are the advantages of defining subnets:

1. The routing table size in the Internet core decreases because it is unnecessary to specify each host in an organization. A router can be delegated the task of forwarding a packet originating or destined to any host on the subnet. Normally, at least one router is assigned for each subnet.

2. Subnets are used to contain some types of IP traffic, such as IP broadcasts. There are packets that are sent to all the hosts on a subnet. If an organization has a network ID 125.126, a broadcast

packet would be sent to all the 65,000 hosts! If subnets are used, these packets are restricted just to the subnet.

IP supports three kinds of addresses—unicast, multicast, and anycast. Unicast addressing is where an IP address is uniquely a host. Any IP address in the range 1.0.0.1 to 223.255.255.255 represents a unicast address. Address range 224.0.0.0 to 239.255.255.255 represents a multicast address and address range 240.0.0.0 to 247.255.255.255 represents an anycast address, and 248.0.0.0 to 255.255.255.255 is reserved for future use. Anycast address is still a research topic, and is not covered in this book.

As there are 32 bits in an IPv4 address, one can address up to 2^{32} hosts[6]! One would imagine that this should be more than sufficient to address hosts in the Internet. However, the Internet is running out of address spaces and this has led to the design of IPv6.

IPv4 Header   The IPv4 header is shown in Figure 2.5

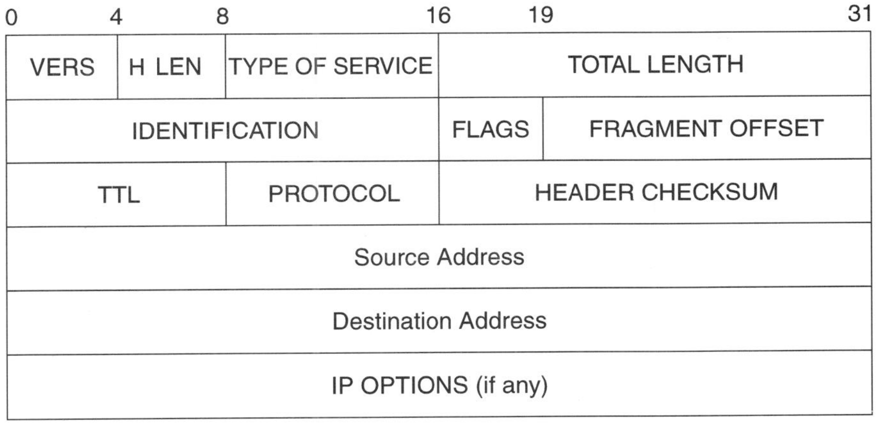

Figure 2.5   IPv4 header.

The usage of various fields is described below.[7]

Version field: This 4-bit field is used to indicate the version. This value is 4 for IPv4. The version field is normally used for backward com-

---

6.   In reality, the number of addressable hosts is less than this number because some addresses are reserved.

7.   We describe in detail only those fields that are used by IPSec. For example, the options field is not discussed in detail.

patibility. When new versions are defined, they may be required to inter-operate with the legacy systems.

Header length: The header length indicates the length of the header in 32 bits (4 bytes). This limits the maximum length of the IPv4 header to 60 bytes. This is one of the limitations of IPv4 that led to the development of a newer version of IP discussed in the next section.

Type Of Service (TOS): TOS is used to indicate the traffic requirements of the packet. This field is currently under review at the IETF.

Length: The length of the datagram in bytes (including the header) in the network byte order.[8] THIS FIELD INDICATES THE SIZE OF THE DATAGRAM TO THE NETWORK LAYER AT THE RECEIVING END.

Identification: The 16-bit identification field is used to uniquely identify an IP datagram. The term IP datagram refers to the transport payload plus IP header, and is used in the context of end hosts. The identification field is used mostly in the context of fragmentation that is described later. The identification field is used to uniquely identify which IP packets belong to an IP datagram.

Flags: Only 2 out of the 3 bits in the flag are defined. The first bit is used to specify not to fragment the IP packet. When this is set, a router sends back a control message to the host indicating its MTU (Maximum Transfer Unit). This bit is used in Path MTU. This is a process by which the end host discovers what size the IP packets it generates should be so that the packets do not get fragmented en route to the destination. This is necessary because fragmentation is detrimental to the operation of the network. The transport layer has to send the entire datagram if a fragment is lost. The second bit is used to indicate if the packet is the last fragment of a fragmented datagram or if there are more to follow. This bit is used in reassembling fragmented packets.

Fragmentation offset: This field indicates the offset of the IP packet in the IP datagram. The utility of this field is discussed in the fragmentation section.

Time To Live (TTL): This field is used to avoid packet looping and also to administratively scope the transmission of a packet. The host sets this field to a certain default value and each router along the path decrements this field by 1. If a router sees a packet with a TTL of 1, it drops the packet. This is crucial in case of routing loops as the packet will be roaming in the network forever if nobody drops it.

---

8.   In the rest of the book, the network byte order is assumed. There are two types of representation of integers— big endian and little endian. In big endian, the most significant byte of an integer is in the most significant byte (Motorola chips use big endian). In little endian, the most significant byte of an integer is in the least significant byte (Intel). Network byte order corresponds to big endian.

Protocol: This 8-bit field is used to indicate the transport protocol carried by this IP packet. This field is used by the end host to demultiplex the packet among various transport protocols.

Checksum: The checksum is calculated on the IP header and is used to guarantee the integrity of the IP header. The checksum is not a cryptographic checksum and can be easily forged.

Source address: This 32-bit field indicates the IP address of the source that generated this packet.

Destination address: This 32-bit field indicates the IP address of the destination host.

Options: An IP header can optionally carry additional information. As options are not important in understanding IP security, they are not discussed in this book.

IPv6

IPv4 limits the address space to 32 bits. To avoid the address crunch, the IETF started working on the next version of IP and called it IPv6. One of the main advantages of IPv6 is that it increased the address space from 32 bits to 128 bits (16 bytes).

Other modifications include:

- No fragmentation support for transit packets in routers. The end hosts are required to perform PMTU now.

- Richer options support. The options are treated as separate headers instead of being part of the IP header. This is called header chaining and is more flexible. In this case, the IP extension headers (options) are inserted between the IP header and the transport layer header.

Addressing   Conceptually, both the address and subneting of IPv6 are similar to that of IPv4. IPv6 address is 128 bits long and their representation is different. Instead of the dotted decimal notation used in IPv4, IPv6 uses a different notation—hexadecimal numbers separated by colons:

0123:4567:89AB:CDEF:0123:4567:89ab:cdef

There are a number of variations to compress the address. The reader is encouraged to refer to IPv6 addressing architecture IETF documents for a more detailed discussion.

The concept of network mask and subnet in IPv6 is similar to what exists in IPv4. IPv6 implements a much richer hierarchy for addressing to ease the problem of routing and addressing.

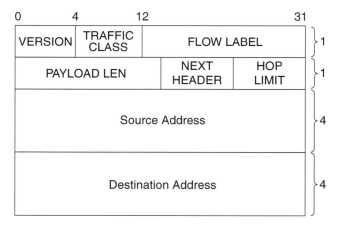

Figure 2.6   IPv6 header.

IPv6 Header   The IPv6 header is shown in Figure 2.6.
The usage of various fields is described below.

Version: This 4-bit field indicates the version. For IPv6 this value is 6.
Traffic Class: This 8-bit field is used to indicate the traffic requirements of the packet and is similar to the TOS field in the IPv4 header.
Flow Label: This 20-bit field is still experimental and it is still not clear how this will be used in the future. One possible usage is to identify a flow that requires special processing by the routers.
Payload Length: This 16-bit field indicates the length of the payload excluding the IPv6 header.
Next Header: This 8-bit field is similar to the next protocol field in IPv4 header, the only difference being that the option header may appear in this field unlike IPv4.
Hop Limit: This 8-bit field is the same as TTL field in the IPv4 header.
Source and Destination Address: These 128-bit fields represent the source and destination IPv6 addresses respectively.

Extension Headers   As mentioned before, IPv6 defines option headers to provide the capabilities that IPv4 option fields provide. These are called extensions. The option extensions are inserted between the IPv6 header and the transport header as shown in Figure 2.7.

IPV 6 HEADER	OPTION 1 HEADER	OPTION 2 HEADER	TRANSPORT HEADER	DATA

Figure 2.7   IPv6 header with options.

Each option header is assigned a unique protocol ID and is encoded using the same format as shown in Figure 2.8.

OPTION TYPE	OPTION DATA LEN	OPTION DATA	. . .

Figure 2.8   IPv6 options format.

There are two kinds of options—hop by hop and destination-based. Hop-by-hop options can change along the path and are normally included immediately following the IPv6 header. Destination-based options do not change along the path and are inserted after the hop-by-hop options.

Fragmentation

Fragmentation is the process whereby an IP packet is fragmented into multiple IP packets at the source or in a router. After fragmentation, each packet is transmitted independently and is reassembled at the destination. The question that immediately comes to mind is: Why should we fragment IP packets?

The IP layer accepts any transport layer payloads. The transport layer payloads can be of any size (restricted only by the buffer limitations on the system). The IP layer does not have the ability to restrict the data that is passed to it from the upper layers. However, as the network layer (IP) has to transmit the packet over a physical interface, there are limitations with respect to the size of the packet it can transmit. These limitations arise because of the physical limitations of the medium over which a packet is transmitted. For example, over Ethernet the maximum size of the packet cannot exceed 1518 bytes. If the IP layer's transport payload is more than 1480 bytes (assuming there are no options), it has to fragment the packet before it is transmitted. Otherwise, the length of the packet will exceed 1518 bytes—1480 + 20 bytes for IP header + 14 bytes for Ethernet layer header + 4 bytes of CRC used for detecting errors.

The network layer packets can also be fragmented in any router where there is a mismatch in the maximum length of the packets between two physical layers. For example, the incoming interface can be a token ring that has a maximum packet size of 4096 and the outgoing interface can be Ethernet that has a maximum packet size of 1518. If the IP packet coming in on the token ring is greater than 1500 bytes, the router has to fragment the packets even though it did not generate the packet.

On the destination, the IP layer has to reassemble all the fragmented packets before it passes the payload to the transport layer. Referring to Figure 2.3, the transport layer on the destination should see the same information that was passed from the transport layer down to the network layer on the source. Hence, it is up to the IP layer to reassemble all the fragmented packets, construct the transport payload, and pass it up to the transport layer.

The IP layer achieves this process of fragmentation and reassembly by using the flags, length, and fragmentation offset fields in the IP header.

Fragmenting a packet is considered detrimental to the operation of the network. This is because, even if one packet is lost, the transport payload has to be retransmitted by the reliable transport layer as the IP layer does not cache packets. The IP layer avoids fragmentation by monitoring the MTU along the path from the source to the destination. This process is called Path MTU discovery or PMTU. After the IP layer discovers the PMTU, it never sends a packet that exceeds the PMTU.

ICMP

ICMP (Internet Control Message Protocol) is used to ensure the proper operation of the network and for debugging. The protocol runs on top of a network protocol such as IPv4 or IPv6.

ICMP messages are generated both by hosts and routers to monitor the network and to ensure proper operation of the network. For example, if a router does not have a route to a particular network, it sends an ICMP message back to the host indicating the network is unreachable. If the router drops the packet without any indication, monitoring the network becomes a nightmare. ICMP is used to determine if a host is reachable or not. ICMP is used in PMTU discovery. If a router needs to fragment a packet but the *do not fragment* bit is set, then the router sends back an ICMP message to host indicating the MTU of its link so that the host can generate packets whose size does not exceed this MTU.

Multicast

IP also provides the ability to send a packet to multiple hosts anywhere on the Internet. This is a special case of broadcasting where only interested hosts receive a packet. Consider the example of pay-per-view broadcast. If a cable company intends to telecast a program over the Internet to all its subscribers, it has three options:

- Telecast individually to each subscriber. This process has a very high overhead as the same data is duplicated to all the subscribers. It has lot of undesired side effects. It increases the Internet traffic substantially and also increases tremendously the load on the server that is distributing data.

- Telecast by sending a broadcast to the whole Internet. This process is unacceptable because even nonsubscribers get to see the pay-per-view program. Moreover, Internet-level broadcast is very bad.

- Telecast only to subscribers by using a technique called multicast. Multicast is an intelligent packet distribution mechanism where only subscribers get the packet. The data is distributed on only those links with subscribers. The traffic is delivered only to those nodes that have subscribed to the traffic.

Multicast packets have the same format as unicast IP packets. However, the destination field in the IP header has a multicast address and not a unicast address. The obvious question that comes to mind is, How do you know where to send the packet if you cannot uniquely identify a host? That is the beauty of multicast. There is support from the routing layer that has the knowledge of the hosts that are listening on a particular multicast address. A detailed discussion of multicast is out of the scope of this book. In fact, multicast discussion is a whole topic in itself.

Transport Layer

The TCP/IP protocol suite implements two protocols at the transport layer—Transmission Control Protocol (TCP) and User Datagram Protocol (UDP).

TCP is a connection-oriented protocol ensuring ordered and guaranteed delivery of packets. It has mechanisms built into it to provide these services to the application layer. In addition, TCP also implements mechanisms such as flow control, that ensures that the destination is not bombarded with packets. UDP is a connectionless protocol that does not ensure either guaranteed or ordered delivery of the packets nor does it ensure flow control. The choice of using TCP or UDP is entirely up to the application.

Although we will not discuss the TCP and UDP headers in detail, we will briefly discuss two fields that are present in both the headers—the source port and the destination port. These two fields are critical in identifying how to process the data once the destination receives it.

The TCP/IP protocol suite identifies the application a packet is destined to by a five tuple: <source address, destination address, source port, destination port, protocol>. This tuple must be unique for each application running on a host. We have already discussed the source and destination address fields. These fields are set in the network header. The source and destination ports are 16-bit fields set in the transport header. The source port is allocated by the source host and the destination is allocated by the destination host. For an application to communicate with another application on another host, it needs to know three things—the address of the destination, the port number on which the application is running, and the protocol over which to communicate. For example, most Web servers are listening on port 80 and use TCP protocol. An application binds to the source and destination port and also specifies the transport protocol to use for the transmission. The transport protocol uses this tuple to identify the application that receives the data.

Domain Name System

Domain Name System (DNS) is a simple and scalable directory system for the Internet. Its most important function is to translate a machine name that is in the form www.xyz.com into an IP address. It is not possible for humans to remember hundreds of addresses, particularly when there are no semantics associated with the address. Also, IP addresses are allocated dynamically and hence remembering IP addresses may be meaningless. On the other hand, the network layer can handle only addresses. This necessitates a scalable system that can translate a name to an IP address.

DNS achieves this by defining a domain name hierarchy. There is the concept of a root. The root server address is well known. In fact, there are few well-known root servers. Under the root there are a few well-defined domains as shown in Figure 2.9.

Under each of these well-known domains exists one or more organizations belonging to that domain. In our example, com domain is registered under the root server and the company xyz is registered under com domain. Registering implies that the organization is running a domain name server that can answer to queries.

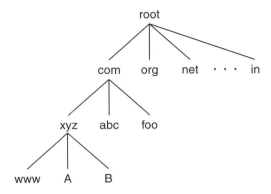

Figure 2.9   DNS hierarchy.

When a client wishes to talk to a host, it requests the resolver (software that resolves the domain name to an IP address) to resolve the domain name to an IP address. For example, when you enter www.xyz.com in your browser, the browser requests the resolver to map www.xyz.com to an IP address. The resolver goes through a well- defined process to resolve the domain name to an IP address. This algorithm is beyond the scope of this book. After the domain name is resolved, the client is ready to communicate with the www.xyz.com Web server.

In addition to resolving DNS names, DNS is also used to resolve the mail host, that is, where to send all the mail destined to the company xyz.com. DNS is also being enhanced to perform other directory services. The reader is urged to refer to it for a better understanding of DNS and its capabilities.

Security—at What Level?

In today's Internet, there are a lot of protocols designed to secure traffic at various levels in the network. It depends on the security requirements of the application and the user to decide where in the stack security should be implemented. Irrespective of where in the stack security is implemented, the following basic services have to be provided:

- Key management (This includes negotiation of keys and storage of keys.)
- Confidentiality
- Nonrepudiation

- Integrity/authentication
- Authorization

Depending on where in the stack the security is implemented, it is possible to provide some or all of the services above. In some cases, it does make sense to provide some capabilities at one layer and other capabilities at a different layer.

This section discusses the advantages and disadvantages of providing security at various layers in the stack.

Application Layer

Application-level security has to be implemented in end hosts. Providing security at the application layer has the following advantages:

- Executing in the context of the user enables easy access to user credentials such as private keys.
- Complete access to the data the user wants to protect. This simplifies the task of providing services such as nonrepudiation.
- An application can be extended without having to depend on the operating system to provide these services. Normally, applications have no control over what gets implemented in the operating system.
- Application understands the data and can provide appropriate security.

The downside to application layer security is that the security mechanisms have to be designed independently for each application. This implies existing applications have to be enhanced to provide security. As each application has to define its own security mechanisms, there is a greater probability of making mistakes and hence opening up security holes for attacks.

In implementing security mechanisms in applications, applications integrate with a system providing the security mechanisms. Examples of such systems are PGP, Kerberos, and Secure Shell. These systems are application-level protocols that provide the capability of key negotiation and other security services. Applications are enhanced to call into this system to use their security mechanisms. One example is the e-mail clients that use PGP to provide e-mail security. In this case, the e-mail clients are extended the following capabilities:

- ability to look up public keys in a local database that correspond to a particular user,
- ability to provide security services such as encryption/decryption, nonrepudiation, and authentication for e-mail messages.

Applications should design their own security mechanisms when their needs are specific and they cannot depend on the lower layers to provide those services. One such example is nonrepudiation. It is difficult for lower layer to provide nonrepudiation services as they do not have access to the data.

Transport Layer

Providing security at the transport layer has a definite advantage over the application-layer security as it does not mandate enhancements to each application. Existing applications get security services seamlessly.

However, obtaining the user context gets complicated. In order to provide user-specific services, assumptions are made that a single user is using the system, which is becoming a popular paradigm. Like application-level security, transport-layer security can only be implemented on an end system.

Transport-layer security is protocol specific. Transport Layer Security (TLS) is a protocol that provides security services such as authentication, integrity, and confidentiality on top of TCP. TLS needs to maintain context for a connection and is not currently implemented over UDP as UDP does not maintain any context. As the security mechanism is transport-protocol specific, security services such as key management may be duplicated for each transport protocol.

The World Wide Web currently provides security services using TLS. However, if security services were implemented at the network layer, this can be moved down to the network layer. Another limitation of transport-layer security as it is currently defined is that the applications still need modification to request security services from the transport layer.

Network Layer

Implementing security at this layer has many advantages. First off, the overheads of key negotiation decrease considerably. This is because multiple transport protocols and applications can share the key management infrastructure provided by the network layer. Also, if security is implemented at lower layers, fewer applications need changes. It reduces the explosion in the implementation of security protocols at the higher layer. If security is implemented at higher layers, each application has to design its own security mechanism. This is overkill and the probability of someone making a mistake is much higher. Also, security is provided seamlessly for any transport protocol.

One of the most useful features of network layer security is the ability to build VPNs and intranets. Because VPNs and intranets are subnet based, and network layer supports subnet-based security, it is easy to implement VPNs and intranets.

The disadvantage of implementing security at the network layer is the difficulty in handling issues such as nonrepudiation of data. This is better handled in higher layers. It is more difficult to exercise control on a per user basis on a multiuser machine when security is implemented at network layer. However, mechanisms can be provided to perform user-based security on end hosts. On the routers, there is no context of user and this problem does not arise.

IP Security, the focus of this book, provides security at the network layer. IPSec is the only protocol that can secure all and any kind of Internet traffic. IPSec also allows per flow or per connection security and thus allows for very fine-grained security control.

Data Link Layer

If there is a dedicated link between two hosts/routers and all the traffic needs to be encrypted for the fear of snooping, one can use hardware devices for encryption.

The advantage of this solution is speed. However, this solution is not scalable and works well only on dedicated links. Moreover, the two entities involved in communication have to be physically connected.

This type of model is useful in automatic teller machines where all the machines are connected via dedicated links to a central office. If ATM machines were connected to an IP network instead of dedicated secure links, the data link layer security would not suffice and one would have to move up one layer to provide security services.

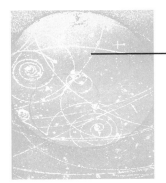

IP Security Overview

IP Packets have no inherent security. It is relatively easy to forge the addresses of IP packets, modify the contents of IP packets, replay old packets, and inspect the contents of IP packets in transit. Therefore, there is no guarantee that IP datagrams received are (1) from the claimed sender (the source address in the IP header); (2) that they contain the original data that the sender placed in them; or (3) that the original data was not inspected by a third party while the packet was being sent from source to destination. IPSec is a method of protecting IP datagrams. This protection takes the form of data origin authentication, connectionless data integrity authentication, and data content confidentiality.

IPSec provides a standard, robust, and extensible mechanism in which to provide security to IP and upper-layer protocols (e.g., UDP or TCP). A default, mandatory-to-implement suite of algorithms is defined to assure interoperability between different implementations, and it is relatively straightforward to add new algorithms without breaking interoperability.

IPSec protects IP datagrams by defining a method of specifying the traffic to protect, how that traffic is to be protected, and to whom the traffic is sent. IPSec can protect packets between hosts, between network security gateways (e.g., routers or firewalls), or between hosts and security gateways. Since an IPSec-protected datagram is, itself, just another IP packet, it is possible to nest security services and provide, for example, end-to-end authentication between hosts and send that IPSec-protected data through a tunnel which is, itself, protected by security gateways using IPSec.

The method of protecting IP datagrams or upper-layer protocols is by using one of the IPSec protocols, the Encapsulating Security Payload (ESP) or the Authentication Header (AH). AH provides proof-of-data origin on received packets, data integrity, and antireplay protection. ESP provides all that AH provides in addition to optional data confidentiality. Since ESP provides all that AH provides, one may ask, "Why use AH?" That's a good question, and is the topic of debate in the security community. The debate has shown no signs of subsiding though and AH may be deprecated in the future. One subtle difference between the two is the scope of coverage of authentication. This will be discussed more fully in later chapters.

It should be noted that the ultimate security provided by AH or ESP is dependent on the cryptographic algorithms applied by them. Mandatory-to-implement algorithms are defined for conformance testing and to insure interoperability among implementations. These algorithms are generally secure, although recent advances in cryptography and the continued demonstration of Moore's law (the observation that every 18 months computing power doubles) continue to whittle away at the effective security of ciphers. The Digital Encryption Standard (DES) has deprecated for just this reason. The new Advanced Encryption Standard (AES) is taking its place.

The security services that IPSec provides requires shared keys to perform authentication and/or confidentiality. A mechanism to manually add keys for these services is mandatory to implement. This ensures interoperability of the base IPSec protocols. Of course, manual key addition scales poorly so a standard method of dynamically authenticating IPSec peers, negotiating security services, and generating shared keys is defined. This key management protocol is called IKE—the Internet Key Exchange.

The shared keys used with IPSec are for either a symmetric cipher (when confidentiality is needed) or for a keyed MAC (for data integrity) or for both. IPSec must be fast and existing public key technologies, such as RSA or DSS, are too slow to operate on a packet-by-packet basis. Presently, public key technology is limited to initial authentication during key exchange.

The Architecture

The Architecture Document for IPSec, RFC2401, defines the base architecture upon which all implementations are built. It defines the security services provided by IPSec, how and where they can be used, how packets are constructed and processed, and the interaction of IPSec processing with policy.

The IPSec protocols—AH and ESP—can be used to protect either an entire IP payload or the upper-layer protocols of an IP payload. This distinction is handled by considering two different "modes" of IPSec (Figure 3.1). Transport mode is used to protect upper-layer protocols; tunnel mode is used to protect entire IP datagrams. In transport mode, an IPSec header is inserted between the IP header and the upper-layer protocol header; in tunnel mode the entire IP packet to be protected is encapsulated in another IP datagram and an IPSec header is inserted between the outer and inner IP headers. Both IPSec protocols, AH and ESP, can operate in either transport mode or tunnel mode.

Because of the method of construction, transport mode can only be used to protect packets where the communications endpoint is also the cryptographic endpoint. Tunnel mode may be used in place of transport mode, and in addition may be used by security gateways to provide security services on behalf of other networked entities (for example, a virtual private network). In this latter case, the communications endpoints are those specified in the inner header that's protected and the cryptographic endpoints are those of the outer IP header. A security gateway decapsulates the inner IP packet upon the conclusion of IPSec processing and forwards the packet to its ultimate destination.

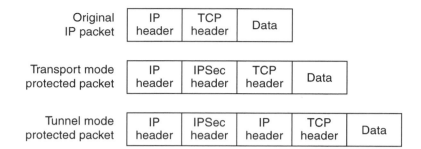

Figure 3.1   IP packets protected by IPSec in transport mode and tunnel mode

As noted, IPSec may be implemented in end systems or on security gateways such as routers and firewalls. Typically this is done by directly modifying the IP stack to support IPSec natively. When access to the IP stack of a machine is not possible, IPSec may be implemented as a "Bump in the Stack" (BITS) or "Bump in the Wire" (BITW). The former is typically a shim that extracts and inserts packets from the IP stack. The latter is typically an external, dedicated crypto device that may be independently addressable.

Security Association

To properly process IPSec packets it is necessary to have a way to associate security services and a key, with the traffic to be protected, and the remote peer with whom IPSec traffic is being exchanged (in other words, how to protect the traffic, what traffic to protect, and with whom the protection is performed). Such a construct is called a "Security Association" (SA). An SA contains the state necessary to do IPSec processing on an IP packet.

An IPSec SA is unidirectional. That is, it defines security services for one direction, either inbound for packets received by the entity, or outbound, for packets that are sent by the entity. SAs are identified by a Security Parameter Index (SPI)—which exists in IPSec protocol headers, the IPSec protocol value—either AH or ESP, and the destination address to which the SA applies—which dictates the direction. Typically, SAs exist in pairs, one in each direction. They may be created manually or dynamically. SAs reside in the Security Association Database (SADB).

When created manually, an SA has no lifetime. It exists until it is manually deleted. When created dynamically, an SA may have a lifetime associated with it. This lifetime is generally negotiated between the IPSec peers by the key management protocol. A lifetime is important because the amount of traffic protected by a key, or similarly the time that a key remains active and in use, must be carefully managed. Excessive use of a key can give an attacker an entry into your work.

Policy

The IPSec Architecture defines the granularity by which a user may specify his or her policy. This allows for certain traffic to be identified coarsely and have one level of security applied while allowing other traffic to be identified more finely and have a completely different level of security applied. (Figure 3.2) For example, one may specify IPSec policy on a network security gateway that requires all traffic between its local protected subnet and the subnet of a remote peer be encrypted with AES and authenticated with HMAC-MD5, while all telnet traffic to a mail server from the remote subnet requires encryption with 3DES and authentication with HMAC-SHA, and all Web traffic to another server requires encryption with IDEA and authentication with HMAC-RIPEMD.

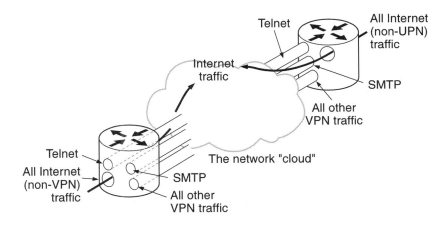

Figure 3.2   IPSec protected flows between separate networks

IPSec policy is maintained in the Security Policy Database (SPD). Each entry of the SPD defines the traffic to be protected, how to protect it, and with whom the protection is shared. For each packet entering or leaving the IP stack, the SPD must be consulted for the possible application of security. An SPD entry may define one of three actions to take upon traffic match: *discard*—do not let this packet in or out; *bypass*—do not apply security services to an outbound packet and do not expect security on an inbound packet; and *protect*—apply security services on outbound packets and require inbound packets to have security services applied. SPD entries that define an action of *protect* will point to an SA or bundle of SAs that identifies the state used to protect the packet.

IP traffic is mapped to IPSec policy by *selectors*. A selector identifies some component of traffic and may be either coarse or fine. IPSec selectors are: destination IP address; source IP address; name; upper-layer protocol; source and destination ports; and a data sensitivity level (if an IPSec system also provides for flow security). The values of these selectors may be specific entries, ranges, or "opaque." A selector in a policy specification may be opaque because that information may not be available to the system at that time. For example, a security gateway that has an IPSec tunnel with a remote security gateway peer may specify that (some of) the traffic that goes through that tunnel is IPSec traffic between two hosts behind the gateways. In this case, neither gateway would have access to, say, the upper-layer protocol or ports, since they would be encrypted by the end hosts. Opaque may also be used as a wild card, indicating the selector applies to any value.

If an SPD entry defines *protect* as an action and does not point to any existing SAs in the SADB, those SAs will have to be created before any traffic may pass. If this rule is applied to inbound traffic and the SA does not exist, the IPSec Architecture requires the packets to be dropped; if this rule is applied to outbound traffic the SAs can be created dynamically using the Internet Key Exchange (IKE).

The IPSec Architecture defines the interaction of the SPD, the SADB, with the IPSec processing functions—encapsulate, encrypt, integrity protect and decapsulate, decrypt, integrity verify—and defines how various IPSec implementations may exist. It does not, though, define how the base IPSec protocols operate. That is left for two different documents, one to define the Encapsulating Security Payload (RFC2406) and one to describe the Authentication Header (RFC2402).

Anti-Replay

Both IPSec protocols provide an antireplay service to prevent against a denial of service attack in which old packets are resent by an attacker to cause the recipient to waste CPU cycles processing them. This protection is not explicitly part of the architecture but is germane to both protocols and, as such, will be described here. IPSec packets are protected against replay attacks by using a sequence number and a sliding receive window. Each IPSec header contains a unique and monotonically increasing sequence number. When a SA is created, the sequence number is initialized to zero and prior to IPSec output processing the value is incremented. New SAs must be created prior to the sequence number wrapping around back to zero—prior to 2^{32} packets since the sequence number is 32 bits long. The receive window can be any size greater than 32 but 64 is recommended. For performance reasons, the window size should be a multiple of the size of a word on the computer on which IPSec is being implemented.

The left end of the window represents the sequence number of the beginning of the window and the right end is *window-size* packets in the future. Received packets must be new and must fall either inside the window or to the right of the window, otherwise they are dropped. A packet is new if it has not yet been seen in the window. If a packet is received that is to the right of the window, it may be dropped if it fails an authenticity test (more on that later). If it passes the authenticity check the window is advanced, to the right, to encompass that packet. Note that packets may be received out of order and still be properly processed. Also note that a packet received too late—that is, received after a valid packet with a sequence number greater than the size of the window—will be dropped.

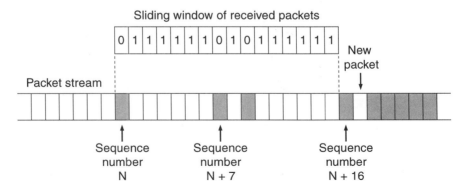

Figure 3.3   A 16 bit sliding replay window

The replay window in Figure 3.3 is only 16 bits and is therefore illegal, but for the sake of illustration will suit us fine. The left end of the window of Figure 3.3 is at sequence number *N*, the right end is therefore at sequence number $N+15$. Packets N, $N+7$, $N+9$, $N+16$, and $N+18$ onward have not been received. If recently received packet $N+17$ is authenticated the window is advanced such that the right end is at $N+17$ and the left end is at $N+2$. This would cause packet N to be irretrievably lost since it's now to the left of the receive window. Notice, though, that packet $N+7$ can still be received provided that packet $N+23$ is not received and authenticated first.

It's important to note that the window must not be advanced until the packet that would cause its advancement has been authenticated. Doing otherwise would allow an attacker to generate bogus packets with large sequence numbers that would move the window outside the range of valid sequence numbers and cause us to drop valid packets.

Encapsulating Security Payload (ESP)

ESP is the IPSec protocol that provides confidentiality, data integrity, and data source authentication of IP packets, and also provides protection against replay attacks. It does so by inserting a new header—an ESP header—after an IP header (and any IP options) and before the data to be protected, either an upper-layer protocol or an entire IP datagram, and appending an ESP trailer. The location of the ESP header and trailer in an ESP-protected packet are shown in figure 3.4. ESP is a new IP protocol and an ESP packet is identified by the protocol field of an IPv4 header and the "Next Header" field of an IPv6 header. If the value is 50 it's an ESP packet and immediately following the IP header is an ESP header. RFC2406 defines ESP.

An older version of ESP from RFC1827 did not provide data integrity and is considered deprecated by the IPSec Working Group. There were several implementations of RFC1827, but they have all been replaced by the current definition of ESP.

Since ESP provides both confidentiality and authentication, it has multiple algorithms defined in its SA—one for confidentiality called a *cipher*; and the other for authentication called the *authenticator*. Each ESP SA will have at most one cipher and one authenticator. It is possible to define NULL ciphers or NULL authenticators and do ESP without encryption or ESP without authentication respectively, but it is illegal to have both a NULL cipher and a NULL authenticator within a single ESP SA. This is illegal because not only is it a pointless burden on the system, but because it provides no security. One thing that cannot be mentioned enough is that doing something insecure with a security protocol is worse than not doing the security protocol in the first place because of the false sense of security provided. ESP provides security and it should not be used in a patently insecure manner.

The ESP header is not encrypted but a portion of the ESP trailer is. Enough is in clear text, though, to allow for a recipient to process the packet. Since the SPI is used, along with the destination IP address of the IP header of this packet, to identify an SA it must be in the clear. In addition, the sequence number and authentication data are also in the clear (this is explained further in chapter 5). This is due to the specified order of processing of ESP packets: First verify the sequence number, then verify the integrity of the data, then decrypt the data. Since decryption is last, the sequence number and authentication data must be in the clear.

Figure 3.4   An ESP-protected IP packet

All encryption algorithms used with ESP must operate in cipher block chaining (CBC) mode. CBC requires that the amount of data to encrypt be a multiple of the block size of the cipher. This requirement is met by adding padding to the end of the data when necessary to encrypt. The pad becomes part of the cipher text of the packet and is stripped off by the recipient after IPSec processing. If the data is already a multiple of the block size of the cipher, padding need not be added. Compliant implementations are required to support the Data Encryption Standard (DES).

Ciphers in CBC mode also require an initialization vector (IV) to jump-start the encryption process. This IV is contained in the payload field generally as the first bytes, although it is up to a specific algorithm specification to define where it obtains its IV, and a size of the IV. For instance, when using 3DES-CBC the IV is the first 8 bytes of the protected data field.

As mentioned, ESP is both a header and a trailer—it encapsulates the data it protects. The header portion contains the SPI and sequence number, the trailer contains the padding (if any), an indicator regarding the length of the pad, the next protocol of the data after ESP, and the authentication data. The size of the authentication data is dependent on the authenticator used. Compliant implementations are required to support both HMAC-MD5 and HMAC-SHA as authenticators with an output of 96 bits. You'll note that these two MACs produce different-sized digests though. HMAC-MD5 produces a 128-bit digest while HMAC-SHA produces a 160-bit digest. This is alright because the high-order 96 bits of the digest are used as ESP's authentication data. Ninety-six bits was chosen because it ensured alignment for IPv6.

There was some discussion about the security of truncating the output of a MAC. It has generally been agreed that such a practice is not inherently insecure and may, in fact, increase security. Regardless of the practice of the two required authenticators, new authenticators may be any length and padding is used to enforce alignment.

The ESP specification defines the format of the ESP header, where that header is placed when doing transport mode or tunnel mode, output data processing, input data processing, and other information such as fragmentation and reassembly. The ESP specification imposes requirements on transforms used with ESP but does not specify what those transforms are. That is left to individual transform specifications. Currently there is one document that describes using AES-CBC as the cipher for ESP, and two documents that describe using the truncated output of HMAC-MD5 and HMAC-SHA as the authenticators for ESP. Other cipher documents include Blowfish-CBC, CAST-CBC, 3DES-CBC, and the depricated DES-CBC (all optional to implement).

Authentication Header (AH)

Like ESP, AH provides data integrity, data source authentication, and protection against replay attacks. It does not provide confidentiality. Because of this the AH header is much simpler than ESP; it is merely a header and not a header plus trailer (figure 3.5). In addition, all of the fields in the AH header are in the clear.

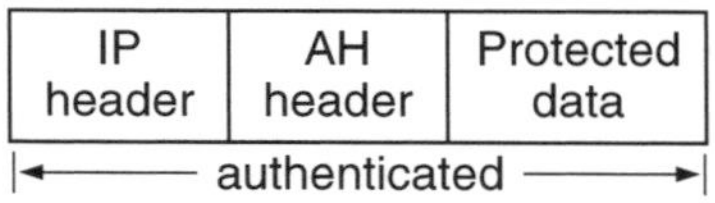

IP header	AH header	Protected data
	← authenticated →	

Figure 3.5   An AH-protected IP Packet

RFC2402 defines the current incarnation of AH while RFC1826 described an older, deprecated version of AH. The important features of AH specified in that RFC remain in the new document—providing data integrity and data source authentication of IP packets—but new features and clarification of some issues raised with RFC1826 were added. For example, antireplay protection is now an integral part of the specification and a definition of using AH in tunnel mode was added. Just as there were several implementations of RFC1827, there were several of RFC1826—usually the same implementations. These deprecated transforms are being replaced by the new suite of IPSec RFCs.

The AH header, like the ESP header, contains an SPI to help locate the SA with which the packet is processed, a sequence number to provide against replay attacks, and an authentication data field to contain the digest from the keyed MAC used to secure the packet. Like ESP, the length of the digest field is defined by the particular transform used. Not too coincidentally, the default, mandatory-to-implement keyed MACs for AH are HMAC-MD5 and HMAC-SHA, both truncated to 96 bits. The same two documents, RFC2403 for HMAC-MD5-96 and RFC2404 for HMAC-SHA-96, used to define how to use these MACs with ESP, are used to define how to use them with AH.

Since AH does not provide confidentiality using a symmetric cipher in CBC mode, there is no explicit padding requirement imposed on it. Some MACs may require padding, for example DES-CBC-MAC, but the technique of addition of the pad is left to the document describing the MAC itself.

The authentication coverage of AH differs from that of ESP. AH authenticates the outer IP header of the IPSec packet. Therefore, the AH document describes the various fields of the IPv4 and IPv6 headers that are mutable—i.e., they may be changed by routers while the packet is in transit from source to destination (this is further explained in chapter 6). These fields must be zeroed prior to computation of the authentication data.

The AH document defines the format of the AH header, where that header is placed when doing transport mode or tunnel mode, output data processing, input data processing, and other information such as handling fragmentation and reassembly.

Internet Key Exchange

Security associations are used with IPSec to define the processing done on a specific IP packet. An outbound packet produces a hit in the SPD and the SPD entry points to one or more SAs—an SA bundle. If there is no SA that instantiates the policy from the SPD it is necessary to create one. That is where the Internet Key Exchange (IKE) comes into play. The whole purpose of IKE is to establish shared security parameters and authenticated keys—in other words, security associations—between IPSec peers.

The IKE protocol is a hybrid of the Oakley and SKEME protocols and operates inside a framework defined by ISAKMP—the Internet Security Association and Key Management Protocol. ISAKMP defines packet formats, retransmission timers, and message construction requirements, in effect, the language. Oakley and SKEME define the steps two peers must take to establish a shared, authenticated key. IKE uses the ISAKMP language to express these and other exchanges.

IKE is actually a general-purpose security exchange protocol and may be used for policy negotiation and establishment of authenticated keying material for a variety of needs—for example, SNMPv3, OSPFv2, etc. The specification of what IKE is being used for is done in a Domain of Interpretation (DOI). There exists a DOI for IPSec, RFC2407, which defines how IKE negotiates IPSec SAs. If and when IKE is used by other protocols, they will each have to define their own DOI.

IKE uses the concept of a security association but the physical construct of an IKE SA is different than an IPSec SA. The IKE SA defines the way in which the two peers communicate; for example, which algorithm to use to encrypt IKE traffic, how to authenticate the remote peer, etc. The IKE SA is then used to produce any number of IPSec SAs between the peers. Therefore, the action that an IPSec implementation takes when an SPD entry has a NULL SADB pointer is to communicate the security requirements from the SPD to IKE and instruct it to establish IPSec SAs.

The IPSec SAs established by IKE may optionally have perfect forward secrecy of the keys and, if desired, also of the peer identity. More than one pair of IPSec SAs may be created at once using a single IKE exchange, and any number of such exchanges may be performed by a single IKE SA. This richness of options makes IKE very extensible but also very complex.

The IKE protocol is performed by each party that will be performing IPSec; the IKE peer is also the IPSec peer. In other words, to create IPSec SAs with a remote entity you speak IKE to that entity not to a different IKE entity. The protocol is a request-response type with an *initiator* and a *responder*. The initiator is the party that is instructed by IPSec to establish some SAs as a result of an outbound packet matching an SPD entry; it initiates the protocol to the responder.

The SPD of IPSec is used to instruct IKE *what* to establish but does not instruct IKE *how* to do so. How IKE establishes the IPSec SAs is based on its own policy settings. IKE defines policy in terms of *protection suites*. Each protection suite must define at least the encryption algorithm, the hash algorithm, the Diffie-Hellman group, and the method of authentication used. IKE's policy database then is the list of all protection suites weighted in order of preference. Since the specific policy suite that the two peers agree upon will dictate how the remainder of their communication is done, this negotiation is the first thing the two IKE peers do.

There is more than one way for two peers to establish a shared secret, but IKE always uses a Diffie-Hellman exchange. The act of doing a Diffie-Hellman exchange is not negotiable, but the parameters to use are. IKE borrows five groups from the Oakley document; three are traditional exchanges doing exponentiation modulo a large prime, and two are elliptic curve groups. The Diffie-Hellman exchange and the establishment of a shared secret is the second step of the IKE protocol.

Upon completion of the Diffie-Hellman exchange the two peers have a shared secret but it is not authenticated. They may use it—or in the case of IKE, a secret derived from it—to protect their communication, but they have no guarantee that the remote peer is, in fact, someone they trust. The next step in the IKE exchange is authentication of the Diffie-Hellman shared secret and, therefore, authentication of the IKE SA itself. There are five methods of authentication defined in IKE: preshared keys; digital signature using the Digital Signature Standard; digital signature using the RSA public key algorithm; an encrypted nonce exchange using RSA; and a "revised" method of authentication with encrypted nonces that is subtly different than the other encrypted nonce method. (A nonce is merely a random number. Each party in an IKE exchange contributes a nonce to the state of the exchange. This concept will be explained fully in Chapter 7.)

Creation of the IKE SA is referred to as phase one. Once phase one is completed, phase two—creation of IPSec SASs—may commence. There are two exchanges that can be performed for phase one, a *Main mode* exchange or an *Aggressive mode* exchange. *Aggressive mode* is faster but *Main mode* is more flexible. There is a single phase two exchange, *Quick mode*. This exchange negotiates IPSec SAs under the protection of the IKE SA, which was created from a phase one exchange.

The keys used for the IPSec SAs are, by default, derived from the IKE secret state. Pseudo-random nonces are exchanged in *Quick mode* and hashed with the secret state to generate keys and guarantee that all SAs have unique keys. All such keys do not have the property of perfect forward secrecy (PFS) since they're all derived from the same "root" key, the IKE shared secret. To provide PFS, Diffie-Hellman public values, and the group from which they're derived, are exchanged along with the nonces and IPSec SA negotiation parameters. The resultant secret is used to generate the IPSec SA keys to guarantee PFS.

To properly construct the IPSec SA, the initiator of the protocol must specify to IKE which selectors from his SPD matched the traffic. This information is exchanged in *Quick mode* using identity payloads and is used to constrain what traffic can be protected by these SAs. At the time of this writing the selector suites in the IPSec Architecture Document was richer than that allowed by the IKE protocol. The IKE protocol cannot express port ranges, nor can it express the "all except" construct—for example, "all TCP ports greater than 1024 except 6000." It is expected that the specifics of selector indication in *Quick mode* exchanges will be changed to allow the full expression of possible selectors.

Upon completion of a *Quick mode* the IKE SA returns to a quiescent state and awaits further instruction from IPSec or further communication from the peer. The IKE SA remains active until its lifetime expires or until some external event—such as an operator command to flush the database of IKE SAs— causes the SA to be deleted.

The first two messages in a phase one exchange (either *Main mode* or *Aggressive mode*) also exchange *cookies*. These resemble pseudo-random numbers but are actually temporal and bound to the peer's IP address. Cookie creation is done by hashing together a unique secret, the peer's identity, and a time-based counter. To the casual observer the result of this hash will be a random number, but the recipient of a cookie can quickly determine whether it generated the cookie or not by reconstructing the hash. This binds the cookie to the peer and provides for limited denial of service protection since the real work—the Diffie-Hellman exchange—is not performed until a complete round trip, and an exchange of cookies, has been accomplished.

It would be trivial to write a routine that constructed bogus IKE messages and send them to a destination with a forged source address. If the responder did some work prior to having a strong belief that it is speaking to a genuine IKE peer and not an attacker forging packets it could easily be overwhelmed. Therefore, in *Main mode*, the responder does not do any Diffie-Hellman work until he has received a second message from the initiator and has verified that message contains a cookie that he generated for the initiator.

Aggressive mode does not have such a protection against denial of service attacks. The parties complete the exchange in three messages (as opposed to *Main mode*'s six) and pass more information in each message. Upon receipt of the first *Aggressive mode* message the responder must do a Diffie-Hellman exponentiation, this before he has had the chance to check the cookie of the next message that he receives (which is actually the last).

These cookies are used to identify the IKE SA. During a phase one exchange the IKE SA progresses from one state to the next upon processing of received messages and the sending of responses. The state advancement is one way. A phase two exchange is different. A phase two exchange is unique to itself. It is protected by the phase one IKE SA but has its own state. Therefore, it is entirely possible for two or more phase two exchanges to be simultaneously negotiated between the peers and under the protection of the same IKE SA. Each phase two exchange, therefore, creates a transient state machine to track the advancement of the protocol. When the exchange finishes, the state is thrown away. Since each of these transient state machines is protected by the same IKE SA, the messages of the exchanges all have the same cookie pair. An identifier unique to each phase two exchange is used to multiplex these exchanges into a single pipe. This identifier is called a Message ID. Figure 3.6 shows two simultaneous phase 2 negotiations, with different Message IDs, taking place under the protection of a single IKE SA.

Figure 3.6   An IKE SA from Phase 1 protecting multiple Phase 2 exchanges

Periodically, it is necessary for an IKE process to send a message to his peer outside of any exchange. This could be to notify the peer that some IPSec SAs which it shares are being deleted, or it could be to report some error. Notification messages and delete messages are sent in another unique exchange called an Informational Exchange. This is a one-way message, no retransmission timer is set upon sending such a message, and no response is expected. These Informational exchanges are similar to a phase two exchange in that they're protected by an IKE SA but are unique and have their own state machine (actually a very simple state machine). Each Informational Exchange therefore has its own unique Message ID to allow it to be multiplexed with *Quick mode* Exchanges and possibly other Informational Exchanges through a single IKE SA.

Implementation of a compliant IKE requires adherence to three documents: the base ISAKMP specification (RFC2408), the Domain of Interpretation for IPSec (RFC2407), and the IKE specification itself (RFC2409).

IPSec Architecture

This chapter discusses the IPSec architecture in detail. This includes various components of IPSec, how they interact with each other, the protocols in the IPSec family, and the modes in which they operate.

The IPSec working group at the IETF has defined 12 RFCs (Request for Comments). The RFCs define various aspects of IPSec—architecture, key management, base protocols, and the mandatory transforms to implement for the base protocols. This chapter concentrates mostly on the architecture. The base protocols and the key management protocols are discussed in greater detail in later chapters.

The IPSec Roadmap

The IPSec protocols include AH, ESP, IKE, ISAKMP/Oakley, and transforms. In order to understand, implement, and use IPSec, it is necessary to understand the relationship among these components. The IPSec roadmap defines how various components of IPSec interact with each other. This is shown in Figure 4.1..

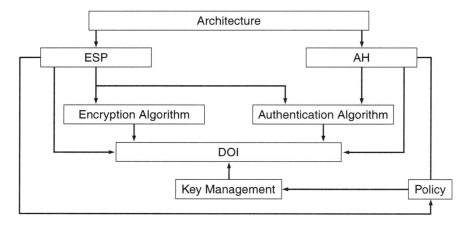

Figure 4.1   IPSec Roadmap (this figure has been reproduced from the draft with permission of the authors)

IPSec is a suite of protocols and it is important to understand how these protocols interact with each other and how these protocols are tied together to implement the capabilities described by the IPSec architecture.

The IPSec architecture, as described in the previous chapter, defines the capabilities the hosts and gateways should provide. For example, IPSec architecture requires the host to provide confidentiality using ESP, and data integrity using either AH or ESP and antireply protection. However, the architecture document does not specify the header formats for these protocols. The architecture discusses the semantics of the IPSec protocols and the issues involved in the interaction among the IPSec protocols and the rest of the TCP/IP protocol suite.

The ESP and the AH documents define the protocol, the payload header format, and the services they provide. In addition these documents define the packet processing rules. However, they do not specify the transforms that are used to provide these capabilities. This is because the new transforms can be defined when the algorithms used by the older transforms are proved to be cryptographically insecure. However, this does not mandate any change to the base protocols.

The transforms define the transformation applied to the data to secure it. This includes the algorithm, the key sizes and how they are derived, the transformation process, and any algorithmic-specific information. It is important to be specific about the necessary information so that different implementations can interoperate. Let us consider the DES-CBC transform that is defined for ESP. If we do not specify how the Initialization Vector is derived, the two implementations end up deriving the Initialization Vector in different ways, and they will never be able to interoperate.

IKE generates keys for the IPSec protocols. IKE is also used to negotiate keys for other protocols that need keys. There are other protocols in the Internet that require security services such as data integrity to protect their data. One such example is OSPF (Open Shortest Path First) routing protocol. The payload format of IKE is very generic. It can be used to negotiate keys for any protocol and not necessarily limit itself for IPSec key negotiation. This segregation is achieved by separating the parameters IKE negotiates from the protocol itself. The parameters that are negotiated are documented in a separate document called the IPSec Domain of Interpretation.

An important component that is not yet a standard is "policy." Policy is a very important issue because it determines if two entities will be able to communicate with each other and, if so, what transforms to use. It is possible, with improperly defined policies, for two sides to be unable to communicate with each other.

The issues with policy are representation and implementation. Representation deals with definition of policy, storage, and retrieval. The IETF is currently working on defining the policy standards. The implementation addresses the application of policy for actual communication. It is important that the keys established by the key management protocol are applied appropriately in the communication. It is equally important to apply the appropriate filters and rules. This chapter discusses the implementation issues of policy and how these rules are applied to the IPSec traffic. The policy representation is discussed later.

IPSec Implementation

IPSec can be implemented and deployed in the end hosts or in the gateways/routers or in both. Where in the network IPSec is deployed depends on the security requirements of the users.

This section discusses the capabilities and implications of implementing IPSec in various network devices (hosts and routers). There are merits in implementing IPSec in both routers and end hosts as they address different problems. The host implementation is most useful when end to end security is desired. However, in cases when security is desired over a part of a network, router implementation is desirable. This includes VPNs, Intranets, and Extranets.

Host Implementation

The proper definition of a host in this context is the device where the packet is originating. The host implementation has the following advantages:

- Provides security end to end
- Ability to implement all modes of IPSec security
- Provides security on a per flow basis
- Ability to maintain user context for authentication in establishing IPSec connections

Host implementations can be classified into:

1. Implementation integrated with the operating system (OS). We call it host implementation (for lack of a better term).
2. Implementation that is a shim between the network and the data link layer of the protocol stack. This is called the "Bump in the Stack" implementation.

OS Integrated

In the host implementation, IPSec may be integrated with the OS. As IPSec is a network layer protocol, it may be implemented as part of the network layer as shown in Figure 4.2. IPSec layer needs the services of the IP layer to construct the IP header. This model is identical to the implementation of other network layer protocols such as ICMP.

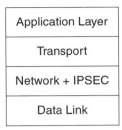

Figure 4.2   IPSec stack layering.

There are numerous advantages of integrating the IPSec with the OS. A few key advantages are listed below.

- As IPSec is tightly integrated into the network layer, it can avail the network services such as fragmentation, PMTU, and user context (sockets). This enables the implementation to be very efficient.
- It is easier to provide security services per flow (such as a Web transaction) as the key management, the base IPSec protocols, and the network layer can be integrated seamlessly.
- All IPSec modes are supported.

Bump in the Stack

For companies providing solutions for VPNs and intranets, OS integrated solution has one serious drawback. On the end hosts, they have to work with the features provided by the OS vendors. This may limit their capabilities to provide advanced solutions. To overcome this limitation, IPSec is implemented as a shim, and inserted between the network and the data link layer as shown in Figure 4.3. This is commonly referred to as Bump in the Stack (BITS) implementation.

Application
Transport
Network
IPSEC
Data Link

Figure 4.3   BITS IPSec stack layering.

As you may notice, the major issue in this implementation is duplication of effort. It requires implementing most of the features of the network layer, such as fragmentation and route tables. Duplicating functionality leads to undesired complications. It becomes more difficult to handle issues such as fragmentation, PMTU, and routing. An advantage of BITS implementation is the capability of an implementation to provide a complete solution. Vendors providing integrated solutions such as firewalls, prefer to have their own client as the OS vendor and may not have all the features required to provide a complete solution.

Router Implementation

The router implementation provides the ability to secure a packet over a part of a network. For example, an organization may be paranoid about the Internet but not its own private network. In this case, it may want to secure only those packets destined to the geographically distributed branchs as these packets traverse the Internet. The IPSec implementation provides security by tunneling the packets.

The router implementation has the following advantages:

- Ability to secure packets flowing between two networks over a public network such as the Internet.

- Ability to authenticate and authorize users entering the private network. This is the capability that many organizations use to allow their employees to telecommute over the Internet to build its VPN or intranet. Previously, this was possible only over dial-ups (dialing through modem directly into the organization).

There are two types of router implementation:

1. Native implementation: This is analogous to the OS integrated implementation on the hosts. In this case, IPSec is integrated with the router software.

2. Bump in the Wire (BITW): This is analogous to BITS implementation. In this case, IPSec is implemented in a device that is attached to the physical interface of the router. This device normally does not run any routing algorithm but is used only to secure packets. BITW is not a long-term solution as it is not viable to have a device attached to every interface of the router.

The network architectures for these implementations is shown in Figure 4.4.

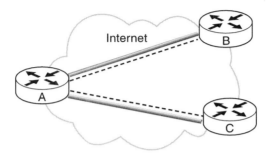

Figure 4.4a   Native implementation deployment architecture.

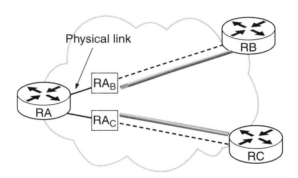

Figure 4.4b   BITW deployment architecture.

The IPSec implementation on routers has many implications on the packet-forwarding capabilities of the router. The routers are expected to forward packets as fast as possible. In fact, we are already seeing core routers that can forward up to 30 million packets per second! Although IPSec may not be used in the core of the Internet, the implementations should still be concerned about efficiency. The packets that do not require security should not be affected because of IPSec. They should still be forwarded at normal rates. Many implementations make use of some hardware assists to perform public key operations, random number generation, encryption/decryption, and calculating hashes. There are specialized chipsets that assist the basic router hardware with security operations.

Another issue with router implementation is IPSec contexts. Memory on the routers is still a scarce commodity, although this is changing fast with memory prices falling rapidly. As the router has to store huge routing tables and normally does not have huge disks for virtual memory support, maintaining too many IPSec contexts is an issue.

IPSec Modes

We have talked about IPSec in transport mode and tunnel mode without explaining when and how IPSec protocols are used in these modes. In this section, we describe how the IPSec protocols, AH and ESP, implement the tunnel and transport modes. There are four possible combinations of modes and protocol: AH in transport mode, AH in tunnel mode, ESP in transport mode, and ESP in tunnel mode. In practice, AH in tunnel mode is not used because it protects the same data that AH in transport mode protects.

The AH and ESP header do not change between tunnel or transport mode. The difference is more semantic in nature—what it is they are protecting, IP packet or an IP payload. The guidelines for deciding what mode to use and some examples of using IPSec in various modes is discussed in later chapters.

Transport Mode

In transport mode, AH and ESP protect the transport header. In this mode, AH and ESP intercept the packets flowing from the transport layer into the network layer and provide the configured security.

Let us consider an example. In Figure 4.5, A and B are two hosts that have been configured so that all transport layer packets flowing between them are encrypted. In this case, transport mode of ESP is used. If the requirement is just to authenticate transport layer packets, then transport mode of AH is used.

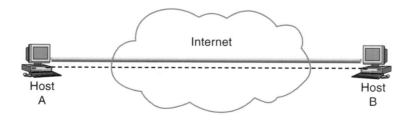

Figure 4.5   Hosts with transport ESP.

When security is not enabled, transport layer packets such as TCP and UDP flow into the network layer, IP, which adds the IP header and calls into the data link layer. When security in transport layer is enabled, the transport layer packets flow into the IPSec component. The IPSec component is implemented as part of the network layer (when intergrated with OS). The IPSec component adds the AH, ESP, or both headers, and invokes the part of the network layer that adds the network layer header.

The transport mode of IPSec can be used only when security is desired end to end. As stated earlier, the routers look mostly at the network layer in making routing decisions and the routers do not and should not change anything beyond the network layer header. Inserting transport mode IPSec header for packets flowing through a router is a violation of this rule.

When both AH and ESP are used in transport mode, ESP should be applied first. The reason is obvious. If the transport packet is first protected using AH and then using ESP, the data integrity is applicable only for the transport payload as the ESP header is added later on as shown in Figure 4.6.

IP	ESP	AH	TCP hdr	Data

Figure 4.6   Packet format with ESP and AH.

This is not desirable because the data integrity should be calculated over as much data as possible.

If the packet is protected using AH after it is protected using ESP, then the data integrity applies to the ESP payload that contains the transport payload as shown in Figure 4.7.

IP header	AH header	ESP header	TCP payload

Figure 4.7   Packet format with AH and ESP

The transport mode for BITS implementation is not as clean, as the ESP and AH headers are inserted after the IP payload is constructed. This implies the BITS implementation has to duplicate the IP functionality because it has to recalculate the IP checksum and fragment the packet if necessary. Many BITS implementations may not support transport mode but support only tunnel mode.

Tunnel Mode

IPSec in tunnel mode is normally used when the ultimate destination of the packet is different from the security termination point as shown in Figure 4.8 or in case of BITS or BITW implementations. The tunnel mode is also used in cases when the security is provided by a device that did not originate packets as in the case of VPNs.

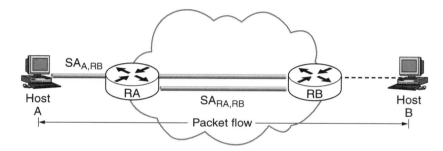

Figure 4.8   IPSec in tunnel mode.

It is also used when a router provides security services for packets it is forwarding. The operation of tunnel mode is discussed in detail in the IPSec implementation chapter.

In the case of tunnel mode, IPSec encapsulates an IP packet with IPSec headers and adds an outer IP Header as shown in Figure 4.9.

IP header	ESP	IP header	Network payload

Figure 4.9   IPSec tunneled mode packet format.

An IPSec tunneled mode packet has two IP headers—inner and outer. The inner header is constructed by the host and the outer header is added by the device that is providing the security services. This can be either the host or a router. There is nothing that precludes a host from providing tunneled mode security services end to end. However, in this case there is no advantage to using tunnel mode instead of transport mode. In fact, if the security services are provided end to end, transport mode is better because it does not add an extra IP header.

IPSec defines tunnel mode for both AH and ESP. IPSec also supports nested tunnels. The nested tunneling is where we tunnel a tunneled packet as shown in Figure 4.10a.

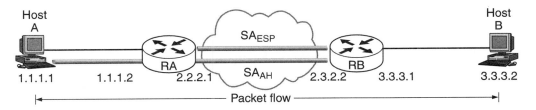

Figure 4.10a **Nested tunnel example.**

IP header	ESP	IP header	AH	IP header	data
Src = 2.2.2.1 Dst = 2.3.2.2		Src = 1.1.1.1 Dst = 2.3.2.2		Src = 1.1.1.1 Dst = 3.3.3.2	

Figure 4.10b **Nested packet format.**

In this example, host A is sending a packet to host B. The policy says it has to authenticate itself to router RB. In addition, there is a VPN between the two networks bordered by RA and RB. The packet seen by router RB is shown in Figure 4.10b. The outermost header is the tunneled ESP packet. It is carrying a tunneled AH packet. The tunneled AH packet is carrying the IP packet destined for the host B generated by host A.

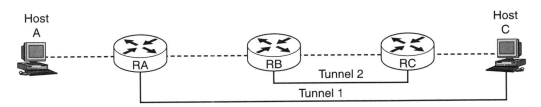

Figure 4.11a **Valid tunnel.**

Host
A
Host
C
RA
RB
RC
Tunnel 2
Tunnel 1

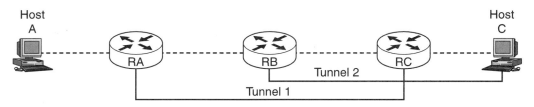

Figure 4.11b Invalid tunnel.

The requirement for the tunnel is that inner header is completely encompassed by the outer header. The valid and invalid tunnels examples are shown in Figures 4.11a and b.

The example shown in Figure 4.11a is valid as the inner tunnel (tunnel 2) is completely encompassed by tunnel 1. The example shown in Figure 4.11b is invalid because neither tunnel completely encompasses the other. To understand why this is invalid, let us trace the packet flow. After RA constructs the tunneled packet, the packet format is as shown in Figure 4.12a.

Encrypted
IP header
ESP
IP
Data
Src = RA
Dst = RC
Src = Host A
Dst = Host C

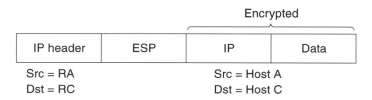

Figure 4.12a Tunneled packet.

When the packet reaches RB, it tunnels the packet to host C. The packet format when the packet leaves RB is shown in Figure 4.12b.

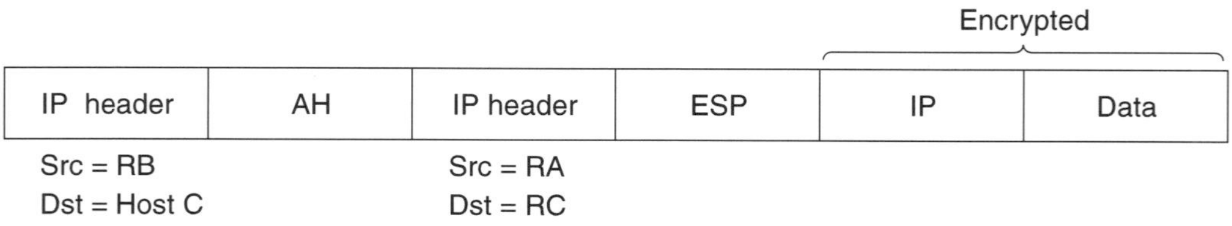

Encrypted
IP header
AH
IP header
ESP
IP
Data
Src = RB
Dst = Host C
Src = RA
Dst = RC

Figure 4.12b Invalid tunnel packet.

Clearly, this is incorrect because the packet now reaches host C before it reaches RC. When the packet reaches host C, it processes the AH header. When the second IP header is exposed, the host drops the packet because the destination is RC and not itself. Nested tunnels are difficult to build and maintain and should be used sparingly.

Security Associations

The Security Associations, or SAs as they are normally referred to in IPSec terminology, form the basis for IPSec. The SAs are the contract between two communicating entities. They determine the IPSec protocols used for securing the packets, the transforms, the keys, and the duration for which the keys are valid to name a few. Any IPSec implementation always builds an SA database (SADB) that maintains the SAs that the IPSec protocols use to secure packets.

The SAs are one way, i.e., simplex. If two hosts, A and B, are communicating securely using ESP, then the host A will have an SA, SAout, for processing outbound packets and will have a different SA, SAin, for processing the inbound packets. The host B will also create two SAs for processing its packets. The SAout of the host A and the SAin of the host B will share the same cryptographic parameters such as keys. Similarly, SAin of the host A and the SAout of the host B will share the same cryptographic parameters. As SAs are unidirectional, a separate table is maintained for SAs used for outbound and inbound processing.

The SAs are also protocol specific. There is an SA for each protocol. If two hosts A and B are communicating securely using both AH and ESP, then each host builds a separate SA for each protocol.

There is another component in the IPSec architecture called the security policy database (SPD). The SPD works in conjunction with the SADB in processing packets. The policy is an extremely important component of IPSEC architecture. The policy defines the security communications characteristics between two entities. It defines what protocols to use in what modes and the transforms to use. It also defines how the IP packets are treated. This is discussed in detail in later sections.

Security Parameter Index (SPI)

The SPI is a very important element in the SA. An SPI is a 32-bit entity that is used to uniquely identify an SA at the receiver. It was mentioned before that the security context or SA is a contract between two hosts communicating securely and indicates the parameters, such as keys and algorithms. However, there has to be some mechanism for the source to identify which SA to use to secure the packet and for the destination to identify which SA to use to check the security of the received packet. The source identifies the SA by using the selectors. However, the destination does not have access to all the fields in the selectors as some of the fields in the selectors belong to the transport layer.

To solve the problem of identifying the SA on the destination, the SPI that uniquely identifies the SA on the destination is sent with every packet. The destination uses this value to index into the receiving SADB and fetch the SA. The obvious questions are who guarantees the uniqueness of the mapping between the SPI and SA and what is the domain of uniqueness on the destination for each protocol—global, per source, or per address on the host. It is up to receiver/destination to guarantee this uniqueness. It is a requirement to maintain a separate SPI domain for each protocol. The destination can use any consistent mechanism to guarantee uniqueness inside each domain. The IPSec architecture specifies that the <spi, destination address> in the packet should uniquely identify an SA.

The receiver allocates the SPI that is stored as part of the SA on the sender. The sender includes this in every packet under the assumption that the receiver can use this to uniquely identify the SA. If the receiver does not guarantee uniqueness, packets will fail security checks as invalid keys and transforms may be used.

The sending host uses the selectors to uniquely index into the sending SADB. The output of this lookup is an SA that has all the negotiated security parameters, including the SPI. The host that allocates the SPI guarantees uniqueness. The SPI is reused once the SA expires but it is guaranteed that at any point the mapping between <spi, dst>, and SA is one to one. The src address is used in cases where the host is multihomed, that is, a host with more than one IP interface. This can be because there is more than one network card on the host or because of the fact that multiple IP interfaces are configured on the same network card (the host has multiple IP addresses). In this case, it is possible that the index <spi, dst> is not unique and src is used to resolve the ambiguity.

The SPI is transmitted as part of AH and ESP headers. The receiving host uses the tuple <spi, dst, protocol> (where dst is the destination address in the IP header) to uniquely identify the SA. It is possible to use the source address in addition to <spi, dst, protocol> to uniquely identify an SA to conserve the SPI space. However, this is not part of the standards and is something specific to an implementation.

SA Management

The two most important tasks of the SA management are creation and deletion. The management of SAs can be either manual or through an Internet standard key management protocol such as IKE. The SA management requires an interface for the user applications (which includes IKE) to communicate with kernel to manage the SADB. The management aspect is discussed in greater detail in the chapter on policy.

Creation

The SA creation is a two-step processānegotiating the parameters of the SA and updating the SADB with the SA.

Manual keying is mandatory to support and it was used extensively during the initial development and testing of IPSec. In manual keying, two sides agree on the parameters of the SA offline, either by phone or over e-mail (although unsecured e-mail is dangerous!). The process of allocating the SPI, negotiation of parameters is all manual. Needless to say, this process is error prone, cumbersome, and insecure. The other limiting factor is that these SAs never expire. Once they are created they stay good until they are deleted. Manual keying is a useful feature for debugging the base IPSec protocols when the key management protocols are failing. However, with a stable key management protocol, the use of manual keying is questionable.

In an environment where IPSec is deployed, the SAs are created through an Internet standard key management protocol such as IKE. IKE is invoked by the IPSec kernel when the policy mandates that the connection should be secure but the SA's are not yet established. IKE negotiates the SA with the destination or intermediate host/router, depending on the policy, and creates the SA. Once the SA is created and added to the SADB, secure packets start flowing between the two hosts.

In the previous sections, we discussed nested or chained implementations of IPSec. For example, a host creates a transport AH to end to end, but also creates a tunneled ESP to the gateway/firewall. In this case, for the packet to be processed properly, the source has to create two SAs, one for the gateway and another for the end host. When the policy requires establishment of multiple SAs for two hosts to communicate securely, the collection of SAs is called SA bundle.

Deletion

The SA is deleted for various reasons:

- The lifetime has expired.
- The keys are compromised.
- The number of bytes encrypted/decrypted or authenticated using this SA has exceeded a certain threshold set by the policy.
- The other end requests that the SA be deleted.

The SAs can be deleted manually or through the IKE. It is important to renew or refresh keys in security to reduce the chance of someone breaking the system. IPSec does not provide the ability to refresh keys. Instead, we have to delete existing SA and negotiate/create a new SA. Once the SA is deleted, the SPI it was using can be reused.

To avoid the problem of stalling the communication, a new SA is negotiated before the existing SA expires. For a small duration of time, until the soon-to-expire SA is deleted, the two entities have multiple SAs that can be used for secure communication. However, it is always desirable to use the newly established SA instead of the older SA.

Parameters

The SA maintains the context of a secure communication between two entities. The SA stores both protocol-specific and generic fields. This section discusses the fields that are used by both AH and ESP. The protocol-specific fields are discussed in AH and ESP chapters. These fields are used in processing each IP packet. Some of the fields are used for outbound processing, some for inbound processing, and some for both, depending on the usage of the field. Certain fields are updated when the SA is used to process a packet. Semantics associated with the parameters in an SA are discussed below.

Sequence Number   The sequence number is a 32-bit field and is used in outbound processing. The sequence number is part of both AH and ESP header. The sequence number is incremented by 1 every time the SA is used to secure a packet. This field is used to detect replay attacks by the destination. When the SA is established this field is set to 0. Normally, SAs are renegotiated before this field overflows as it is unsafe to send more than 4 Giga (4,000,000,000) packets using the same keys.

Sequence Number Overflow This field is used in outbound processing and is set when the sequence number overflows. The policy determines if the SA can still be used to process additional packets.

Antireplay Window This field is used in inbound processing. One of the concerns in networks today is replay attack. In replay attacks, applications get bombarded with the same packets. IPSec overcomes this by detecting packets replayed by rogue hosts. This is discussed in greater detail where the inbound processing of packets is described in the implementation chapter.

Lifetime There is a lifetime associated with each SA beyond which the SA cannot be used. The lifetime is specified either in terms of number of bytes that has been secured using this SA or the duration for which the SA has been used or both. When the lifetime of the SA expires, it cannot be used anymore. In order to avoid the problem of breaking the communication when the SA expires, there are two kinds of lifetimesãsoft and hard. The soft lifetime is used to warn the kernel that the SA is about to expire. This allows the kernel to negotiate a new SA before the hard lifetime expires.

Mode IPSec protocols can be used either in tunnel or transport mode. The payload is processed differently depending on the value of this field. This field is set to tunnel mode, transport mode, or a wild card. In the cases where this field is set to wild card, the information as to whether it is IPSec in tunnel or transport mode is gleaned from someplace else, that is, sockets. When this field is set to a wild card, it implies that the SA can be used either for tunnel or transport mode.

Tunnel Destination For IPSec in tunnel mode, this indicates the tunnel destinationãthe destination IP address of the outer header.

PMTU parameters When IPSec is used in tunnel mode, it has to maintain the PMTU information so that it can fragment the packets accordingly. As a part of PMTU field, the SA maintains two valuesãthe PMTU and the aging field. This is discussed in greater detail in the implementation chapter.

Security Policy

The security policy determines the security services afforded to a packet. As mentioned earlier, all IPSec implementations store the policy in a database called the SPD. The database is indexed by selectors and contains the information on the security services offered to an IP packet.

The security policy is consulted for both inbound and outbound processing of the IP packets. On inbound or outbound packet processing, the SPD is consulted to determine the services afforded to the packet. A separate SPD can be maintained for the inbound and the outbound packets to support asymmetric policy, that is, providing different security services for inbound and outbound packets between two hosts. However, the key management protocol always negotiates bidirectional SAs. In practice, the tunneling and nesting will be mostly symmetric.

For the outbound traffic, the output of the SA lookup in the SADB is a pointer to the SA or SA bundle, provided the SAs are already established. The SA or SA bundle will be ordered to process the outbound packet as specified in the policy. If the SAs are not established, the key management protocol is invoked to establish the packet. For the inbound traffic, the packet is first afforded security processing. The SPD is then indexed by the selector to validate the policy on the packet. We will discuss this in greater detail when we talk about IPSec in action.

The security policy requires policy management to add, delete, and modify policy. The SPD is stored in the kernel and IPSec implementations should provide an interface to manipulate the SPD. This management of SPD is implementation specific and there is no standard defined. However, the management application should provide the ability to handle all the fields defined in the selectors that are discussed below.

Selectors

This section defines the various selectors used to determine the security services afforded to a packet. The selectors are extracted from the network and transport layer headers.

Source Address   The source address can be a wild card, an address range, a network prefix, or a specific host. Wild card is particularly useful when the policy is the same for all the packets originating from a host. The network prefix and address range is used for security gateways providing security to hosts behind it and to build VPNs. A specific host is used either on a multihomed host or in the gateways when a hostðs security requirements are specific.

Destination Address   The destination address can be a wild card, an address range, a network prefix, or a specific host. The first three are used for hosts behind secure gateways. The destination address field used as a selector is different from the destination address used to look up SAs in the case of tunneled IP packets. In the case of tunneled IP packets, the destination IP address of the outer header can be different from that of the inner header when the packets are tunneled. However, the policy in the destination gateway is set based on the actual destination and this address is used to index into the SPD.

Name   The name field is used to identify a policy tied to a valid user or system name. These include a DNS name, X.500 Distinguished Name, or other name types defined in the IPSec DOI. The name field is used as a selector only during the IKE negotiation, not during the packet processing. This field cannot be used as a selector during packet processing as there is no way to tie an IP address to a name currently.

Protocol   The protocol field specifies the transport protocol whenever the transport protocol is accessible. In many cases, when ESP is used, the transport protocol is not accessible. Under these circumstances, a wild card is used.

Upper Layer Ports   In cases where there is session-oriented keying, the upper layer ports represent the src and dst ports to which the policy is applicable. The wild card is used when the ports are inaccessible.

IPSec Processing

In this section, the processing of the IPSec packets, both inbound and outbound, is discussed briefly. The interactions between the kernel and the key management layer is discussed in the IPSec implementation chapter. The header processing, both IPv4 and IPv6, are discussed in the IPSec implementation chapter.

The IPSec processing is classified into outbound processing and inbound processing.

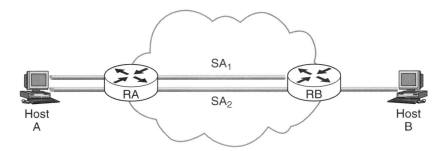

Figure 4.13   Outbound IPSec processing.

Outbound

In outbound processing, the transport layer packets flow in to IP layer. The IP layer consults the SPD to determine the security services afforded to this packet. The input into the SPD is the selectors defined in the previous section. The output of the SPD is one of the following:

- Drop the packet, in which case the packet is not processed and dropped.
- Bypass security, in which case the IP layer adds the IP header to the payload and dispatches the IP packet.
- Apply security, in which case, if an SA is already established, the pointer to it is returned. If SA is not established, then IKE is invoked to establish the SA. If the SAs are already established, SPD has a pointer to the SA or the SA bundle, depending on the policy. If the output of the policy mandates applying IPSec to the packets, the packets are not transmitted until the SAs are established.

The IPSec implementation waits until the SAs for this packet are established, if they are not already established. After the SAs are established, it processes the packet by adding the appropriate AH and ESP headers. The SAs have all the pertinent information and are ordered so that the IPSec headers are constructed appropriately. For example, let us consider the network shown in the Figure 4.13.

In this case, the host is tunneling a packet to the gateway using ESP but is authenticating to the end host B. The correct header is shown in Figure 4.14.

IP header	ESP	IP header	AH	Network payload

Src = HA   Src = HA
Dst = RB   Dst = HB

Figure 4.14   Packet format.

In this case, IKE establishes four SAs—two for sending and two for receiving. As we are discussing the outbound processing, we will ignore the SAs established for processing inbound packets. The two outbound SAs are SA1 and SA2, where SA1 is the SA between A and the gateway and SA2 is the SA between the host and the destination. The ordering of IPSec processing is very important. If SA2 is applied after SA1, the packet is formed incorrectly. It is very important to maintain ordering in the SA bundle so that IPSec processing is applied in the correct order for outbound packets.

This section gave a very brief overview of the processing of the outbound packets. There are lot of other issues with constructing the header in handling fields such as sequence numbers and insertion of headers that is deferred to the implementation chapter.

Inbound

The inbound processing differs from the outbound processing. On the receipt of the IP packet, if the packet does not contain any IPSec headers, the security layer checks the policy to determine how to process the packet. It indexes the SPD using the selector fields. The output of the policy will be one of three values—discard, bypass, or apply. If the output of the policy is discard, the packet is dropped. If the output of the policy is apply, but SAs are not established, the packet is dropped. Otherwise, the packet is passed up to the next layer for further processing.

If the IP packet contains IPSec headers, the packet is processed by the IPSec layer. The IPSec layer extracts the SPI, the source addr, and the destination addr from the IP datagram. It indexes into the SADB using the tuple <SPI, dst, protocol> (additionally the source address is used, depending on the implementation). The protocol value is either AH or ESP. Depending on the protocol value, the packet is handled either by the AH or the ESP layer. After the protocol payload is processed, the policy is consulted to validate the payload. The selectors are used to retrieve the policy. The validation process consists of checking that the SA was used appropriately, that is, the source and destination in the SA corresponds to what the policy says and the SA is protecting the transport layer protocol it was supposed to protect. In case of tunneled packets, the source and destination selector fields are that of the inner header and not the outer header. Indexing into the SPD based on the outer source and destination values yields invalid results because the entry is constructed for the true source and destination and not the tunnel end point.

Let us consider the example where the gateway is tunneling a packet for host B to host A. On the host A, the policy says, packets arriving from B have tunneled ESP and the tunnel source will be the secure gateway. In this case, indexing into the SPD using the gateway as source instead of host B is incorrect.

Once the IPSec layer validates the policy, it strips off the IPSec header and passes the packet to the next layer for further processing. The next layer is either a transport layer or a network layer. For example, if the packet is IP[ESP[TCP]]], then the next layer is a transport layer. If the packet is IP[AH[ESP[TCP]]] the next layer will be the IPSec layer that belongs to the network layer. This process is repeated until the packet reaches the application layer where the data is delivered to the application.

Fragmentation

IPSec does not fragment or reassemble packets. On outbound processing, the transport payload is processed and then passed on to the IP layer for further processing. On inbound processing, the IPSec layer gets a reassembled packet from the IP layer.

However, as IPSec does add IPSec header, it impacts the PMTU length. If IPSec does not participate in PMTU discovery, the IP layer ends up fragmenting a packet as the addition of the IPSec header increases the length of the IP datagram beyond the PMTU.

It is important for IPSec to participate in the PMTU discovery process. This is discussed in greater detail in the chapter on IPSec implementation.

ICMP

ICMP processing is critical to the operation and debugging of a network. When IPSec is used end-to-end, it does not impact ICMP. However, when IPSec is used in tunnel mode, it impacts ICMP and the operation of the network. The problem arises in the tunnel mode, particularly when the tunnel header is added by an intermediate gateway. This is because ICMP messages are required to send only 64 bits of the original header. When the gateway adds the tunneled header and the IPSec header, the inner IP header and hence the actual source is not present in the ICMP error message. The gateway will not be able to forward the message appropriately.

In order to handle ICMP error messages correctly, IPSec needs to maintain some state and perform extra processing. This is discussed in greater detail in the implementation chapter.

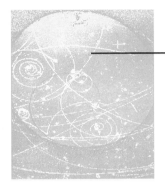

The Encapsulating Security Payload (ESP)

The Encapsulating Security Payload (ESP) is a protocol header inserted into an IP datagram to provide confidentiality, data origin authentication, antireplay, and data integrity services to IP. ESP may be applied in different modes in which it is inserted between the IP header and the upper-layer protocol header (e.g., a TCP or UDP header) or it may be used to encapsulate an entire IP datagram.

ESP provides confidentiality with an *encryptor* and data integrity with an *authenticator*. The specific algorithm used by both the encryptor and authenticator is determined by the corresponding components of an ESP security association. By divorcing the base ESP definition from the actual algorithms that provide its services, ESP is a generic and extensible security mechanism. Antireplay services are optionally provided by ESP. The decision whether antireplay is provided or not is up to the recipient of the packet. A unique and monotonically increasing sequence number is always inserted by the sender of an ESP-protected datagram but the recipient is not required to check it. Since this protection is for the benefit of the receiver, it is usually employed.

The ESP Header

When ESP is used to protect an IP packet the ESP header (figure 5.1) immediately follows an IP header. In the case of IPv4, the ESP header immediately follows the IP header (including any options). The protocol field of that IP header will be 50 to indicate that following the IP header is an ESP header. In case of IPv6, the placement of the ESP header depends on the presence of extension headers. The ESP header is always inserted after the extension headers, which can change en route to the destination. This includes the hop-by-hop, routing, and the fragment headers. The ESP header should be inserted before the destination options header because it is desirable to protect the destination options. If extension headers are present, the next header field of the extension header immediately preceding the ESP header is set to 50. In the absence of any extension header, the next header field in the IPv6 header is set to 50.

ESP provides both confidentiality and integrity to the packet it is protecting. The scope of these two services on the ESP packet are not identical. This is due to a desire to authenticate as much information in the packet as possible but also allowing for efficient processing.

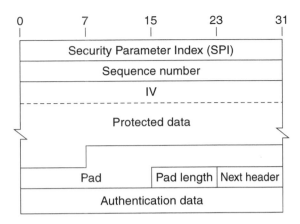

Figure 5.1   The ESP Header (and trailer)

Being an IPSec header, the ESP header contains an SPI field. This value, combined with the destination address and protocol in the preceding IP header, identifies the appropriate security association to use in processing the packet. The SPI itself is an arbitrary number and is selected by the destination, usually during an IKE exchange (more on this in Chapter 7). Note that the SPI is authenticated but not encrypted. This is a necessity because the SPI is used to identify the state—encryption algorithm and key—used to decrypt the packet. If the SPI were encrypted we'd have a serious chicken-and-egg problem!

The sequence number provides antireplay services to ESP. As described in Chapter 3, this value is a unique and monotonically increasing number inserted into the header by the sender. The sequence number is authenticated but not encrypted. This is because we want to determine whether a packet is a duplicate, and hence that we will drop this packet, without expending resources to decrypt it. Since the sequence number does not really require confidentiality—it does not expose any secrets in cleartext form—a safety check can be accomplished by doing the antireplay check prior to decryption.

The actual data being protected by ESP is contained in the payload data field. The length of this field therefore depends on the length of the data. The protected data field is also used to contain any initialization vector that an encryption algorithm may require. The specific transform document that describes how to use ESP with a particular algorithm must define the location of the IV and address any alignment issues that may arise due to the addition of the IV in the payload data field. For all of the encryption algorithms defined for use with ESP, the IV is the first 8 octets of data in the *protected data* field. Note, though, that this is not encrypted.

Padding is used in ESP to maintain boundaries. Certain modes of encryption algorithms require that the input to the cipher be a multiple of its block size. Padding accomplishes this. Also, if confidentiality is not employed by the SA, padding is still used to right-justify the *pad length* and *next header* fields of the ESP header. Certain payloads may not require padding if the payload data already provides the necessary alignment, but up to 255 bytes of padding can still be added. This technique can be used to hide the actual length of the payload data. The contents of the padding is dependent on the encryption algorithm used to provide confidentiality. If the algorithm defines a certain value in its pad that value must be used. If the algorithm does not specify any required pad value, ESP dictates that the first byte of the pad be the value 1 and that all subsequent bytes have a monotonically increasing value. The value of the pad should be checked by the receiver as an additional check for proper decryption and also as an additional protection against certain cut-and-paste attacks if authentication is not employed.

The pad length field simply defines how much pad has been added so that the recipient can restore the actual length of the payload data. The pad length field is mandatory, so even if there is no pad, the pad length field will indicate that. In this case its value should be self-evident.

The authentication data field is used to hold the result of the data integrity check—usually a keyed hash function—done on the ESP packet (note the coverage of the integrity check from Figure 3.1). The length of this field depends on the authentication algorithm employed by the SA used to process this packet. If an authenticator is not specified in the SA used to process an ESP packet there is no authentication data field.

ESP Modes

The next header field indicates the type of data that is contained in the payload data field—what ESP is actually protecting. If ESP is applied in *transport mode* (Figure 5.2), the ESP header is placed between the IP header and the upper-layer protocol header and the *next header* field will indicate the type of upper-level protocol that follows, for example TCP would be six (6).If ESP is applied in *tunnel mode* (Figure 5.3), an entire IP datagram is encapsulated by another IP datagram and the ESP header is placed between the two. In *tunnel mode* the *next header* field with therefore be the value four (4) for IPv4 or fourty-one (41) for IPv6, indicating IP-in-IP encapsulation.

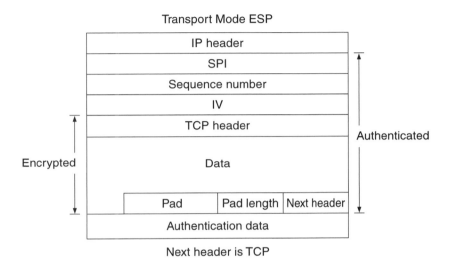

Figure 5.2   An IP Packet protected by ESP in Transport Mode

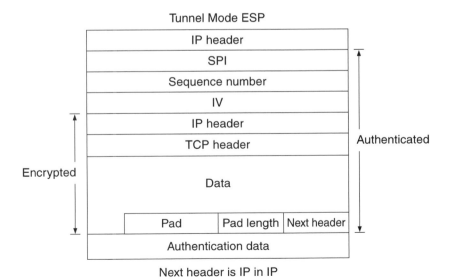

Figure 5.3   An IP Packet protected by ESP in Tunnel Mode

ESP Processing

Processing of an IP packet with ESP depends partly on the mode in which ESP is being employed. In either case, though, one thing to remember is that with ESP, the cipher text is authenticated. The authenticated plaintext is not encrypted. What this means is that, for outbound packets encryption happens first and for inbound packets authentication happens first.

For interoperability purposes mandatory-to-implement algorithms have been defined for ESP. The must-implement authenticators are HMAC-MD5-96 and HMAC-SHA-96, RFC2403 and RFC2404, respectively. Originally the must-implement cipher was DES-CBC with an explicit IV, as defined in RFC2405 but after the IPSec documents advanced from Internet-Draft to RFC status a (relatively) low-cost DES cracker was built. This cracker, named Deep Crack, was able to determine a DES key in merely 56 hours. Several months later, at a conference in San Jose, California, DES was broken in just 22 hours! Because of this, the RFCs all have statements indicating the deprecated nature of DES and suggest using stronger cipher algorithms for ESP, such as AES. Deep Crack has no impact on the mandatory-to-implement authenticators and they are believed to be secure.

Outbound Processing

For transport mode application running over IPv4, the ESP header is inserted into an outbound IP packet immediately after the IP header (including any options the IP header may have). The protocol field of the IP header is copied into the next header field of the ESP header and the remaining fields of the ESP header are filled in—the SPI field is assigned the SPI from the particular SA in the SADB used to process this packet, the sequence number field is filled with the next value in the sequence, the pad is inserted and its value assigned, and the pad length value is assigned. The protocol field of the IP header is then given the value of ESP, or 50.

The rules for IPv6 processing are similar to IPv4 processing except for the insertion of the header. The ESP header is inserted after any extension headers that may be modified en route.

For tunnel mode application, the ESP header is prepended to the IP packet. The next header field of the ESP header is assigned the value four (4) if it is encapsulating an IPv4 packet and a value 41 if it is encapsulating an IPv6 packet. The remaining fields are filled in in the same manner as in transport mode. Then a new IP header is prepended to the ESP header and the appropriate fields are filled in—the source address is the device itself which is applying the ESP, the destination address is taken from the SA used to apply ESP, the protocol is set to fifty (50), and the rest are filled in according to local IP processing.

Regardless of mode, the next steps are identical. The packet, from the beginning of the payload data to the next header field, is encrypted using the cipher and encryption key in the appropriate SA. Then the packet, from the ESP header, through the encrypted ciphertext, to the ESP trailer, is authenticated using the authenticator and the authenticator key in the appropriate SA. The result of the authenticator is then inserted into the *authentication data* field of the ESP trailer.

The final step in outbound processing is to recompute the checksum of the IP header that precedes the ESP header.

Note that a fragmentation check need not be employed when adding the ESP header. If the resulting packet (after ESP has been employed) is larger than the MTU of the interface from which it is traveling, it will merely be fragmented. This is no different than if a whole, complete, ESP packet left the device and was fragmented somewhere in the network. We'll let the input processing deal with that.

Input Processing

Upon receipt of an ESP packet the receiver has no way of knowing whether the packet is in tunnel mode or transport mode without processing it. Based upon the SA used to process the packet, he'll know what it *should* be, but until it is decrypted there is practically no way to know what ESP is protecting. This is a good thing because any person doing traffic analysis would not know either!

If a received IPSec packet is a fragment, it must be retained until all fragments have been received. A fragmented IPSec packet cannot be processed because it would fail the first check made upon it—a data integrity check.

The first thing the recipient of an ESP packet does is check whether an SA exists to process it—this is a basic IPSec requirement and not particular to ESP. If there is no SA the packet must be dropped. Input processing can begin only if an SA exists.

Once a valid SA has been identified, it is used to process the packet. The sequence number is checked first. If the sequence number of the packet is valid—that is, it is not a duplicate and is not to the right of the sequence number window contained in the SA—processing proceeds. Since ESP authenticates ciphertext and not plaintext, the next thing to do is authenticate the packet. The entire ESP packet, minus the authentication data of course, is passed with the appropriate key to the authenticator algorithm from the SA. If the resulting digest matches the data contained in the Authentication Data field (taking into account any truncation that the authentication algorithm may require), the packet is authenticated. The next step is decryption. The ESP packet, from the beginning of the payload data to the next header field, is decrypted using the key and cipher algorithm from the SA. A simple check to determine whether decryption was successful is a check of the pad. Since the content of the pad is deterministic—it's either a monotonically increasing number starting at one or it's dependent on the encryption algorithm—verifying the contents of the pad will determine whether the packet has decrypted successfully.

There is a clever optimization that can be made in ESP input processing. The ciphertext is authenticated, not the other way around, so neither the decryption nor verification steps depend on each other. It is therefore easy to parallelize ESP input processing by giving a copy of the authenticated and encrypted packet to the verification engine and the decryption engine. One engine doesn't have to wait until the other engine is finished and the packet is processed more quickly.

After successfully passing both authentication and decryption checks, a preliminary validity check of the resulting packet can be made. If the SA used to process the packet dictates that only ESP packets in a particular mode—either transport or tunnel mode—can be processed, the packet must be checked for compliance. If the packet does not correspond to the required mode it must be dropped. In Chapter 7 we'll discuss how IKE can create IPSec SAs for an explicit mode.

The packet can now be rebuilt without the ESP header. For transport mode, the upper-layer protocol header is synced up with the IP header, the next header field from the ESP header is copied into the protocol field of the IP header, and a new IP checksum computed; for tunnel mode the outer IP header and the ESP header can merely be thrown away—the decapsulated packet is what we need. At this point, regardless of the ESP mode, another validity check has to be made with the SPD entry that corresponds with the SA used to proces the packet. The SPD may require that packets protected by this SA be only for a particular host and/or for a particular port or protocol. If the packet does not correspond to the required address and/or port and/or protocol dictated by the SPD, it must be dropped.

A reconstructed and validated packet can now be forwarded for further processing. If it is a transport mode packet, it is given up to a higher layer—like TCP or UDP—for processing; if it is a tunnel mode packet, it is reinserted into the IP processing stream and forwarded on to its ultimate destination (which may be the same host).

If the reconstructed and validated packet is a fragment, it may be necessary to hold on to this packet until all fragments are received, reconstructed, and validated, and all the fragments have been reassembled. This would be necessary if IPSec was being applied by a network entity, in tunnel mode, on behalf of another host, and the SA that was used to process the packet(s) dictated that only packets for a particular port are allowed. Because any fragments would not have that information in them the only choice besides retaining fragments and reassembling a whole packet would be to forward all fragments on to the destination. Because the destination would not have the SA information, it would not know if the reconstructed packet was valid or not (from a security policy point of view). For processing speed reasons, it is recommended that network entities (such as routers) applying IPSec to transient traffic not retain decrypted and validated fragments if it is not required. Note that this case is different than receiving fragmented IPSec packets that must always be retained until a complete IPSec packet can be reassembled.

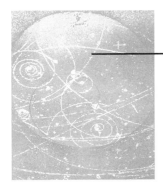

The Authentication Header (AH)

The Authentication Header (AH) is an IPSec protocol used to provide data integrity, data origin authentication, and limited antireplay (the antireplay is optional) services to IP. AH does not provide any encryption services.

Since AH does not provide confidentiality, it does not require a cipher algorithm. It does, though, require an authenticator. AH defines the method of protection, the placement of the header, the authentication coverage, and input and output processing rules, but it does not define the authentication algorithm to use. Like its sibling protocol, ESP, AH does not mandate antireplay protection. The use of the antireplay services are solely at the discretion of the recipient and there is no way for a sender to know whether a receiver will check the sequence number. Consequently, the sender must always assume that antireplay services is being employed by the recipient.

AH can be used to protect an upper-layer protocol (transport mode) or an entire IP datagram (tunnel mode), just like ESP. In either case the AH header immediately follows an IP header. AH is defined over IP and an AH-protected IP packet is just another IP packet. Therefore, AH can be used alone or in conjunction with ESP. It can protect a tunneling protocol like L2TP or GRE or it can be used to tunnel packets. Like ESP, AH is a versatile security service for IP.

The data integrity that AH provides is subtly different than that provided by ESP; AH authenticates portions of the outer IP header as well.

The AH Header

AH is another IP protocol and has been assigned the number fifty-one (51). The protocol field of an AH-protected IPv4 datagram is 51 indicating that following the IP header is an AH header. In case of IPv6, the value of the next header field depends on the presence of extension headers. In the absence of extension headers, the next header field in the IPv6 header will be 51. In the presence of extension headers prior to the AH header, the next header field in the extension header immediately preceding the AH header is set to 51. The rules for inserting the AH header in IPv6 is similar to that described for ESP. When AH and ESP are protecting the same data, the AH header is always inserted after the ESP header. The AH header is much simpler than the ESP header because it does not provide confidentiality. There is no trailer as there is no need for padding and a pad length indicator. There is also no need for an initialization vector. The AH header is shown in Figure 6.1.

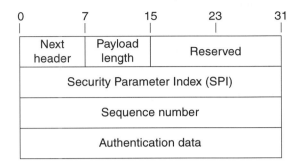

Figure 6.1   The AH header.

The next header field indicates what follows the AH header. In transport mode it will be the value of the upper-layer protocol being protected, for instance UDP or TCP. In tunnel mode, the value is 4 indicating IP-in-IP (IPv4) encapsulation or 41 for IPv6 encapsulation.

The payload length field indicates the length of the payload itself in 32-bit words minus two. AH is an IPv6 extension header, and according to RFC2460 its length is calculated by subtracting one 64-bit word from the length of the header in 64-bit words. But AH is measured in 32-bit words so we subtract two 32-bit words (or one 64-bit word). The reserved field is not used and must be set to zero.

The SPI field contains the SPI that, along with the destination address of the outer IP header, is used to identify the security association used to authenticate this packet.

The sequence number is a monotonically increasing counter that is identical to that used in ESP. Chapter 3 describes the antireplay function that the sequence number provides.

The authentication data field is a variable length field that contains the result of the integrity checking function. AH does not define an authenticator, but there are two mandatory-to-implement authenticators: HMAC-SHA-96 and HMAC-MD5-96. Like ESP, these are keyed MAC functions whose output is truncated to 96 bits. No public key authentication algorithms (like RSA or DSS) have been defined for use with AH. This is due to the cost; public key algorithms are too slow for bulk data authentication. In certain situations, such as network bootstrapping or the sending of SNMP traps, there is no bulk data protection and this limitation may not apply. For just this reason there is work being done to define the use of DSS with AH.

AH Modes

AH can be used in either transport or tunnel mode, just like ESP. The difference is the data being protected, either an upper-layer protocol or an entire IP datagram.

Transport Mode

When used in transport mode, AH protects end-to-end communication. The communications endpoint must be IPSec endpoint. The AH header is inserted into the datagram by placing it immediately following the IP header (and any options) and before the upper-layer protocol header.

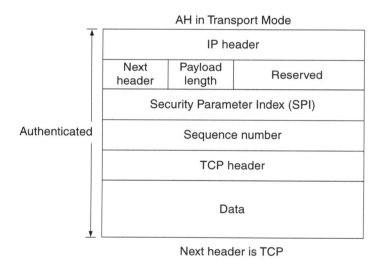

Figure 6.2   An IP packet before and after protection with transport mode AH.

Tunnel Mode

When used in tunnel mode, AH encapsulates the protected datagram. An additional IP header is added before the AH header after that. The "internal" IP datagram maintains the original addressing of the communication and the "outer" IP datagram contains the addresses of the IPSec endpoints. Tunnel mode can be used as a replacement to transport mode for end-to-end security. However, as there is no confidentiality and therefore no protection against traffic analysis, it is pointless. AH is used only to guarantee that the received packet was not modified in transit, that it was sent by the party claiming to have sent it, and, optionally, that it is a fresh, nonreplayed packet.

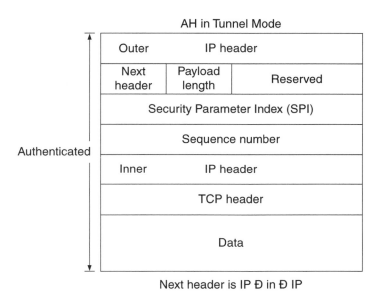

Figure 6.3   An IP packet before and after protection with tunnel mode AH.

AH Processing

When an outbound packet matches an SPD entry indicating protection with AH, the SADB is queried to see whether a suitable SA exists. If there is no SA, IKE can be used to dynamically create one. If there is an SA, AH is applied to the matched packet in the mode dictated by the SPD entry. If there is an SPD bundle, the order of application depends on the protocols involved. AH always protects ESP, not the other way around.

Output Processing

As mentioned in Chapter 3, when an outbound SA is created—either manually or by IKE—the sequence number counter is initialized to zero. Prior to construction of an AH header using this SA, the counter is incremented. This guarantees that the sequence number in each AH header will be a unique, nonzero, and a monotonically increasing number.

The remaining fields of the AH header are filled in with their appropriate value—the SPI field is assigned the SPI from the SA; the next header field is assigned the value of the type of data following the AH header; and the payload length is assigned the number of 32-bit-words-minus-two value discussed above; and the authentication data field is set to zero.

Unlike ESP, AH extends its protection to immutable or predictable fields of the outer IP header. It is therefore necessary to zero out the mutable fields prior to computation of the Integrity Check Value (ICV). The mutable fields of an IPv4 header that are not included in the authenticating ICV (and are therefore "unprotected") are the shaded fields in Figure 6.4.

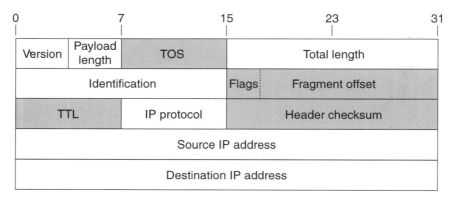

Figure 6.4   Mutable and immutable fields of an IPv4 header.

For IPv4 options or IPv6 extension headers, if they are immutable or predictable, they are included in the computation of the ICV. Otherwise, it is necessary to zero them out before computing the ICV.

Padding may be needed depending on the requirements of the authenticator or for alignment reasons. Some MACs—for instance, DES-CBC MAC—require the data over which the MAC is applied be a multiple of the algorithm's block size. In this case padding must be added to properly use the MAC. (Note that neither of the mandatory algorithms have this requirement.) This padding is implicitly added. It must be entirely of the value "zero", and its size is not included in the payload length and is not transmitted with the packet.

The AH header must be a multiple of 32 bits for IPv4 and 64 bits for IPv6. If the output of the MAC is such that this requirement is not met, the AH header must be padded. There is no requirement on the value of the pad, but it must be included in the ICV calculations and the pad size must be reflected in the payload length. The mandatory-to-implement authenticators are properly aligned, so no padding is needed when using HMAC-MD5-96 or HMAC-SHA-96.

The ICV is calculated by passing the key from the SA and the entire IP packet (including the AH header) to the algorithm identified as the authenticator in the SA. Since the mutable fields have been zeroed out the actual values are not included in the ICV. The ICV value is then copied into authentication data field of the AH and the mutable fields in the IP header can be filled in.

AH processing is now complete and the AH-protected IP packet can be transmitted. Depending on the size of the packet, it might be fragmented prior to placing on the wire or it might be fragmented in transit by routers between the two IPSec peers. This is not a problem and is taken care of during input processing.

Input Processing

Reassembly may be required prior to AH input processing if the protected packet was fragmented prior to its receipt. This is a fairly obvious requirement since the ICV check will fail unless it is done on exactly the same data from which the ICV was generated. The Authentication Header document (RFC2402) notes that the current specification of IPv4 does not require the offset field to be zeroed or the more fragments flag to be cleared after reassembly. AH therefore imposes this requirement on reassembly to guarantee that the inbound packet resembles the outbound packet the peer sent. A fully-formed, AH-protected IP packet can then be passed on to AH input processing.

The first thing to do when processing any IPSec packet is to find the SA that was used to protect it, and AH is no different than ESP in this respect. The SA is, again, identified by the destination address of the IP header, the protocol (in this case 51), and the SPI from the AH header. If no SA is found, the packet is discarded.

Once the SA is found, a sequence number check is made. This step is optional but the cost-to-benefit ratio is so low that there is really no reason not to perform an antireplay check. The antireplay check (described in Chapter 3) determines whether this packet is new or received too late. If it fails this check it is discarded.

The ICV must now be checked. First, the ICV value in the authentication data field of the AH header is saved and that field is zeroed. All mutable fields in the IP are also zeroed (these are the same fields, described above, that were zeroed prior to ICV calculation). If the authenticator algorithm and payload length are such that implicit padding is required to bring the size of the data authenticated up to the requirements of the algorithm, implicit padding is added. This implicit padding must contain the value zero. The authenticator algorithm is then applied to the entire packet and the resulting digest is compared to the saved ICV value. If they match, the IP packet has been authenticated; if they do not match the packet must be discarded.

Once the ICV has been verified, the sequence number of the sliding receive window can be advanced if necessary. This concludes AH processing. The saved IP header can then be restored—remember that the mutable fields were zeroed out and this would prevent further processing—and the entire authenticated datagram can be passed to IP processing.

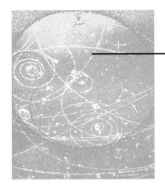

The Internet Key Exchange

Prior to an IP packet being secured by IPSec, a security association (SA) must exist. The Internet Key Exchange (IKE) creates SAs dynamically on behalf of IPSec and populates and manages the Security Association Database (SADB).

IKE, described in RFC2409, is a hybrid protocol. It is based on a framework defined by the Internet Security Association and Key Management Protocol (ISAKMP), defined in RFC2408, and implements parts of two key management protocols—Oakley and SKEME. In addition IKE defines two exchanges of its own.

Oakley is a protocol developed by Hilarie Orman, a cryptographer from the University of Arizona. It is a free-form protocol that allows each party to advance the state of the protocol at its own speed. From Oakley, IKE borrowed the idea of different modes, each producing a similar result—an authenticated key exchange— through the exchange of information. In Oakley, there was no definition of what information to exchange with each message. The modes were examples of how Oakley could be utilized to achieve a secure key exchange. IKE codified the modes into exchanges. By narrowing the flexibility of the Oakley model, IKE limits the wide range of possibilities that Oakley allows yet still provides multiple modes, albeit in a well-defined manner.

SKEME is another key exchange protocol, designed by cryptographer Hugo Krawczyk. SKEME defines a type of authenticated key exchange in which the parties use public key encryption to authenticate each other and "share" components of the exchange. Each side encrypts a random number in the public key of the peer and both random numbers (after decryption) contribute to the ultimate key. One can optionally do a Diffie-Hellman exchange along with the SKEME share technique for Perfect Forward Secrecy (PFS), or merely use another rapid exchange, which does not require public key operations, to refresh an existing key. IKE borrows this technique directly from SKEME for one of its authentication methods (authentication with public key encryption) and also borrows the notion of rapid key refreshment without PFS.

ISAKMP was developed by researchers at the National Security Agency (NSA). The NSA used to be a super-secret organization whose existence was even denied by the United States government. Recently, the NSA has come out of the shadows and its considerable expertise in cryptography and security has been put to visible use. ISAKMP is one such output.

It is upon these three protocols—ISAKMP, Oakley, and SKEME—that IKE is based. It is a hybrid protocol; it uses the foundation of ISAKMP, the modes of Oakley, and the share and rekeying techniques of SKEME to define its own unique way of deriving authenticated keying material and negotiating shared policy. The contributions of Oakley and

SKEME can be seen in the discussion of IKE itself, but the contributions of ISAKMP are considerable enough to warrant a separate discussion.

IKE is a generic protocol that can establish security associations for multiple security services. IPSec is one such service. The specification of how to use IKE to establish IPSec Sas is in the Domain of Interpretation (DOI) for IPSec. This specification is described in RFC2407.

ISAKMP

ISAKMP defines how two peers communicate, how the messages they use to communicate are constructed, and also defines the state transitions they go through to secure their communication. It provides the means to authenticate a peer, to exchange information for a key exchange, and to negotiate security services. It does not, however, define *how* a particular authenticated key exchange is done, nor does it define the attributes necessary for establishment of security associations. That is left to other documents, namely a key exchange document (such as the Internet Key Exchange) and a Domain of Interpretation (such as the Internet IP Security Domain of Interpretation).

Messages and Payloads

Messages exchanged in an ISAKMP-based key management protocol are constructed by chaining together ISAKMP payloads to an ISAKMP header (Figure 7.1).

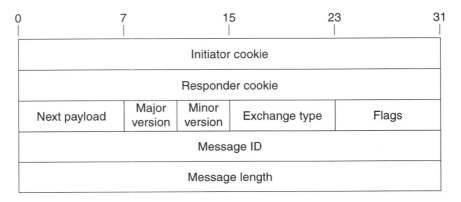

Figure 7.1   The ISAKMP Header

The initiator cookie and responder cookie are created by each peer and are used, along with the message ID, to identify the state that defines an ISAKMP exchange in progress. The next payload field indicates which of the various ISAKMP payloads immediately follows the header. ISAKMP versions are identified by major/minor number in the major version and minor version fields. The specific type of ISAKMP exchange is identified by the *exchange* field. The entire length of the ISAKMP message, including the length of the header itself, is denoted in the message length field. The flags field gives the recipient additional information pertinent to the message. Flags are represented by a bit mask where each bit signifies the presence of an option. There are 3 flags defined (in an 8-bit field, which allows for growth): encryption, which signifies that the payloads following the header are encrypted; the commit flag, which signifies that a peer wishes a notification of exchange completion (more on this in the description of IKE); and the authentication-only bit, used primarily by those who wish to add key recovery to ISAKMP.

There are 13 distinct payloads defined in ISAKMP. They all begin with the same generic header, as shown in Figure 7.2.

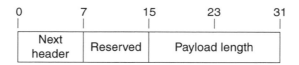

Figure 7.2   The ISAKMP Generic Header

The type of ISAKMP payload that follows the current payload is denoted by the next payload field. The entire length of an ISAKMP payload, including the header, is denoted by the payload length field. The reserved field is not used and must be set to zero.

Some payloads are dependent on each other. For instance, a transform payload is always encapsulated by a proposal payload that in turn is always encapsulated by a security association payload. Several payloads also define attributes specific to their type. For instance, a certificate payload defines what sort of certificate it is—an X.509 signature certificate, or a CRL, or a PKCS#7 wrapped certificate, etc.

ISAKMP defines payloads to express certain constructs during an exchange. Some of these are generic, like hash digests or pseudo-random nonces, or specific, like certificates or security associations. The generic payloads are all syntactically identical and differ only in what they contain. These include:

- a hash payload, which contains the digest output of a particular hash function.
- a signature payload, which contains a digital signature.
- a nonce payload, which contains some pseudo-random information necessary for the exchange.
- a vendor ID payload, which is, in effect, an opaque blob. Each vendor defines his own and is therefore able to identify his own implementations on the network.
- a key exchange payload, which contains information necessary to perform a key exchange, for instance, a Diffie-Hellman public value.

Some payloads are syntactically different. The construct construct they represent are different enough to have a unique payload specification. These include:

- a security association payload, which defines a security association—both an ISAKMP SA and one for other security protocols like IPSec.
- a certificate payload.
- a certificate request payload.
- an identification payload.

There are two other payloads that are dependent on and encapsulated by a security association payload and may not appear alone. These are the proposal payload, which describes a single proposal of a security association, and a transform payload, which describes a single transform for a proposal.

Each transform payload contains a set of attributes that apply to the transform. These attributes are quite flexible and therefore also quite complicated. An attribute is basically a type/value pair. Each attribute is identified by its type and that type has a value. For instance, an attribute of type "encryption algorithm" may have an attribute value of "CAST." (Of course these type/value pairs are not English words but are numbers whose values are assigned by IANA—the Internet Assigned Number Authority). Attribute types are represented by simple 16-bit words while their values may be variable length or also a 16-bit word. The high-order bit of the type field denotes whether the attribute is a basic attribute whose value is a single 16-bit word, or a variable-precision integer, or VPI attribute, whose length is a single 16-bit word and whose value is contained in a variable length field. The remainder of the attribute type field is the actual numeric definition of the type. A basic attribute value immediately follows the attribute type, a VPI attribute value follows the length field. The attribute payload is shown in Figure 7.3.

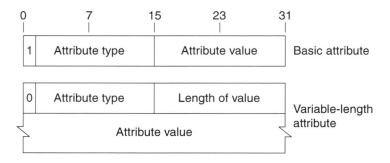

Figure 7.3   The Attribute Payload

where the first bit is the attribute format, A/F, flag which signals whether the low-order two bytes of the four-byte payload is the value of the attribute (A/F = 1) or whether they are the length of the value that follows the four-byte payload (A/F = 0). If A/F equals 1 the entire attribute is four bytes; if A/F equals 0 the entire attribute is four bytes plus the length of the value. These variable length attributes are necessary to express values that may be too large to hold in a 16-bit word, like Diffie-Hellman exponentials.

Other payloads are defined to enable notification data, such as error conditions to be passed to a peer and delete messages to be passed instructing a peer to delete a specific security association. These payloads are the notify payload and the delete payload.

In addition, certain payloads define attributes that are specific to the payload. For instance, the certificate payload has a certificate type field that is used to specify what type of certificate is being conveyed in the payload.

The ISAKMP specification has a complete description of payload formats and payload-specific attributes.

Messages

Payloads are chained together in a message by using the next payload field in the generic header (see Figure 7.4). The ISAKMP header describes the first payload following the header, and each payload describes which payload comes next. The last payload in the message is zero. ISAKMP communication is done via UDP port 500. Other port/protocol combinations are possible, but UDP port 500 has been reserved by IANA for ISAKMP and all ISAKMP implementations are required to support communication over UDP port 500.

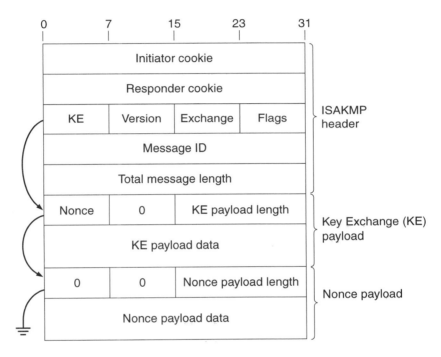

Figure 7.4   ISAKMP Payloads Chained to Form a Message

Exchanges and Phases

ISAKMP describes two separate phases of negotiation. In the first phase, peers establish an authenticated and secure channel between themselves. In the second phase that authenticated and secure channel is used to negotiate security services for a different protocol—such as IPSec.

A phase one exchange establishes an ISAKMP "security association." The concept of this SA—an abstraction of security policy and a key—has some similarities to an IPSec SA but it is decidedly different. To establish this SA the peers must first negotiate the desired attributes for the SA, and a method to authenticate each other. After the peers have authenticated each other his SA is then used to protect subsequent phase two exchanges. There is no limit to the number of ISAKMP SAs two peers can share, but practically, one will do.

A phase two exchange establishes security associations for other protocols. Since the ISAKMP SA is already authenticated, it can be used to provide source authentication, integrity, and confidentiality to all messages in a phase two exchange. Once a phase two exchange finishes the state associated with it in the ISAKMP process it is destroyed but the ISAKMP SA can live on to secure subsequent phase two exchanges. There is no limit to the number of phase two exchanges, but one generally wants to limit the use of any secret derived from a single key exchange. This will be discussed further when we talk about IKE.

ISAKMP describes five exchanges. These exchanges are neither strictly phase one nor phase two exchanges, but are merely generic examples of how to use ISAKMP to negotiate a security association and perform an authenticated key exchange. These are not full exchanges in that the method of authentication is not described; authentication data is exchanged but the generation and processing of this data, the actual authentication step, is not described. Each exchange has slightly different goals and accomplishes them in differing numbers of steps. For instance, the identity protection exchange has the goal of hiding the identity of the peers from any eavesdroppers; it accomplishes this in six messages. The authentication only exchange is only concerned with authenticating the peers and not establishing a shared secret; it accomplishes this in three messages and does not include a key exchange.

Cookies

The first step of any exchange is an exchange of cookies. These are 8 byte pseudo-random numbers generated by each ISAKMP entity and assigned to each remote peer. Each cookie is unique to the remote peer and also to the particular exchange in which it is defined. The purpose of the cookies is to identify the ISAKMP SA and also to provide some anti-clogging protection against certain denial of service attacks. While no method of cookie generation is proscribed in ISAKMP, the technique proposed by Karn and Simpson (in the *Photuris* key exchange) is the preferred method: The cookie is the result of hashing a unique identifier of the peer (e.g., his IP address and a port and protocol), a secret known only to the generator, and some timestamp. In this manner, each cookie is bound to the remote peer and it is trivial to check that the cookie presented by a peer is the one given to him. The cookies reside in the ISAKMP header.

To achieve the most anticlogging protection out of the cookies, an exchange will generally delay expensive and intensive operations—such as exponentiation for a Diffie-Hellman exchange—until cookies have been exchanged. In this way, some protection against rudimentary denial-of-service attacks is possible. For instance, an attacker who generates thousands of bogus ISAKMP messages with false return addresses would not cause his target to do any significant work because the second message that contains the cookie unique to the (bogus) address would not be received.

The cookie exchange takes place in the first two messages exchanged. The first message is from the *initiator* of the protocol to the *responder*. The initiator creates a cookie unique to the responder and the exchange he wishes to begin and inserts it into the initiator cookie portion of the ISAKMP header. Since this is the first message there is no responder cookie and that field is zero. After the message has been received and processed the responder generates a cookie for this exchange. To formulate a reply he copies this to the responder cookie portion of the header of his reply and copies the cookie provided by the initiator into the initiator cookie field of the header of his reply. The responder is able to create a larval ISAKMP security association identified by the cookies and send the message back to the initiator. Upon receipt of this response the initiator is able to update her larval SA with the responder's cookie and the exchange continues.

Obviously the initiator must create some state prior to sending out the first message. At a minimum, this state must contain the peer to which the message was sent and the cookie created for him. Since he sent out the message before he knew the responder's cookie, he must be prepared to identify this state based solely on his own cookie. After receiving the responder's first message, though, he's able to update that state to include the responder's cookie.

The responder also creates some state in the form of the larval ISAKMP SA. It does not do any significant work until it has received it's cookie back from the initiator and verified that that cookie is correct based on the peer's IP address.

After the cookie exchange the concatenation of the two cookies identifies the SA in the same manner in which an SPI identifies an IPSec SA. Since the cookies are passed as part of the ISAKMP header it is straightforward for an entity to look up the state associated with the message—the ISAKMP SA—upon receipt of the message. After a message is processed, the state of the ISAKMP SA is updated and a response, if required, is sent. In this manner, the exchange proceeds until the ISAKMP SA has been completed.

Policy Negotiation

Establishing a shared security association entails negotiation of security policy. Since policy may be complex (e.g., A and B or C), a flexible parsing of security association, proposal, and transform payloads must be allowed that in turn allows for the construction and processing of complex policy offers. ISAKMP accomplishes this with security association, proposal, and transform payloads (figure 7.5). A single security association may contain one or more proposals and each proposal may contain one or more transforms.

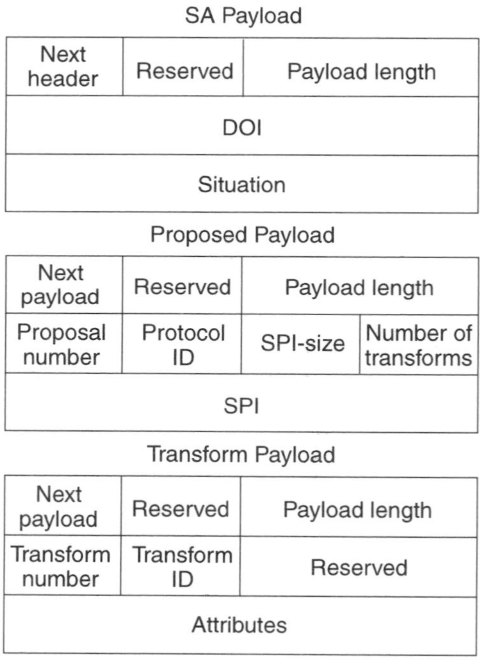

SA Payload

Next header	Reserved	Payload length
DOI		
Situation		

Proposed Payload

Next payload	Reserved	Payload length	
Proposal number	Protocol ID	SPI-size	Number of transforms
SPI			

Transform Payload

Next payload	Reserved	Payload length	
Transform number	Transform ID	Reserved	
Attributes			

Figure 7.5   Security Association Payload, Proposal Payload, and Transform Payload

The DOI field of the security association payload defines the domain of interpretation to which the payload applies. A DOI value of zero is used for ISAKMP. Different DOI values are used for different security services. A separate DOI defines how ISAKMP is used to establish SAs for that particular service. The DOI for IPSec is described later in this chapter. The situation field of the SA payload contains information necessary to allow the recipient to make policy decisions during negotiation and is DOI-specific. Since multiple proposal payloads per SA payload are possible, the proposal payload contains a proposal number. Each proposal can result in a security association and therefore has an SPI, and an SPI size, and the protocol of the SA. Following a proposal payload is one or more transform payloads, and the proposal payload must therefore include a field to denote how many transform payloads follow. The transform payload contains a transform number and a transform identifier that indicates the type of transform. Following a transform are any attributes (encoded using the attribute payload) specific to that transform.

As mentioned, a single SA payload may contain multiple proposal payloads. The proposal number of the proposal payload is used to express the logical operators OR and AND. Matching proposal numbers are taken as a logical AND and differing proposal numbers are taken as a logical OR. For instance, if IPSec policy requires AH *and* ESP, the proposal payloads for each separate proposal—one for each protocol—would have identical proposal numbers. If IPSec policy required AH *or* ESP, the proposal payloads for each separate proposal—one for each protocol—would be different. In this manner it is possible to construct quite complex offers. If we include the IP payload compression protocol (more on that in section 11) in our policy, it is possible to express things such as: "authenticate everything and if possible also encrypt it, and if possible also compress it." Since order of preference in offers counts, this would be expressed as "[AH-1 or ESP-2 or (ESP-3 and PCP-3)]" where *protocol-n* is a proposal for *protocol* with proposal number *n*.

Each proposal may be, in fact, an offer of multiple transforms. Each of these transforms are a different way of accepting the proposal and each transform is the logical OR of the others. Continuing with our complex policy expression, we could add multiple transforms per proposal and desire 3DES over AES and SHA over MD5 and LZS over Deflate (for PCP) and our offer would be:

Proposal 1: AH
    Transform 1: HMAC-SHA
    Transform 2: HMAC-MD5
Proposal 2: ESP
    Transform 1: 3DES with HMAC-SHA
    Transform 2: 3DES with HMAC-MD5
    Transform 3: AES with HMAC-SHA
    Transform 4: AES with HMAC-MD5
Proposal 3: ESP
    Transform 1: 3DES with HMAC-SHA
    Transform 2: 3DES with HMAC-MD5
    Transform 3: AES with HMAC-SHA
    Transform 4: AES with HMAC-MD5
Proposal 3: PCP
    Transform 1: LZS
    Transform 2: Deflate

What we're offering here is ((AH-HMAC-SHA OR AH-HMAC-MD5) OR (3DES w/HMAC-SHA OR 3DES w/HMAC-MD5 OR AES w/HMAC-SHA OR AES w/HMAC-MD5) OR [(3DES w/HMAC-SHA OR 3DES w/HMAC-MD5 OR AES w/HMAC-SHA OR AES w/HMAC-MD5) AND (PCP-LZS OR PCP-DEFLATE)]). That's quite a complex offer!

Security association payload construction and parsing are complex because security policy is complex. Thankfully, other payloads are not so complicated.

IKE

ISAKMP doesn't define a key exchange. That is left to other protocols. For IPSec the defined key exchange is IKE—the Internet Key Exchange. IKE uses the language of ISAKMP to define a key exchange and a way to negotiate security services. IKE actually defines a number of exchanges and options that can be applied to the exchanges. The end result of an IKE exchange is an authenticated key and agreed-upon security services—in other words, an IPSec security association. But IKE is not only for IPSec. It is generic enough to negotiate security services for any other protocol that requires them, for instance routing protocols which require authenticated keys like RIP or OSPF.

IKE is a two-phase exchange. The first phase establishes the IKE security association and the second uses that security association to negotiate security associations for IPSec. Unlike ISAKMP, IKE defines the attributes of its security association. It doesn't define the attributes of any other security association, though. That is left up to a domain of interpretation (DOI). For IPSec there exists the Internet IP Security domain of interpretation. Other protocols are free to write their own DOI for IKE.

A DOI defines the optional and required attributes that IKE will negotiate in a phase two exchange. IKE doesn't define its own DOI per se, but it does define the terms and conditions surrounding the use of its security association.

IKE defines two phase one exchanges, one phase two exchange, and two extra exchanges for proper maintenance of its security association. For the phase one exchanges IKE uses the identity protect exchange, and aggressive exchange from the base ISAKMP document and calls them main mode and aggressive mode, respectively. But unlike the ISAKMP exchanges, IKE has fully defined the exchange—the contents of all payloads and the steps taken to process them. For phase two, IKE defines a Quick Mode exchange. This negotiates security services for protocols other than IKE—primarily IPSec, but, again, IKE is generic enough for a Quick Mode exchange to establish the necessary security services for RIPv2 or OSPF or any other protocol requiring security. The two other exchanges IKE defines are an informational exchange in which IKE peers can communicate error and status information to each other, and a new group exchange that allows IKE peers to negotiate the use of a new Diffie-Hellman group among themselves.

IKE Exchanges

The two phase one exchanges—main mode and aggressive mode—each accomplish the same thing: establishment of a secure and authenticated communications channel (the IKE SA) and authenticated keys used to provide confidentiality, message integrity, and message source authentication to the IKE communications between the two peers. All the other exchanges defined in IKE have an authenticated IKE SA as a prerequisite. Therefore a phase one exchange, either main mode or aggressive mode, must be performed before any other exchange.

The IKE SA has various parameters that define how it was created and authenticated and how it is to protect phase 2 exchanges. For all these negotiated parameters, IKE defines attributes and the range of values that these attributes may have.

The parameters—encryption algorithm, hash algorithm, authentication method, and Diffie-Hellman group—are referred to as a protection suite. Protection suites are negotiated as a unit by exchanging ISAKMP SA payloads. Each of the attributes of the protection suite are contained in transform payloads. In addition to those mandatory attributes there are also optional attributes that may be negotiated as part of a protection suite. Foremost among these optional attributes is a lifetime. The lifetime attribute determines how long the IKE SA exists. The longer an IKE SA exists, the greater the risk of leakage of its key, so an implementation is encouraged to include lifetimes in the protection suites offered to peers.

A hash algorithm is negotiated as part of a protection suite, but its use is usually in HMAC form. IKE uses an HMAC version of the hash algorithm as a pseudo-random function (PRF) to generate a seemingly random bitstream. It is possible to negotiate other PRF functions with IKE, but usually an HMAC version of the negotiated hash algorithm is used.

The encryption algorithm and hash algorithm attributes are straightforward. They determine which algorithm will be used for message encryption and authentication. But what about the rest?

The Diffie-Hellman group is a basic attribute that determines the parameters to use when the peers engage in a Diffie-Hellman exchange. You're probably wondering how a single basic attribute can express the required parameters to perform a Diffie-Hellman exchange. This is because IKE defines five groups and assigns unique values to them. Therefore, when a peer refers to "group number 2" the other peer knows the generator and prime modulus of the group implicitly and the two can participate in a Diffie-Hellman exchange. There are three types of Diffie-Hellman groups that can be expressed in IKE—traditional exponentiation over a prime modulus (MODP), and two types of elliptic curves, one over $G[P]$ (ECP) and another over $G[2^N]$ (EC2N). The groups IKE defines are:

1. an MODP group with a 768-bit modulus
2. an MODP group with a 1024-bit modulus
3. an EC2N group with a 155-bit field size
4. an EC2N group with a 185-bit field size
5. a MODP group with a 1680-bit modulus

More groups can be easily defined and using the New Group Exchange two peers can define their own. Only group two is mandatory to implement. It is generally felt that groups 1 and 3 provide roughly similar amounts of security to an exchange, one using a prime modulus and the other an elliptic curve. Similarly, groups 2 and 4 also provide roughly similar amounts of security. The difference between the two is the speed considerations that can be realized by using elliptic curve cryptography (groups 3 and 4) over traditional exponentiation in a finite field (groups 1 and 2). Currently there is no Elliptic Curve analog to group 5.

The attribute with the most impact on the IKE exchange is the authentication method. The other attributes will determine the contents of payloads and how messages are protected, but the authentication method determines which payloads are exchanged and when they are exchanged. An IKE exchange may actually change depending on the authentication method negotiated by the two peers! The acceptable methods of authentication are: (1) preshared keys; (2) digital signatures using the Digital Signature Algorithm; (3) digital signatures using the Rivest-Shamir-Adelman algorithm; and (4) two similar methods of authenticating via exchange of encrypted nonces.

These attributes are negotiated between the peers as part of the first messages they exchange. These are the external and visible characteristics of the IKE SA—their negotiation takes place "in the clear". But each side also maintains some secret information that will not be visible to a casual observer (or an active attacker!) of an IKE exchange. This secret information is the keys that are authenticated used to protect IKE messages and also derive keys for other security services. The peers generate a secret, SKEYID, and then three other secrets based on SKEYID: SKEYID_d, which is used to derive keying material for IPSec (and others) SAs, SKEYID_a, which is used to provide data integrity and data source authentication to IKE messages; and, SKEYID_e which is used to encrypt IKE messages. The generation of SKEYID is dependent on the authentication method negotiated. All other SKEYID-based secrets are generated identically, regardless of authentication method.

Each side contributes a cookie and a nonce to SKEYID state generation: The initiator contributes his cookie, CKY-I, and his nonce, Ni; similarly, the responder contributes CKY-R and Nr. These are used as a "liveliness" proof: Each side demonstrates to the other that it possesses the other's nonce and cookie and is therefore "live" and not "Memorex." They also provide some additional freshness to each secret. As a result of the Diffie-Hellman exchange the peers share the Diffie-Hellman shared secret, g^{xy}, which is also used in SKEYID generation. Using '|' to denote concatenation, SKEYID state is generated as follows:

> For preshared key authentication:
> > SKEYID=PRF(preshared-key, Ni | Nr)
> For signature authentication:
> > SKEYID=PRF(Ni | Nr, g^{xy})
> For encrypted nonce authentication:
> > SKEYID=PRF(hash(Ni | Nr), CKY-I | CKY-R)

where PRF, the aforementioned pseudo-random function, usually the HMAC-version of the negotiated hash function. Once SKEYID has been generated the remainder of the secrets can be generated:

> SKEYID_d = PRF(SKEYID, g^{xy} | CKY-I | CKY-R | 0)
> SKEYID_a = PRF(SKEYID, SKEYID_d | g^{xy} | CKY-I | CKY-R | 1)
> SKEYID_e = PRF(SKEYID, SKEYID_a | g^{xy} | CKY-I | CKY-R | 2)

Note that all SKEYID state is generated by PRF functions. The block size of the PRF function will therefore determine the resulting size of the SKEYID state. For cases where the output of the PRF is too small to be used as an encryption key, SKEYID_e must be expanded. For example, a PRF of HMAC-MD5 will produce 128-bits of output but the Blowfish cipher can require 448 bits of keying material. In this case, SKEYID_e is expanded by using a feedback and concatenation technique until the requisite number of bits has been achieved. Using our MD5 and Blowfish example, SKEYID_e would be the first (high-order) 448 bits of K, where:

> K = K1 | K2 | K3 | K4
> K1 = PRF(SKEYID, 0)
> K2 = PRF(SKEYID, K1, 1)
> K3 = PRF(SKEYID, K1, 2)
> K4 = PRF(SKEYID, K2, 3)

Phase one exchanges are authenticated by each side computing a hash that only they could know. Since it is impossible to determine the inputs to a hash function from the output of the hash function, and the same inputs will always produce the same output, the production of the appropriate digest authenticates the peer. The computation of the hash is identical regardless of the authentication method negotiated, but the initiator and responder compute their respective digests differently. The initiator's authenticating hash is:

> HASH-I = PRF(SKEYID, g^i | g^r | CKY-I | CKY-R | SA-offer | ID-I)

The responder's authenticating hash is:

HASH-R = PRF(SKEYID, g^r | g^i | CKY-R | CKY-I | SA-offer | ID-R)

Where g^i and g^r are the Diffie-Hellman public numbers of the initiator and responder, respectively, SA-offer is the entire SA payload with all protection suites offered by the initiator to the responder, and ID-I and ID-R are the identities of the initiator and responder respectively.

Inclusion of the entire SA payload is important to prevent a man-in-the-middle attack where an attacker could modify the protections suites offered down to their lowest or weakest protection suite. For instance, if both peers would prefer to use Triple-DES as the encryption algorithm but would reluctantly settle for DES, an attacker could modify a request of "Triple-DES or DES" to merely "DES." The responder would reluctantly accept it and neither party would be aware that they could have been communicating more securely. By including the entire offered SA payload in the authenticating hash, such an attack is prevented.

The IKE SA differs from an IPSec SA in that it is bidirectional. There are specific roles assumed by the participants of an exchange. Specifically, one party is the initiator and the other is the responder, but once the SA has been established it may be used to protect both inbound and outbound traffic. Also, regardless of who initiated the phase one exchange that established the IKE SA, either party may initiate a phase two exchange and protect it with the IKE SA. The cookies in the ISAKMP header are not swapped if the responder in phase one becomes the initiator in phase two since the cookie pair is used to identify the appropriate SA in the IKE SADB.

In the following exchange diagrams, payloads encrypted using SKEYID_e as the key are italicized. All ciphers used in IKE must be in CBC mode and therefore require, in addition to a key, an initialization vector (IV). The initial IV is generated by hashing the two Diffie-Hellman public values together, and after each successive encryption and decryption the IV becomes the last ciphertext block processed. In this way the IV chains cipher operations together and "runs" from block to block.

Main Mode Exchange

Main mode uses six messages, in three round trips, to establish the IKE SA. These three steps are SA negotiation, a Diffie-Hellman exchange and an exchange of nonces, and the authentication of the peer. The features of main mode are identity protection and the full use of the

ISAKMP's negotiation capabilities. Identity protection is important when the peers wish to hide their identities. The breadth of negotiation capabilities will become apparent when we discuss aggressive mode. As mentioned, the authentication method can influence the composition of payloads and even their placement in messages, but the intent and purpose of the messages—the steps taken in Main Mode—remain regardless.

When used with preshared key authentication, main mode is the exchange of messages shown in Figure 7.6.

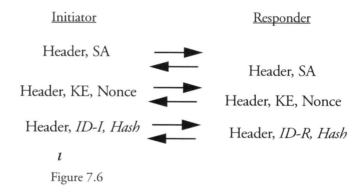

Figure 7.6

In the first exchange of messages the peers negotiate the parameters of the IKE SA and agree on what the rest of the exchange will look like. They also exchange cookies in the ISAKMP header of each message—the initiator chooses his in his first message, placing it in the initiator cookie portion of the ISAKMP header, the responder chooses his in the second message, placing it in the responder cookie portion of the ISAKMP header. In the second exchange of messages the peers exchange Diffie-Hellman public values (computed in the group negotiated as part of a protection suite in the first message exchange) and pseudo-random nonces. At this point the peers can complete their Diffie-Hellman exchange and generate the SKEYID secrets. In the last message exchange the peers identify themselves and exchange the authenticating hash digest. The final two messages exchanged are encrypted with SKEYID_e.

An observant reader will notice that since SKEYID_e must be used before the ID payloads are exchanged, a preshared key can be based only on the IP address of the peer. This is an acknowledged limitation of preshared keys with Main Mode. For most situations this is not an issue, but for remote-access environments where the initiator of the protocol is coming from an IP address that cannot be known a priori there is a problem. The responder cannot maintain preshared keys for addresses that it does not know. An easy way out of this problem is for remote-access environments to use a public key signature-based authentication method and not use preshared keys. If preshared keys must be used, aggressive mode can be used as a phase one exchange since it does not have this limitation. More on aggressive mode later.

Main mode can also be authenticated with public key signatures, either DSS or RSA. Public keys are usually obtained from certificates and IKE allows for certificates to be exchanged and also for certificates to be requested from a peer. Using public key signatures, main mode is the exchange of messages shown in Figure 7.7.

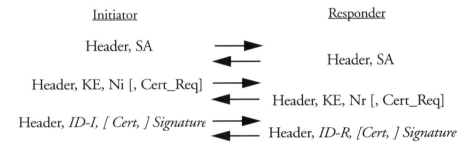

Figure 7.7

where optional payloads are bracketed. Notice the similarity to main mode with preshared keys. Excluding the optional payloads, the one difference is that the authentication is accomplished by a digital signature and not a hash digest. The optional payloads allow for certificates to be requested—the Cert_Req payload—and be exchanged—the Cert payload.

There are two types of authentication methods that use an exchange of encrypted nonces—a standard public key encryption method, and a revised method of public key encryption. The revised method arose because of a criticism against the standard method, that it requires two separate, and expensive, public key encryptions. The revised mode only requires a single public key encryption and encrypts the other payloads with a symmetric cipher. During development of the IPSec and IKE standards there was discussion of removing the standard mode, but since several implementations of it were already in existence another method was added.

Both of these methods have the feature of being repudiable. That is, each side could deny that they were a party to the exchange even if all the messages and state associated with the IKE session are saved. If you've ever done something you don't want anyone to know about, these are the exchanges you should've used to establish your IPSec SAs! The proof of authentication is ability of the peer to decrypt the key and reconstruct the authenticating digest is proof that the peer holds the corresponding private key—after all, he was able to decrypt the nonce—and therefore is proof of identity. The reason these are deniable is because the nonces exchanged in main mode are encrypted in the peer's public key—the initiator's nonce is encrypted with the responder's public key and vice versa. Since anyone can encrypt anything in your public key and since both sides know the entire contents of each side of the exchange, the entire exchange can be faked! Of course, when two parties are actively engaged in one of these exchanges, they have proof of identity via the ability of the peer to compute the right digest, but either party could deny the exchange to a third party at a later date.

Since both these methods use public key encryption it is not possible to use DSS with them. The most common manner of implementing these methods is to use RSA public keys that provide for a way to encrypt with a public key. The El-Gamal variant of the Diffie-Hellman public key cryptosystem is also a viable possibility for use with these methods.

The standard method of public key encryption is the exchange of messages shown in Figure 7.8.

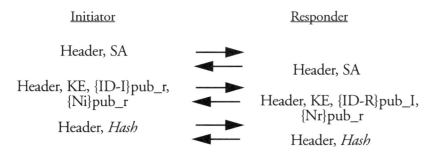

Figure 7.8

where {}pub_x is used to denote encryption with the public key of "x." Notice that in this exchange the ID payloads are exchanged with the second message. This is because the initiator has to give the responder some indication of his identity so the responder can properly locate his public key and encrypt the response to him. The ID protection feature of main mode is ensured by each peer also encrypting his identity with the public key of the peer.

Two public key encryptions are a drawback of this method. Another is that it does not allow for certificates to be requested or exchanged. To exchange a certificate would be to lose the identity protection of main mode. The initiator must know the identity of the responder prior to initiation of this exchange. This is generally not an issue since the initiator knows where he wants to go on the network and knows to whom he must talk to get there. Since there is no way to pass a certificate in this authentication method each side must support some other method of obtaining certificates.

You're probably asking, why not just encrypt the two payloads together? If both payloads were encrypted together the header of the nonce payload would be hidden. To properly parse the message then, the payload length of the ID payload would have to include the encrypted nonce payload. Such behavior would have a detrimental impact on the receiver of such a packet. A sanity check on the received message would be precluded since there would be no way to check the nonce payload's generic header for correctness. Also, the true length of the ID payload could not be determined. The receiver would have to guess where the ID stops and the generic header of the nonce begins! So, two public key encryptions are required.

As mentioned, the revised method of public key encryption does not have the drawbacks of the standard method. It requires half the public key operations and also provides for a capability for the initiator to provide a certificate to the responder. The initiator must still use some means outside of IKE to obtain the certificate of the responder, though. The revised method of authentication with public key encryption is the exchange of messages shown in Figure 7.9.

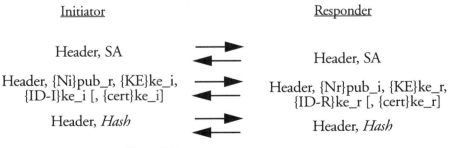

Figure 7.9

where {}ke_x indicates symmetric key encryption with the key "Ne_x." Now you're probably asking: Where does the key for the symmetric cipher come from and which algorithm do you use? Well, the algorithm is the same as that used fo rthe IKE SA, the one negotiated in the exchange of SA payloads. The keys are generated as follows:

Ne_i = PRF(Ni, CKY-I)
Ne_r = PRF(Nr, CKY-R)

So, upon decryption of the nonce, it is possible to compute the appropriate symmetric key and decrypt the remainder of the payloads.

Aggressive Mode Exchange

The purpose of an aggressive mode exchange is the same as a main mode exchange—the establishment of an authenticated security association, and keys, which IKE can then use to establish security associations for other security protocols. The major difference is that aggressive mode takes half the number of messages as main mode. By limiting the number of messages, aggressive mode also limits its negotiating power and also does not provide identity protection.

In an aggressive mode exchange, the initiator offers a list of protection suites, his Diffie-Hellman public value, his nonce, and his identity, all in the first message. The responder replies with a selected protection suite, his Diffie-Hellman public value, his nonce, his identity, and an authentication payload—for preshared key and encrypted nonce authentication this would be a hash payload, for signature-based authentication it would be a signature payload. The initiator sends his authentication payload as the final message.

The rich negotiation capabilities of IKE are constrained in aggressive mode. This is because the initiator must provide his Diffie-Hellman public value and his nonce in the first message. Obviously, he cannot therefore offer different Diffie-Hellman groups in different protection suites. Also, if he desires to offer authentication based on encrypted nonces this must be his only offer, since the nonce must be encrypted for such an exchange. In addition, if he wishes to do authentication using the revised method of encrypted nonces he cannot offer multiple protection suites with differing encryption or hash algorithm options.

Aggressive mode is decidedly limited! So what use is it then? For remote access situations where the address of the initiator cannot be known by the responder a priori, and both parties desire to use preshared key authentication, this is the only exchange possible to establish the IKE

SA. Also, for situations where the initiator knows the policy of the responder, or has a very good idea what that policy is, they may use this exchange to create the IKE SA more quickly. If an employee wishes to remotely access the corporate resources of his company he will most likely know the policies under which access is granted—for example, encryption with AES, hashing with SHA, authentication with RSA signatures using certificates signed by the corporate Certification Authority—and, therefore, the full power of IKE negotiation is not necessary.

Quick Mode Exchange

Once an IKE SA is established, via a Main Mode or Aggressive Mode exchange, it can be used to generate SAs for other security protocols such as IPSec. These SAs are established via a Quick Mode exchange. A Quick Mode exchange is done under the protection of a previously established IKE SA. Many Quick Modes can be done with a single Main Mode or Aggressive Mode exchange. In fact, simultaneous Quick Modes can be performed under the protection of a single IKE SA!

In a Quick Mode exchange the two peers negotiate the characteristics of, and generate keys for, an IPSec security association. The IKE SA protects a Quick Mode exchange by encrypting it and authenticating the messages. The messages are authenticated via the PRF function, most likely the HMAC version of the negotiated hash function. The SKEYID_a value from the IKE SA state is used as a key to authenticate the entire message of a Quick Mode exchange. This authentication provides data integrity protection as well as data source authentication: Upon receipt we'll know that the message could only have come from our authenticated peer and that the message did not change in transit. Encryption, using SKEYID_e, provides confidentiality to the exchange.

Since multiple Quick Mode exchanges can be performed simultaneously there must be some way to multiplex the IKE messages and determine which message refers to which exchange. The message ID of the ISAKMP header is used for this purpose. Each Quick Mode exchange has a unique message ID which is used with the cookies in the ISAKMP header, to identify the state to which a particular message refers. Also, since all the Quick Mode messages are protected by the same IKE SA, there must be some way to coordinate the initialization vector (IV) for encryption and decryption to prevent two IKE peers from getting out of sync and not being able to decrypt messages the other party encrypted. The message ID is used for this purpose too. Each Quick Mode exchange begins with a unique IV that is derived from the IV from the finished phase one exchange and the message ID of the phase two exchange. The IV for a particular Quick Mode is a running IV similar to that from the phase one exchanges. The initial IV is derived from a deterministic algorithm and subsequent IVs are defined to be the last ciphertext block from the last message. When a Quick Mode exchange is finished, and IPSec SAs have been created, the state—the running IV, the nonces, the Diffie-Hellman values—that was created to handle this exchange can be deleted. Obviously the state created for the IKE SA is not deleted because it is used to protect subsequent Quick Mode messages.

Quick Mode derives the keys used for the IPSec SAs from its SKEYID_d state. That key is used in the pseudo-random function (same one from phase one) with the nonces passed in the exchange and the protocol and SPI from the IPSec SA offers. This guarantees unique keys for each SA: the inbound SA will have a different SPI and therefore a different key than the outbound SA. All IPSec keys are derived from the same source and are therefore all related. If an attacker was able to determine SKEYID_d from the IKE SA he would have an easy time determining all the keys of all the IPSec SAs derived from that SKEYID_d, and all the keys that are derived in the future too! This is a problem. None of the keys have what is referred to as "perfect forward secrecy," or PFS. Quick Mode has a PFS option to satisfy these concerns.

To provide PFS to a Quick Mode exchange an additional Diffie-Hellman exchange is performed and the resulting shared secret is used in generation of keys for IPSec. Obviously that secret is not retained once the exchange is finished. The memory in which it resides must be zeroed and freed immediately upon completion. Negotiation of the Diffie-Hellman group is not possible in a Quick Mode exchange for the same reason as in an aggressive mode exchange. The initiator must offer his Diffie-Hellman public value derived from the group he is offering. If he offered multiple groups, the responder would have a difficult time correlating public values to SA offers.

In addition to the SA offer(s), the nonce, and the optional Diffie-Hellman public value (if PFS is desired), identity information can also be exchanged by both parties. Both parties have already determined and authenticated each other's identity as part of the phase one exchange, so what are these additional identities for? They're used to exchange selector information that describes the purposes of the SA payloads being established. The IPSec DOI defines identity types and port and protocol fields of the ISAKMP ID payload. Since the DOI deals with phase two exchanges, and, specifically, how to establish SAs for IPSec, these definitions come into effect.

These identities can be a simple address, a range of addresses, or a subnet. Recall in our discussion of IPSec that valid policy could be "all telnet traffic to network 132.239.4.0/255.255.255.0" or "all Web traffic to 132.239.4.24." Using ID payloads in Quick Mode, it is possible to express this policy to the IKE peer. Selector information, in the form of ID payloads, is sent by the initiator of the Quick Mode along with SA offers to the responder. This selector information refers to all SAs negotiated in the single Quick Mode exchange. The responder can use this information to check his own policy and decide whether the initiator is allowed to establish SAs for this purpose. If this policy check passes, the selector information derived from the ID payloads must be provided to the IPSec SADB along with the specifics of the SA. This information constrains the IPSec SA. The SA can only be used for traffic identified by the ID payloads. If the phase 2 identities indicated that negotiation was for telnet to a particular host, the resulting SAs could not be used for any other traffic. Passing the selector information, derived from the phase 2 identities, to the SADB allows the IPSec processing to determine whether the traffic protected by the particular IPSec SA is allowed. Recall the discussion of AH input processing and ESP input processing.

We've described Quick Mode as a simple request/response exchange, but there is more to it than that. The initiator needs a liveness proof that the responder is on-line and has actually processed his initial Quick Mode message. To accomplish this the responder includes the initiator's nonce and the message ID of the exchange in the authenticating hash payload. This digest now not only provides message integrity and source authentication to the initiator, it also provides a liveness proof.

The responder also needs a liveness proof. The message from the initiator could have been an old message replayed by an adversary. The adversary might not have known the contents of the message but he would know through traffic analysis that it was a Quick Mode message. Replaying that message would result in the unnecessary creation of SAs by the responder. This would be considered a denial of service attack, albeit a mild one, because of the memory and SA management overhead that the responder would unnecessarily expend on this message. To prevent such an attack a third message is added to the Quick Mode exchange. In it the initiator includes both nonces and the exchange's message ID in an authenticating hash payload, proving to the responder that he is a real live and active participant in the exchange. At this point the responder may add the SAs to his IPSec SADB as shown in Figure 7.10.

Initiator   Responder

Header, *HASH1, SA, Ni [, KE]* ━━━▶
     [, ID-ci, ID-cr]

                          ◀━━━ Header, *HASH2, SA, Nr [, KE]*
                                         [, ID-ci, ID-cr]

Header, *HASH3*   ━━━▶

Figure 7.10

Where:

HASH1 = PRF(SKEYID_a, M-ID | SA | Ni [| KE] [| IDci | IDcr])
HASH2 = PRF(SKEYID_a, M-ID | Ni | SA | Nr [| KE] [| IDci | IDcr])
HASH3 = PRF(SKEYID_a, 0 | M-ID | Ni | Nr)

Notice how the initiator has all the information necessary to add his IPSec SAs to his SADB before the responder does. After receiving the responder's only message he knows what the responder chose from his offer; if the exchange had PFS he has the responder's Diffie-Hellman public value, and he has a liveness proof. But the responder must wait until he receives the initiator's final message before he's ready. Because of this, the initiator may begin sending IPSec-protected packets prior to the receipt of his final message. In fact, due to network latencies or processor priorities—the initiator may choose to give IPSec processing a higher priority to IKE processing—the IPSec packets may even arrive at the responder before the final IKE message does! If this happens the responder will drop all the IPSec packets until it is able to process the final IKE message.

Depending on the traffic, this may or may not be a problem. If the traffic is a TCP-based protocol these initial messages would, most likely, be the TCP syn packets and they'll be retransmitted until they're acknowledged. For UDP-based protocols these packets could be irretrievably lost. To prevent this from occurring, IKE uses the commit bit from the ISAKMP header to extend a Quick Mode exchange by one message. Either party can set the commit bit and if one does, the responder must send a final message consisting of an authenticating hash payload followed by a notify payload containing a "connected" message. In this case, the initiator does not add the SAs to his SADB until he receives the "connected" message. This will allow the responder to add his SAs first and be ready when the first IPSec packets begin to flow.

As mentioned earlier, the IKE SA is bidirectional. Either party may initiate a Quick Mode exchange regardless of who initiated the main mode or aggressive mode exchange. When this happens, the roles for phase 2 reverse but the role-specific information from phase 1 does not. The initiator cookie and responder cookie *in that order* continue to identify the IKE SA used to protect the phase 2 SAs regardless of the role being played in phase 2.

Other IKE Exchanges

All of the exchanges in IKE described so far have been for the creation of SAs—the phase one exchanges create the IKE SA and the phase two exchange creates IPSec SAs. IKE defines two other exchanges that provide for maintenance of the IKE SA and for negotiation of private Diffie-Hellman groups.

The IKE informational exchange allows IKE peers to send status and error messages to each other. This is not an exchange per se, but just a single message that is not acknowledged nor, due to the UDP-based nature of IKE, guaranteed to arrive. Because of the unreliability of informational exchange messages, they are not mandatory to send. Implementers are strongly encouraged to be "good citizens" and use them, but they should not design their code to expect them. The most common use of the informational exchange is to tell a peer that a particular SA, either the IKE SA or an IPSec SA, has been deleted and to refrain from using it.

Informational exchanges are similar to Quick Mode messages in that they all have a unique message ID and generate a unique IV to use for encrypting the message. They are also authenticated with a hash payload, which is the result of the keyed PRF function taking SKEYID_a as the key and a concatenation of the message ID and the entire notify or delete payload. Since this is a single, unacknowledged message the state associated with this exchange can be freed after sending the message.

Another exchange IKE defines is a new group exchange. IKE defines five Diffie-Hellman groups that peers can use, three groups using exponentiation over a prime modulus, and two groups using elliptic curves. The new group exchange allows peers to negotiate private groups for their use and define a group identifier that they can subsequently use in a later exchange to identify the group. This exchange must be protected by the

IKE SA due to the sensitive nature of the data being exchanged. Therefore, a new group exchange, while not strictly being a phase two exchange, must follow a phase one exchange and must be protected by the IKE SA. Similar to a Quick Mode and informational exchange, the protection takes the form of encryption using SKEYID_e and an authenticating hash function keyed with SKEYID_a.

The new group exchange is a request-response exchange in which the initiator sends an SA payload that contains the characteristics of the group being proposed and an identifier out of the range of numbers reserved for private use. For instance, to propose a new group that uses exponentiation over a prime modulus, the initiator would send the prime number and the generator. If this group is acceptable to the responder it responds with an identical response. It is strongly recommended that the responder test the group for strength and not blindly accept any offer. For instance, in an offer of a group using exponentiation over a prime modulus, the modulus offered should be checked for primality. If it is not prime, the offer should be refused.

The IPSec DOI

As mentioned, IKE defines how security parameters are negotiated and shared keys are established for other protocols. What it does not define is *what* to negotiate. That is up to a Domain of Interpretation (DOI) document. A DOI document defines many things: a naming scheme for DOI-specific protocol identifiers, the contents of the situation field of the ISAKMP SA payload, the attributes that IKE negotiates in a Quick Mode and any specific characteristics that IKE needs to convey. For instance, the IPSec DOI defines new fields in the ISAKMP ID payload—in effect overloading it—and new values of possible identities. This is necessary to convey selector information used to constrain the negotiated IPSec SAs.

The attributes defined in the IPSec DOI are those required to be part of an IPSec SA. Separate attribute spaces for AH and ESP are not necessary since the proposal and transform payloads in ISAKMP already allow for separate specification of the protocol. The DOI need merely define what the various protocols are that can be negotiated in its DOI—in the case of IPSec, it's AH, ESP—and the attributes necessary. Any DOI that uses IKE must designate the IKE document as the source for attribute information when negotiating in phase 1. The IPSec DOI is no different.

Summary

This chapter gives a good overview of ISAKMP, IKE, and the IPSec DOI. It also explains how they work and how they all fit together. This is not a substitute, though, for reading the actual specifications. Left out of this chapter (intentionally) are actual payload format specifications and attribute value definitions necessary to develop a compliant IKE.

The reader is encouraged to obtain the relevant specifications and use them to round out his or her knowledge of how key management for IPSec (and more!) works.

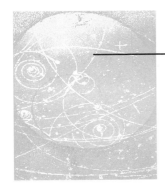

8

Policy

It was mentioned in previous chapters that policy determines the security services afforded to a packet and the treatment of a packet in the network. However, the issue of policy representation and management of IPSec connections were not discussed. We will address some of these issues in this chapter.

Policy is difficult to describe and define. It is the fuzzy middle between a human desire ("I want to encrypt and authenticate all access that my subcontractors have to my network") and a machine's definition ("encrypt tcp packets from 10.3.86.5 to 10.4/16 with CAST and authenticate them with HMAC-SHA"). Because it is the security interface between human and computer, it is extremely important. The transition from human to computer involves policy definition, policy representation, policy management, and finally, the interactions between the policy and the various components of an IPSec system—IKE, the IPSec process itself, the SADB, and the SPD.

Policy is not a standard. IPSec protocol standards define various capabilities of policy. However, IETF does not mandate any particular representation of policy nor does it enforce any particular implementation. The policy issues such as definition and representation are left to implementations. Standards bodies typically refrain from dictating how policy is implemented. For instance, the IPSec working group of the IETF discusses the policy issues mostly from IPSec implementation perspective. However, the main challenge with policy is its definition and representation at a higher level, and then mapping it so that IKE and IPSec protocols can access it efficiently and unambiguously.

Another issue associated with policy is its deployment and management. This involves how policy is defined and communicated among various nodes in a network and how the policy is synchronized among various nodes. Network security is complex, and the larger the network being secured the more complex the policy that dictates how that security is achieved. There is, therefore, an obvious scaling problem with policy definition and deployment. If a network manager must visit each and every network entity and manually configure it in compliance with his or her system security policy, it will take an excessive amount of time. It also opens up the network to subtle errors that can manifest themselves as massive holes in the overall security of the network. Obviously, as networks grow, policy management for them will have to be centrally managed.

Policy is not solely the domain of security. Any network service that desires to identify certain classes of traffic (or =flows= of traffic) and apply different services to them require a policy. Network services such as traffic engineering, where certain flows are identified and given a higher quality of service or allocated specified bandwidth, are a prime example of this. In this chapter, we will discuss the capabilities of an IPSec policy system, its representation, distribution, and address the support the policy system has to provide for the kernel and IKE. The implementation issues are discussed in the next chapter.

Policy Definition Requirement

Chapters 3 and 4 discussed the IPSec architecture and the relationship between the various protocols that are traditionally referred to as "IPSec" and databases such as the SADB and SPD, but omitted the details of how the policies are enumerated in the SPD and get defined and installed. IPSec allows for very complex policy definitions. Because of its notion of selectors, the policy rules applied to inbound and outbound packets is very rich. Selectors can be gross—an entire subnet—or fine—a specific port and protocol to a specific host.

The design for a policy definition and management system must not constrain the richness of IPSec. Therefore, there are several requirements imposed on any policy system. These requirements are very high level because there is no single mechanism for policy definition and management. Different IPSec implementations will have different constraints imposed on them—for instance, most routers do not have a hard disk or a floppy drive—and these constraints will dictate how policy is managed.

As IPSec is neither host-oriented nor router-oriented, the requirements for policy definition should be broad enough to encompass both of them. These are not an all-encompassing set of policy requirements but merely a large set that any system will abide by:

- Ability to configure multiple policies per host: It must be possible to specify security policy for an individual host. The policy may reside on the host or it may reside on a router or firewall in the network. The policy may specify end-to-end security (that is, it is policy between two hosts) or it may specify policy for this host to another network. What is important is that policy with the granularity of a host must be able to be expressed.

- Ability to configure policy per network: It must be possible to specify security policy for an entire network. This policy may, likewise, reside on a host or it may reside on a router or firewall in the network. The network policy may take the form of a network and subnet (this is the most important representation because this is how routing decisions are made on both hosts and routers), or the form of a range of addresses. The important thing is that uniform security policy can be assigned to all entities on a network.

- Ability to configure security at the granularity of an application: Application's traffic is uniquely identified on a network by the tuple <source and destination address, source and destination port, and protocol>. The addresses themselves may be explicit addresses or subnets. For instance, it must be possible to protect all telnet (tcp port 23) traffic destined for a particular subnet. What is important is that it must be possible to specify security policy to the granularity of port and protocol.

- Ability to specify multiple protocols per flow[1]: It must be possible to specify that, for instance, AH and ESP and IPPCP (see Chapter 11) be used on a targeted flow. Previous requirements dealt with how to identify targeted traffic. This requirement deals with specifying what to do to that traffic once its been identified. It must be possible to apply more than one security protocol to targeted packets that represent a flow.

- Ability to specify the desired action for each flow: drop, protect, or pass.

- Ability to configure tunnels of more than one level deep: It must be possible to specify a policy that requires nested tunnels. While this will usually be the result of combining various distinct policy requirements into a single unified network policy, it may also be desirable to dictate nested tunnels directly.

- Ability to support different IKE identities for access and authentication: IKE can handle IP addresses, Distinguished Names (DNs), and Fully Qualified Domain Names (FQDN). However, IPSec protocols handle only IP addresses and the policy has to be configured per IP node. This ability is useful for access control. A node can be configured to accept connections by a particular user or by a set of users belonging to a particular domain.

- Ability to selectively disable automated key management: Support for manual keying is required by IPSec and it must be possible to define policy such that manually-keyed SAs are used instead of IKE to protect certain traffic.

1.   A flow is always identified by the tuple <src, dst, src port, dst port, protocol>.

- Ability to support multiple security options. This is a very important requirement. IKE provides the ability to offer multiple choices during negotiation so that the two peers can agree on something they both support. For example, host A may want to use ESP and 3DES with nodes that implement 3DES. However, with nodes that do not support 3DES, it may choose to communicate using DES instead of dropping the connection.

- It must be possible to support all of the aforementioned requirements simultaneously.

The various components of a policy system are discussed below.

Policy Representation and Distribution

Policy representation involves two aspects: the physical representation—defining the format in which the policy is represented, where it is stored, how it is updated/modified, and what protocols are used to update the policy; and the interface—defining how the various IPSec components acquire and manage a policy.

The physical representation of policy, to a very large extent, depends on the distribution mechanism. Because of its flexibility and generic design LDAP (Lightweight Directory Access Protocol) has received the most attention as a mechanism to distribute policy. Therefore, the IPSec policy being distributed takes the form of LDAP schemas.

LDAP is an advantageous mechanism because it provides a simple, lightweight (in fact, that's the L in LDAP) method of depositing and retrieving policy from a central repository.

Whatever method is used to represent policy, it should be capable of supporting all the capabilities that were defined in the policy definition section. The policy representation is a database problem. There has been some work in the IETF on the policy representation, specifically discussing a schema. This schema addresses the policy definition requirements. The schema is defined for LDAP. It is not necessary to use this schema for policy representation— any proprietary schema can be used to represent policy. However, using an LDAP schema eases the deployment of IPSec. The LDAP schema provides the ability to define a schema that either a server or a client uses to store the data. If the policy is stored in a central repository, clients can access this data through a well-defined protocol.

If IPSec were to be enabled on individual nodes there are three possible alternatives for configuration:

1. Configure each node individually.
2. Configure in a central repository but use a proprietary distribution mechanism to distribute the policy.
3. Configure in a central repository but use some standard mechanism to distribute the policy.

As corporations begin to deploy IPSec, the first alternative impedes deployment. This is acceptable only for prototyping. The second choice solves the deployment problem. However, using a proprietary mechanism for distribution is questionable. It is always judicious to use standard protocol if one exists.

Storing the policy in a central repository does not solve the problem of modification/update of the policy. An IPSec client has to download all the policy or incrementally update its policy during boot or whenever the server chooses to update the client's policy. The client has to store the policy locally because it needs to know which packets have to be secure and which do not. If the policy is not stored locally, for every packet for which the kernel does not find a policy, it has to invoke the policy client that in turn has to contact the central repository and invoke the key management protocol and also update the kernel policy. This leads to unacceptable delays for the first few packets.

The policy distribution mechanism has to be secure. The server from which the policy is downloaded should be authenticated. In addition, the access to the server should be restricted. If this is compromised, the security of the network is at risk. These are problems associated with any directory system. This is one reason it is better to use a standard directory mechanism such as LDAP for policy storage and retrieval for which security mechanisms have been already defined.

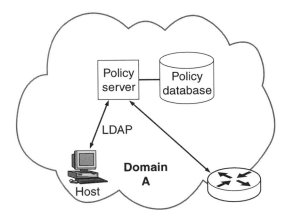

Figure 8.1   Policy deployment architecture.

Figure 8.1 shows the most popular paradigm that currently exists for policy configuration and distribution.

The policy is stored centrally in a policy server. The policy server is responsible for maintaining the policy for all nodes (hosts and routers) in the domain. The policy server provides the capability to configure security for all the nodes in the domain. The policy is either downloaded into the various nodes in the network or is fetched dynamically by the nodes using directory services protocol such as LDAP.

Policy Management System

Policy management defines the following interfaces:

- interface between the directory service and the local database where the policy is stored;
- interface between the User Interface application and the local policy database that allows read, write, and modify access to the database;
- interface between IKE and policy database;
- interface between kernel and the policy database.

The interfaces defined by the policy management should provide the ability to search the database based on one or more selectors. For example, one should be able to look up the policy for a particular <src, dst> pair or the policy for a particular network. It should also be possible to look up both inbound and outbound policy. The policy management should always be deterministic in its matches and should always match the longest prefix.

For example, if you configure a policy for the network 205.15/16 and another policy for the host 205.15.2.1, a search for the policy to 205.15.2.1 should return the policy entry created specifically for the host 205.15.2.1 and not for the network 205.15/16. In cases where it is ambiguous, the policy management should return policy in a deterministic manner. For example, if you configure a policy <205.15/16, 206.1.1.1> (P1) and another policy for <205.15.1.1, 206.1/16> (P2), then a lookup for <205.15.1.1, 206.1.1.1>, you can return either P1 or P2 or both. The proper behavior is to return both and also maintain the same order always.

The interfaces the policy management defines should address all the issues enumerated in the policy definition section. We will not address UI-specific issues in this book as it is impossible to make specific recommendations on UI that are universally acceptable! The interface between the UI application and the database can be similar to the interface between the database and IKE. We will discuss this in the next section.

Kernel Support

The IPSec kernel consults the policy to determine the security services afforded to a packet. If the policy database is maintained in the user space, for every packet, the kernel needs to context switch into the user space to look up the policy. This operation is very expensive. It is almost mandatory for the kernel to maintain its own copy of the security policy database.

It is the policy management application's responsibility to update the kernel's SPD. As an implementor, you can define your own interface between the policy management application and the kernel. There has been some work at the IETF in defining the interface between the policy management application and the kernel. This interface is called PF_KEY, and is modeled after PF_ROUTE socket interface into the Kernel's routing table.

The policy management system should modify/delete/add entries to the kernel's SPD instantaneously. It should also provide the ability for bulk updates and not just one policy record at a time. This is critical for boot performance.

The policy management application should also support manual keying. It should be able to add and delete manual SAs.

IKE Support

IKE is invoked by the kernel or by the policy management application or by another IKE peer to establish keys. The kernel invokes IKE when it needs an SA for secure communication or if an SA has expired and it needs to establish new SA. The policy management application invokes IKE if it establishes keys before the kernel needs it to reduce delays for a new connection.

The kernel or the policy management application can invoke IKE in one of two ways:

1. pass just the selectors, in which case IKE has to consult the user level policy database to determine the policy;
2. pass the full policy.

If you choose option 1, the access to the user-level policy database has to be synchronized between IKE and the policy management application.

When IKE responds to a key negotiation request, it needs an interface to the user-level SPD to choose the parameters for the connection. The policy database lookup is based on selectors.

Another important aspect of policy management for IKE support is certificates. The IETF is working on standards for storage and retrieval of certificates. It is our belief that these technologies are not mature and it will be a few years before we see actual deployment of a large public key infrastructure. During this period, the certificates will be stored locally and fetched from a directory. The policy management system should provide the ability to store/delete certificates in its database and also provide an interface to fetch certificates from its database to IKE. Certificate support in IPSec is discussed in greater detail in Chapter 11.

Deployment

So far, we have discussed the capabilities a policy system should provide and how it may be represented, stored, and managed. In this section, we discuss some of the deployment issues. This includes node level and domain level security, gateway traversal, and some issues associated with policy configuration.

As IPSec provides end-to-end security and can be used to build intranets and VPNs, it is desirable to provide the ability to configure security on a node and a domain level. We discussed node-level security in previous sections. The advantages of domain-level security are discussed here. In the networking world, a domain normally refers to a routing domain. A routing domain is delimited by a set of routers. This implies any packet leaving the domain has to hit one of the routers. It is possible, to a certain extent, to control which routers a particular packet traverses. However, if there is more than one exit point from an organization, it is difficult for the host to control which router is used to exit, particularly if a link goes down. Under these circumstances, defining a domain-level policy and distributing it to all the border routers is extremely important. If all the border routers share the same policy, the security service afforded to a flow is the same irrespective of the border router over which the packet exits or enters the domain.

Policy incompatibility is an issue in policy configuration. Two domains that need to talk securely may configure their policy such that their intersection is NULL set. Consider the network shown in Figure 8.2.

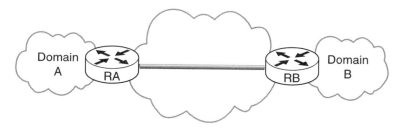

Figure 8.2   Configuring policy between domains.

RA and RB are the edge routers for domain A and B respectively. RA is configured such that all the packets destined to domain B are secured by ESP in tunnel mode using 3DES. However, RB is configured such that all packets it receives from domain A are configured for ESP in tunnel mode using DES. In this case, the two domains never get to talk to each other as IKE negotiation never succeeds.

Setting Up the Policy

In this section, let us try and walk through the steps one has to follow to set up the policy for IPSec.

The first step is to set up the policy for phase I of IKE negotiation. The policy can either be global (i.e., the same IKE phase I policy is used for all the hosts) or it can be host or network prefix-specific, or it can be domain-specific. The following attributes have to be set up for Phase I:

- Phase I mode: main or aggressive
- Protection suite(s)

Once the phase I policy is set up, IKE is ready for phase II, where it can negotiate the security services afforded to an IP packet. The following attributes can be defined:

- The selectors that identify the flow. The granularity can range from being very coarse to being very fine-grained. The spectrum may range from one policy for all packets to a different policy for each flow belonging to a particular identity.
- The security attributes for each flow. This includes the protocols, their modes, the transforms they should be using, and various attributes of these transforms such as lifetime and replay windows.
- Action (secure, drop, or pass) to be taken for each flow.

The phase I and the phase II policies govern the security services afforded to the IP packets originating or destined to the network/domain/host. IPSec provides a very rich set of options. One drawback of providing a rich set of options is that it makes the process of setting and negotiating complicated. If two entities have to negotiate a set of options or choose from a set of options, they need to talk the same language, that is, they should have the same understanding for values passed in the protocol headers. The values that two entities should use to negotiate security parameters are described in the IPSec DOI (see Chapter 7). The IPSec DOI consolidates the various options and values for Phase II negotiation. Any policy system should support all the options described in this document.

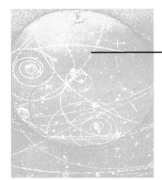

IPSec Implementation

This chapter discusses the implementation issues of IPSec. These include interaction of the various components of IPSec, interfaces that each of these components provide, and a walk through the packet processing for both inbound and outbound packets.

As implementations are specific to a particular platform, the discussions in this chapter are mostly platform-independent so that they can be used as guidelines in implementing IPSec on a specific platform. In places where discussing implementation on a specific OS helps in explanations, the choice is a BSD (Berkeley Software Distribution) variant OS.

We discuss the following components: IPSec base protocols, SADB, SPD, manual keying, ISAKMP/IKE, SA management, and policy management. The implementation and optimization issues that you as an implementor of IPSec should be aware of are highlighted in this chapter.

Implementation Architecture

Most IPSec implementations define the following components:

- IPSec base protocols: This component implements ESP and AH. It processes the headers, interacts with the SPD and SADB to determine the security that is afforded to the packet, and handles network layers issues such as fragmentation and PMTU.

- SPD: The SPD is an important component because it determines the security afforded to a packet. The SPD is consulted for both outbound and inbound processing of the packet. For outbound processing, the SPD is consulted by the IPSec base protocol to decide if the packet needs any security. For inbound packets, the SPD is consulted by the IPSec base protocol component to decide if the security afforded to the packet concurs with security configured in the policy.

- SADB: The SADB maintains the list of active SAs for outbound and inbound processing. Outbound SAs are used to secure outgoing packets and inbound SAs are used to process inbound packets with IPSec headers. The SADB is populated with SAs either manually or via an automatic key management system such as IKE.

- IKE: The Internet Key Exchange is normally a user-level process, except in embedded operating systems. Typically, in nodes such as routers that are running embedded operating systems, there is no distinction between a user space and kernel space. IKE is invoked by the policy engine when the policy mandates an SA or SA bundle exist for two nodes to communicate securely but the SA(s) is yet to be established. IKE is also invoked by its peer when the node needs to communicate securely.

- Policy and SA management: These are applications that manage the policy and SA.

Figure 9.1 indicates the various components of IPSec and the interactions among them.

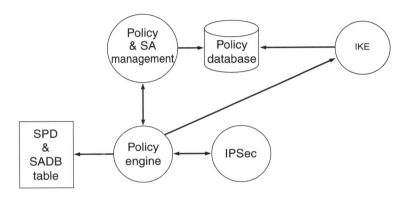

Figure 9.1   IPSec implementation architecture.

In the rest of this section, the interface and design requirements for each of the components are discussed.

IPSec Base Protocols

The IPSec base protocols interact closely with the transport and the network layer. In fact, IPSec base protocol is part of the network layer. The IPSec base protocol module should be designed to efficiently implement the following capabilities:

- Ability to add, possibly multiple, IPSec headers to an outbound packet in both tunnel mode and transport mode.
- Ability to process tunnel mode IPSec packets and pass the decapsulated packet onto IP forwarding.
- Ability to process transport mode IPSec packets and pass them into the appropriate transport layer such as TCP, UDP, or ICMP, depending on the transport payload carried by the IPSec packet.

The IPSec protocol module provides two interface functions—input and output. The input interface function is called for inbound packets and the output interface function is called for outbound packets.

In almost all implementations of IPSec, IPSec is integrated with an existing TCP/IP implementation. The interface between the transport layer and the network layer for both incoming and outgoing traffic is dependent on a particular implementation. For example, in the popular BSD UNIX implementation, the transport layer protocols such as UDP and TCP register with the network layer indicating the input function the IP layer should invoke. TCP registers a function that IP should invoke when the IP layer encounters a TCP payload. The IPSec implementations should not violate the interface between the transport and the network layer. The interface and integration should be seamless. For example, the TCP layer should not be required to know if it was invoked from the IPSec component or the IP component.

SPD and SADB

The choice of the data structure to store the SPD and the SADB is fairly crucial to the performance of IPSec processing. The SPD and SADB implementation depend on the performance requirements of the system and the capabilities of the system. Some of the factors that determine the design of the SPD and SADB are:

- Number of expected entries in the SPD and the SADB
- System throughput both for outbound and inbound packets.
- Cost of allocating memory as needed versus the cost of maintaining large tables, portions of which may be unused.
- Any optimizations the system provides to cache pointers to SAs or SPD entries.

The design of SPD and SADB should satisfy the following requirements:

- Ability to efficiently look up the structure for exact or most specific match based on the selectors—source address, destination address, protocol, and SPI.
- Ability to store wildcards, range, or exact values for the selectors.
- Synchronization mechanisms for the structure when the implementation is optimized by caching pointers to SADB, SPD.
- Ordering of entries so that the match is always deterministic.

As mentioned earlier, the choice of the data structure for SADB or SPD depends, among other things, on the performance requirements and the number of entries in the SADB or the SPD. The lookup for the outbound processing is more complicated than the inbound processing. For outbound processing, the lookups are based on selectors in the SPD. There may not be an exact match, as the selectors for source and destination address can be network prefixes. However, this problem is already solved in routing. In order to find the route to a destination, one has to match the closest network prefix for cases where there are no host routes (host routes have the destination address in the routing table).

The processing can be optimized for SA lookup by caching SA pointers in the SPD entries. If the SA pointers are not cached in the SPD entry, then the lookup for outbound SA is as complicated as the SPD lookup.

The inbound processing of IPSec packets is simpler because the lookups are based on information in the received packet for which the matches are exact. The SPD entry that corresponds to the SA can be cached in the SADB entry. This optimizes the policy checking upon the conclusion of IPSec processing and avoids another lookup.

For inbound IPSec packets, after the IPSec headers are processed, the SPD is consulted to determine if the packet can be admitted based on the security services that were offered. If the policy is not checked, security ofthe system is compromised. Let us consider the example shown in Figure 9.2.[1]

---

1.   For the sake of brevity, all the elements in the SA record are now shown. The lifetime, sequence numbers, and other fields discussed in the security architecture chapter are not shown in these diagrams.

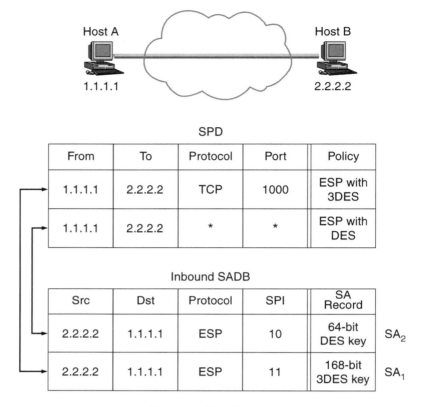

Figure 9.2   Flow-specific IPSec.

Two hosts, A and B, with IP address 1.1.1.1 and 2.2.2.2 have established two SAs, SA1 and SA2. (The SADB shown in the Figure 9-2 does not have all the fields. The sequence number, lifetime, and other fields have been left out.) SA1 is configured for ESP with 3DES and SA2 ESP with DES. This information is stored in the SPD.[2]

SA1 is used for very secure applications, say banking, which runs on a TCP using port 1000. After IPSec processing, if the policy is not checked to determine if the banking application did in fact use 3DES, then security is compromised. The policy can be checked only after the IPSec processing as the selectors are not available before because they may be encrypted.

---

2.   From and to are used instead of source and destination in the SPD intentionally. It was mentioned earlier that IKE does not allow the policy to be asymmetric. This being the case, the terms source and destination are confusing because the inbound and the outbound policies are the same. It does not matter who originated the packet, the same policy is used.

For inbound packets that are not IPSec packets, the SPD has to be consulted to determine the type of processing afforded to the packet. The reason is because, if certain traffic is required to be IPSec-protected, one needs to drop any inbound packets that match the SPD definition of that traffic but that do not have the proper IPSec protection.

The inbound and the outbound processing are completely independent. However, it easier to use the same data structures for the SPD and the SADB for both inbound and outbound processing. There are various choices for the data structures—sorted hash lists, PATRTICIA trees, radix-4 trees, to name a few.

For connection-oriented connections, in the end hosts the lookups can be optimized further by caching the pointer to the SPD entry in the socket data structure, if such a structure exists. This obviates the need to look up the SPD for each outbound packet generated by the application using the socket. Multiple sockets can cache the same SPD. However, caching pointers in end host or router implementations increases the implementation complexity. In multithreaded operating systems, this implies providing locks to synchronize access to these shared data structures. There is also the additional complexity of removing pointers to SAs and SPD entries when the entries themselves are removed from either SADB or SPD.

The SADB and SPD may be implemented in the same module. In fact, it helps to implement them in the same module because of pointer references between the two entities. The module provides the following interfaces:

- Add one or more SA or SPD entries
- Delete one or more SA or SPD entries
- Look up one or more SA or SPD entries

IKE

The Internet Key Exchange is responsible for dynamically populating the SADB. IKE is in a quiescent state until its services are needed. IKE's services can be requested in one of two ways—the SPD requests it to establish an SA or a peer requests it to establish an SA.

IKE provides an interface to the SPD to inform it about establishing new SAs. The physical interface between IKE and the SPD and SADB is completely dependent on the Inter-Process Communications (IPC) capabilities of the platform. For example, it could be a socket, or a message queue. More important is the information passed via the IPC mechanism. Through this interface must pass all the information necessary to begin negotiation: the peer and all transforms with all necessary attributes. Since IPSec policy can be complex, and IKE is capable of expressing complex policy, it is imperative that the information exchanged between IKE and the SPD contain all the required conjunctions to maintain the policy complexity. For example, if the policy states that the SA bundle of AH-HMAC-MD5 and ESP-CAST-CBC (no authenticator), and IPPCP-LZS is needed, then the conjunctive nature of the request ("...and...and...") must be retained. This can be achieved by sending each protocol as an individual IPC message but including a logical operator field in the message, which indicates the relationship this message has to the next, or by passing the entire bundle of information in a single message. Either way, the interface between the SPD and IKE must not hamstring policy declaration and negotiation.

IKE also provides an interface for the remote IKE peer to request SA establishment. The remote peer requests the establishment of a new SA through Phase II negotiation if ISAKMP SA is already established or through Phase I if ISAKMP SA is not established.

The interface between IKE and SPD is bidirectional. This is necessary for IKE to support both ways of the SA establishment. IKE receives policy information from the SPD to present to its peer (in the case of IKE as the initiator) and receives offers from its peer (in the case of IKE as the responder) which it must present to the SPD for a local policy check.

IKE communicates with the SADB either after it has received a message from the SPD (if it is the initiator of the protocol), or after it has received a message from a remote IKE peer (if it is the responder of the protocol). The SADB manages itself and therefore determines which SPIs are used, unused, or in a larval state. When IKE takes part in a quick mode exchange, it must request SPIs from the SADB to be reserved for its negotiation. These SPIs are for SAs that have not yet been fully created and are therefore larval. Upon completion of the quick mode, IKE has all the information necessary to instantiate the SA. This interface must be bi-directional since IKE sends messages to the SADB (SPI request and SA instantiation) and receives messages back from the SADB (SPI response).

IKE provides the following interfaces:

- A bidirectional interface for communicating with the SPD.
- An interface for the SADB to communicate the SPIs IKE can use.

Policy Management System

In the previous chapter, policy requirements, capabilities, and design implications were extensively discussed. The policy management (PM) system module is implemented at the user level. The user interacts with this module for all policy-related processing. This module interacts with the kernel to update the kernel's SPD. This module is also responsible for handling manual keying. This PM module provides the following capabilities and interfaces:

- Add, lookup, and delete policies. This may involve interfacing with a directory protocol to fetch policy from a central repository or provide a UI for the user to manage the policy.
- Add, create, and delete SAs manually.

IPSec Protocol Processing

The IPSec processing is broadly classified into outbound versus inbound processing and AH versus ESP and their variants thereof. Although the interface to the various components of IPSec remains the same, the packet processing is different between input and output processing. The protocol processing can be classified into SPD processing, SA processing, header, and transform processing. The SPD and SA processing are the same for both AH and ESP. The transform and header processing is different between AH and ESP.

Outbound Processing

In most TCP/IP implementations, the transport layer invokes the IP layer to send a packet by calling a function ip_output. One of the parameters to the function will be a pointer to an IP structure that has the elements such as source address and destination address that enables the IP layer to construct the IP header. The transport layer also passes the value of the protocol that IP layer puts in its next header field in its header and a flags field that gives IP layer to support various socket options. It makes most sense to perform SPD processing (i.e., decide if the packet needs any security) at this entry to ip_output.

Let us consider the example network diagram shown in Figure 9.3.[3]

---

3. In this diagram, we show the IP address for only one of the interfaces for each router. This is the interface exposed to the outside world.

For outbound processing, we will consider an HTTP packet (TCP, port 80) generated by host A destined to host B (a Web server) traversing routers RA and RB. The policy on A for packets destined to host B mandates usage of AH in transport mode using HMAC-MD5. The policy on router RA mandates that all packets destined to the network 2.2.2/24 be encrypted with ESP using 3DES and tunneled to RB.

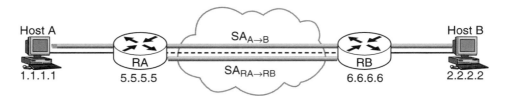

A's SPD

From	To	Protocol	Port	Policy
1.1.1.1	2.2.2.2	Any	Any	Transport AH with HMAC MD5

A's Outbound SADB

Src	Dst	Protocol	SPI	SA record	
1.1.1.1	2.2.2.2	AH	10	MD5 key	$SA_{A \rightarrow B}$

RA's SPD

From	To	Protocol	Port	Policy	Tunnel dst
1.1.1/24	2.2.2/24	Any	Any	Tunnel ESP with 3DES	6.6.6.6

RA's Outbound SADB

Src	Dst	Protocol	SPI	SA record	
5.5.5.5	6.6.6.6	ESP tunnel	11	168-bit 3DES key	$SA_{RA \rightarrow RB}$

Figure 9.3   Example of IPSec processing.

SPD Processing

At the entry point into the ip_output, the policy engine is consulted to determine the security services afforded to a packet. The input to the policy engine will be the selectors from the transport header and the source and the destination address. In our example, the input to the policy engine will be the tuple <1.1.1.1, 2.2.2.2, TCP, 80> (the source port is a wild card). The policy engine determines the security services and performs the following functions:

- If the policy indicates the packet needs to be dropped, it returns to the ip_output function indicating that the packet has to be dropped. The ip_output function is expected to discard the packet.

If the policy indicates that this packet can be transmitted without any extra security processing, the policy engine returns with an indication that the packet can be transmitted in clear. The ip_output function transmits the packet in clear at this point.

- If the policy indicates that the packet needs security, the policy engine checks if the SAs are already established. If the SAs are already established, the SA or SA bundle is passed to the IP output function. If the SAs are not yet established, the policy engine indicates security processing is required but the SAs are not established yet and notifies IKE to establish the required SA(s). At this point, it is up to the ip_output function to decide whether to queue the packet until the SAs are established or to drop the packet.

In our example, the policy engine determines that the packet needs to be secured using transport mode AH HMAC-MD5. The policy engine also determines that the SA is already established and hence does not invoke IKE to establish a new SA.

IKE Processing

IKE requires special processing. It is a requirement that all implementations recognize IKE packets that are locally generated and locally destined, and process them without securing them. Otherwise, we will end up having a chicken and egg problem. As IKE is used to establish the SAs, if the IP layer does not recognize IKE packets and instead "retriggers" IKE to establish SAs for the destination, no packets that require security will ever leave the node!

This is true even after IPSec SAs are established. This is possible as IKE always uses a well-known port (500) and a well-known protocol (UDP).

SA Processing

The next step in the outbound packet processing is the SA processing. This particular SA is fetched from the SADB. In our example, the $SA_{A->B}$ is fetched from the SADB on host. The SA is processed as follows:

- If the SA is using the number of bytes as its lifetime, then the number of bytes fields is increased depending on the size of the payload (not including the padding). For ESP, it will be the number of bytes that are encrypted and not the number of bytes on which we have calculated the hash.

- If the SAs soft lifetime has expired, then invoke IKE to establish a new SA.

- If the SAs hard lifetime has expired, then delete the SA.

- Increment the sequence number field. The sequence number is always incremented before it is copied into the IPSec header. It is initialized to 0 during the SA setup and the first IPSec packet should have a sequence number of value 1. If the sequence number field overflows, it is audited. If the SA was not established using manual keying, IKE is invoked to negotiate a new SA.

After SA processing, the protocol specific component is invoked. Let us consider both cases—transport mode and tunnel mode for both AH and ESP.

Transport Mode Header Processing

So far, we have not distinguished between IPv4 and IPv6. However, the header construction differs between IPv4 and IPv6. This is inevitable because of the format of the headers. There are also some differences between AH and ESP header construction.

In earlier chapters it was mentioned that AH in transport mode protects some parts of IP headers whereas ESP protects only the transport payload. This requires the construction of the AH header after the construction of the partial IP header. We say partial because the length field in the IP header will change once the AH header is added to the payload and this implies that the checksum has to be recalculated. In IPv4, some fields such the TTL and checksum are modified during the flow. In IPv6, hop-by-hop options change. If the hash is calculated over these fields, the authentication will fail at the destination. In order to avoid this, AH zeros out all these fields when it calculates the hash. The rules for calculating the AH were described in the AH chapter.

ESP Processing

The transport mode ESP involves encrypting the transport payload and calculating the hash. As was mentioned while describing ESP, either the encryption or the authentication can be NULL. This is specified in the SA. The transport mode ESP header is constructed before the IP header is added to the payload. This simplifies the implementation because it is not necessary to insert any headers in the middle of a buffer. After the ESP transform is applied to the transport payload and the ESP header is added, the ESP packet is forwarded to the IP layer for IP processing.

AH Processing

AH processing is not as clean as ESP because it expects part of the IP header to be constructed before it calculates the hash. The AH header has to be inserted in the middle of a packet and this leads to inefficient implementations because this involves buffer traversals and potential memory copies that can be very expensive.

The rules for calculating the AH header were described in Chapter 6. Unlike ESP, AH processing cannot be performed at the entry of the ip_output function because it requires part of the IP header be constructed before it can calculate the hash. The ideal place to perform AH processing is just before the fragmentation check is performed. In most IP implementations, the IP header with the mandatory fields for AH calculation is constructed by this point.

Tunnel Mode Processing

Tunnel mode processing involves construction of an extra IP header. Also, tunnels can be nested and can be of any depth as long as they are nested properly. In this section, tunnel implementation when the nesting is only one level deep is discussed.

In our example, when router RA receives the packet, the output of the policy lookup is a pointer to the $SA_{RA->RB}$. The SA indicates that the packet should be protected by a tunnel mode ESP with 3DES. The source and destination fields in the SA record are the source and the destination values in the outer IP header. The router RA constructs a tunnel mode ESP header and forwards the packet to the IP layer for IP processing. The rules for building the IP header follow.

Tunnel mode processing on the hosts is different from that of the router because the host needs to add two IP headers and not one. One possible solution is to perform IPSec processing just before IP fragmentation. It is important to perform IPSec tunnel mode processing before fragmentation. After IPSec processing, the packet is passed back to the IP layer (i.e., call ip_output()). However, this time this function is called with a different destination address. The policy lookup for the tunneled destination indicates that the packets be forwarded without any additional processing. The packet is forwarded to the data link layer after the IP layer adds the IP header.

IPv4 Tunnel Header   The IPv4 tunnel header can carry either an IPv4 or an IPv6 packet. The outer header fields are constructed as follows:

- Version: The value of this field is 4.
- Header length: This value depends on what options are configured on the route. The options are never copied from the inner IP header to the outer IP header.
- TOS: This value is always copied from the inner IP header. If the inner IP header is the IPv6 header, then the class value is mapped to the IPv4 TOS value. The class values for the IPv6 are not standardized. The IETF is in the process of redefining the usage of the TOS byte. Depending on what is standardized at the IETF, in future, the inner TOS byte may not be copied in its entirety.
- Length: This value is constructed for the header after the entire datagram is constructed.
- Identification: This field is constructed.
- Flags: The value for the DF bit is determined based on the configuration. This is dependent on whether the PMTU is turned on or not. The value of MF depends on whether this datagram needs to be fragmented.
- Fragment offset: This field is constructed as is normally done to construct an IP datagram.
- TTL: If a node is forwarding a packet, then the TTL value of the inner header is decremented before the outer header is added. The

TTL value of the outer header depends on the configuration for packets going over a particular interface.

- Protocol: This value is the next immediate protocol IP is carrying. If the tunneled header is constructed to secure a packet, the probable values are 51 for AH or 50 for ESP.
- Checksum: This field is constructed.
- Source address: This is specified in the SA.
- Destination address: This is specified in the SA.
- Options: The options are never copied from the inner header to the outer header.

IPv6 Tunnel Header   The IPv6 tunnel header can carry either an IPv4 or IPv6 packet. The IPv6 tunnel header fields are derived as follows:

- Version: This value is 6 (this represents IP version 6).
- Class: This value is copied from the inner header if the inner header is IPv6, or the TOS byte is mapped to the class value if the inner header is IPv4.
- Flow id: The flow id is copied from the inner header if the inner header is IPv6. If not, a configured value is copied into this field.
- Length: This field is constructed after the packet has been constructed.
- Next header: This value is the next immediate protocol IP is carrying. If the tunneled header is constructed to secure a packet, the probable values are AH or ESP. However, the tunneled header can be constructed to carry non-IPSec traffic as well. In this case the value will be a network protocol, such as routing header or IP header.
- Hop limit: If a node is forwarding a packet, then the TTL value of the inner header is decremented before the outer header is added. The TTL value of the outer header depends on the configuration for packets going over a particular interface.
- Source address: This is either specified in the SA or it is the interface over which the tunneled packet is sent out.
- Destination address: This is specified in the SA.
- Extension headers: The extension headers are never copied.

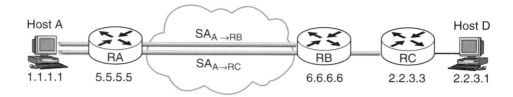

A's SPD

From	To	Protocol	Port	Policy	Tunnel dst
1.1.1.1	2.2.3.1	Any	Any	Tunneled AH using HMACÐMDS	2.2.3.3
1.1.1.1	2.2.3.3	Any	Any	Tunneled ESP using HMACÐMDS	2.2.2.2

A's Outbound SADB

Src	Dst	Protocol	SPI	SA record	
1.1.1.1	2.2.3.3	AH tunnel	11	HMACÐ MD5 key	$SA_{A \to RC}$
1.1.1.1	6.6.6.6	ESP tunnel	12	3DES key	$SA_{A \to RB}$

Figure 9.4   Nested IPSec tunnel headers.

Multiple Header Processing

Multiple header processing is fairly complicated if multiple tunnels have to be constructed from the same node. Consider the example shown in Figure 9.4. Let us say that in order for host A to send a packet to the destination D, it has to authenticate it to firewall RC and send it encrypted to firewall RB.

If all these rules are to be represented in a single policy, the construction of the headers gets fairly complicated. One solution to this problem is to limit the number of tunnels to just one in each policy. In this example, the policy indicates that for the host A to send a packet to the host D, it has to first authenticate to the router RC. The IPSec layer builds a tunneled AH packet to the router RC. After constructing the AH header, the IP layer is invoked to add the tunnel header. It uses the router RC address (2.2.3.3.) as the destination address in the selector field. The policy indicates that the packet has to be encrypted and tunneled to RB (6.6.6.6). IPSec processes the IP packet destined to 2.2.3.3, adding the ESP header and encrypting the payload. It then invokes the IP layer to add an additional header. It uses the router RB address (6.6.6.6) as the destination. At the entry, the IP layer checks the policy for the destination 6.6.6.6. The policy engine indicates that the packet can be sent in clear and this packet with multiple tunnels is dispatched.

The disadvantage of this approach is that the ability to have a policy on a per destination for nested tunnels is lost. For example, if there are two hosts behind router RC, it is not possible to have per host encryption policy from A to D. This is because the policy lookup for encryption is based on the destination address that is RC and not the true destination. Since this information is lost, it will not be possible to define per host encryption from A to D in our example. However, adding support for this increases the complexity of the implementation without providing too much capability.

Inbound Processing

Inbound processing is simpler than outbound processing mainly because header construction is more complicated than header checking. There is also no interaction with the key management system during inbound processing. The focus is more on the generic processing—things that are common to both AH and ESP. In terms of AH and ESP processing, there is not much difference except for the transforms and header processing.

The IP layer is invoked by the layer 2 to process the packet that was received over an interface. This packet is the start of the IP payload and has the IP header at the start. The IP layer processes the packet (reassembly) and invokes the function that handles the input for a particular protocol. Most implementations have a function for each protocol that the IP layer can call to process the packet.

The IPSec layer registers with the IP layer indicating the function that the IP layer has to invoke for both AH and ESP. An implementation may register different functions for AH and ESP or register the same function and perform AH or ESP specific processing in the same function. The IP layer strips the IP header and invokes the IPSec layer with either an AH or ESP header at the beginning of the packet.

The following is the sequence of steps performed by the IPSec layer. Let us continue with the same example we considered for outbound processing. Let us consider the network shown in Figure 9.3. However, this time we will discuss from the perspective of inbound processing. In Figure 9.5, the SADB and the SPD for the receivers are also shown (note that the SPD entries are symmetric). We will first walk through the processing at the host B, a non-tunneled case.

RB's SPD

From	To	Protocol	Port	Policy	Tunnel entry
2.2.2/24	1.1.1/24	Any	Any	3 DES EPS	5.5.5.5

RB's Inbound SADB

Source	Destination	Protocol	SPI	SA record
5.5.5.5	6.6.6.6	ESP	11	168-bit 3DES key

B's SPD

From	To	Protocol	Port	Policy
1.1.1.1	2.2.2.2	AH	Any	Transport AH with HMACÐMD5

B's Inbound SADB

Source	Destination	Protocol	SPI	SA record
1.1.1.1	2.2.2.2	AH	10	HMACÐMD5 key

Figure 9.5   Inbound IPSec processing.

- The IPSec layer extracts the SPI from the AH or the ESP header, and the source and the destination IP addresses and protocol from the IP header. In our example, the AH header has an SPI value of 10 with source and destination being 1.1.1.1 and 2.2.2.2 respectively.

- The IPSec component then fetches the SA from the SADB using the destination (2.2.2.2), protocol (AH), and SPI (10).

- If the SADB does not find the SA, an error is logged and the packet is dropped.

- If the SADB returns the SA, which is true in our example, the IPSec layer processes the packet according to the rules defined in AH and ESP chapters.
- The policy corresponding to the packet is checked to determine if the IPSec processing is applied appropriately. The policy is obtained either by a pointer in the SA or by querying the SPD using the selectors. In the example, the SPD has an entry that specifies that any packets from 1.1.1.1 should have AH in transport mode using HMAC-MD5. The policy engine checks if this is true. In this case, the security afforded to the packet is what was specified in the policy and hence the packet is accepted.

The following failures are possible. In all these cases, the packet is dropped.

- The antireplay option is turned on and the packet fails the replay check.
- The authentication fails.
- The length is incorrect.
- The lifetime for the SA has expired.
- The packet is decrypted but the protocol field contains an invalid value, or if there is a pad, the padding is incorrect.
- If the packet is authenticated and/or decrypted correctly and anti-replay is enabled, the replay window is updated.

In case of tunneling, the IPSec layer has to perform an extra check to determine if the SA that was used to process the packet was in fact established to process the packet from the actual source. This is achieved by using the inner-header destination address for SPD lookup. This check is extremely important. If this check is not performed it is possible to induce a recipient to process and/or forward spoofed packets that may be in violation of its local security policy. IPSec invokes the upper layer to process the packet. In case of tunneled packets, the upper layer is the IP layer itself.

Let us consider the tunneled processing at the router RB. RB receives a tunneled packet from RA. The processing of the packet is the same as the non-tunneled case until the policy is invoked. In our example, RB receives a packet from source 5.5.5.5 with tunneled ESP using 3DES using an SPI value of 11. The lookup in the SADB yields an SA pointer.

However, when the policy engine is invoked, the source and the destination address will be that of the inner IP header. The values in this case are 1.1.1.1 and 2.2.2.2. The lookup in the SPD matches the entry whose from and to fields are network prefixes 2.2.2/24 and 1.1.1/24. They also indicate that the packet was tunneled by 5.5.5.5 that is also live in this case. As the security services afforded to the packet match to that in the SPD, the packet is forwarded to the actual destination.

For non-IPSec packets, the processing is limited to confirming that the packet without any security can in fact be admitted. This requires a lookup into the SPD to determine if the policy requires the packet to be secure.

Fragmentation and PMTU

Generally, IPSec is not affected by fragmentation because the IP packets are fragmented after the IPSec processing and the fragments are reassembled before the IP layer invokes the IPSec layer for further processing. This is true for all implementations of IPSec—host, routers, bump in the stack, or bump in the wire. The general exception to this rule is that IPSec implementations on gateways that have selectors on the granularity of port and protocol may have to assemble enough of the fragments to determine whether the reconstructed packet is permitted.

However, IPSec does affect PMTU. The hosts that generate a packet avoid fragmentation by setting the DF bit in the IP header. This indicates to a router to inform the host that originated the packet about its MTU. If a router gets a packet that is too big for its MTU, it sends an ICMP message to the host that originated the packet, indicating the MTU in the ICMP message. It is up to the host to interpret these ICMP messages and store them appropriately so that future packets generated on this connection should not need fragmentation. The host maintains this information either in the socket, or on a per route basis. It is preferable for the host to maintain PMTU information where possible because it leads to optimal use of bandwidth.

As the IPSec layer introduces extra headers, it should be involved in the PMTU processing. The involvement of IPSec varies, depending on host or router implementation.

Host Implementation

PMTU discovery can be initiated either by the transport layer or by the network layer in host implementations. As hosts do not maintain source routes, it is preferable to maintain the PMTU information at the transport layer. This enables PMTU to be maintained on an end-to-end basis.

When IPSec is enabled end to end, the IPSec implementation on the host should decrease the MTU that the network layer advertises to the transport layer for a particular connection. This value depends on the length and on the kind of IPSec processing afforded to the packet. The various parameters that affect the length are the IPSec protocols afforded to the connection, the transforms (different algorithms produce headers of different length), and the modes (tunnel mode adds an extra IP header).

Before the network layer passes up the MTU to the transport layer, the policy engine has to be consulted to determine the implication on the MTU because of IPSec. The MTU computation should also handle multiple tunnel cases. This computation involves invoking the policy engine multiple times to find the implication on the MTU for each tunnel header that is added. This computation is very expensive and complicated. Host implementations can optimize this process by pre-computing the length of the headers that IPSec protocols add to a packet. Consider the following example where packets from host A to host B are authenticated in transport mode and then tunneled (encrypted) from host A to router R. The host can pre-compute the length of the header from A and B and the length of the header from A to R and store this value packet destined from A to B. However, the implication of this is if the policy changes, the policy engine has to re-compute all the affected header lengths.

Router Implementation

The routers send an ICMP unreachable message to the originating host (this is the source address in the IP packet) with at least the first 64 bits of the packet data, if the DF bit is set and the packet length exceeds the MTU of the interface over which the packet is forwarded. This procedure is essential for PMTU discovery. However, tunneling poses a challenge to the PMTU discovery process.

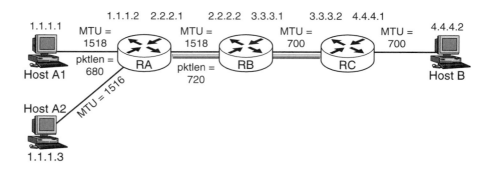

A's Outbound SAPB

Src	Dst	Protocol	SPI	SA record
1.1.1.1	2.2.2.2	AH	10	168-bit 3DES key

A's Outbound SPD

From	To	Protocol	Port	Policy	Tunnel dst
1.1.1/24	4.4.4/24	Any	Any	Tunnel ESP with 3DES	3.3.3.2

Figure 9.6   PMTU discovery.

Let us consider the following scenario shown in Figure 9.6.[4]

There two hosts, A1 and A2, attached to the router RA. A1, A2, and RA are on a network whose MTU is 1518 (Ethernet). RA is connected to RB over Ethernet as well, and hence the MTU is 1518. RB is connected to RC over some other link layer whose MTU is, say, 700. RA has a policy that requires it to tunnel all packets destined to the network 4.4.4/24 to RC (3.3.3.2). Host A1 generates a packet destined to host B and sets the DF bit to prevent fragmentation of the packet. Let us say that the size of this packet is 680 bytes. When the packet reaches RA, RA checks its policy and determines that the packet should be tunneled to RC. Let us say that after adding the tunnel and IPSec header, the packet size increases to 720. RB receives the packet over its interface 2.2.2.2 and determines it has to forward the packet over the interface 3.3.3.1. RB cannot forward the

---

4.   In this diagram, each router is shown with two IP addresses. This is because each interface on the router has a different IP address. The packet comes over one interface and is forwarded over another interface as the router is forwarding packets between different subnets.

packet because the interface over which the packet should be forwarded has an MTU of 700 and the current packet size exceeds that. It cannot fragment the packet as the DF bit is set. It sends an ICMP message with, say, 64 bits of data. The packet that caused the ICMP message and the ICMP error message packet are shown in Figure 9.7.

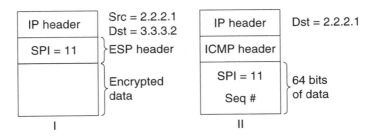

Figure 9.7   PMTU discovery packet format.

In the ICMP error packet, the first 64 bits of the data are the SPI and sequence number values of the ESP header. When RA receives the ICMP packet, it cannot determine the actual source because either A1 or A2 could have generated the packet. This is because the same SPI is used to secure all packets originating from network 1.1.1/24 and destined to 4.4.4/24.

The following guidelines can be used to handle PMTU messages.

- If the routers cannot determine the source, they can use the SPI information to determine the source of the packet and forward the ICMP message to the host. The routers can use the SPI if they are using a different SPI for each host. In our example, if RA was using different SPIs for A1 and A2, it knows by looking at the SPI to whom to direct the PMTU message it receives.

- In cases where the router cannot determine the source, it should remember the SPI and when it sees a packet matching the SPI, it should send the ICMP message indicating the MTU to the host.

The routers should provide the ability to set the DF bit if the DF bit of the inner header is set. However, in some cases, if the data length becomes too small, it may be more efficient to fragment the packet to make better use of the bandwidth. Hence, it may be important for this bit to be configurable in router implementations.

The BITS and the BITW implementation PMTU behavior are similar to the router implementation. As BITS is implemented as a shim, it cannot interact with the stack directly and has to process ICMP as a router. BITW implementations are specialized stand-alone security devices and hence their PMTU behavior is no different than that of a router.

ICMP Processing

ICMP messages are critical to operation of the network. There are different types of ICMP messages. Some of the messages are errors and some are queries used to check the status of the network. The ICMP query messages are end to end and the IPSec processing afforded to these packets is the same as any other IP packets using normal SA processing. The ICMP error messages generated by the end hosts can also be treated as normal IP packets with respect to IPSec processing by performing the selector checks.

However, ICMP error messages generated by the routers need to be handled differently, particularly if a router is tunneling the ICMP packet generated by other routers. The routers at the tunnel origination and destination would have established a tunnel mode SA for their communication. This SA is used to forward ICMP error messages. However, the source address of the inner header will not be the tunnel origination address and the source address check at the destination will fail. The tunnel destination node has to be configured to ignore source address checks for ICMP error packets.

A deployment issue with IPSec is the decision whether to accept non-IPSec ICMP error packets or not. Many routers will not be IPSec-capable for some time to come and if the end host or routers were to drop these packets, it is detrimental to the operation of the network. However, not performing IPSec exposes the nodes to denial of service attacks. Unfortunately, there is no easy answer to this question. It is a matter of policy configuration and one could turn on IPSec processing even for ICMP error packets for offending nodes.

10

IP Security in Action

IPSec is a robust and extensible mechanism for securing IP data-grams. IPSec provides stateless security—data confidentiality, data integrity, data source authentication, protection against traffic analysis, and antireplay protection—and therefore does not make any requirements on the IP protocol to achieve security. As such it is ideal for protecting any type of traffic that can travel on top of IP—basically *any* traffic.

By providing security at the IP layer, IPSec allows any application to take full advantage of its functionality. Security is done in one place, in the stack, instead of in each application that requires security. Authentication and access control are therefore done at the communications aggregation point in the stack. It is important to contrast this with socket-based security—such as SSL—in which every application that desires security must be modified. With IPSec, you just modify your stack and, voila, all applications can be secured.

Different modes of IPSec—tunnel mode and transport mode—allow it to be deployed anywhere an IP stack exists and to protect any type of traffic carried over IP. Transport mode is ideally suited for providing end-to-end security, while tunnel mode is ideally suited for providing protection to transient traffic.

By placing IPSec-enabled hardware at different points in the network—routers, firewalls, hosts, and bump-in-the-wire (BITW) "crypto boxes"—different security deployments can be realized. End-to-end security can be achieved by deploying IPSec-enabled stacks on hosts or by providing a bump-in-the-stack (BITS) solution as a "shim" inserted into the networking stack. A virtual private network (VPN) can be constructed by IPSec-enabled routers protecting traffic between protected subnets. Scenarios such as the roaming road warrior can be achieved by combining host-based and router-based IPSec solutions together.

Since IPSec-protected datagrams are themselves IP datagrams, IPSec can be applied serially or recursively, allowing for hub-and-spoke deployments, or end-to-end IPSec-secured packets being tunneled through an IPSec-protected VPN.

End-to-End Security

When IPSec exists on a host or end system—either natively in the stack or as a bump-in-the-stack implementation—IP packets can be secured from the data source to the data sink (Figure 10.1). The value of this cannot be overstated. When end-to-end security is achieved, every packet that leaves or enters a host can be secured. In addition, it is possible to configure IPSec on a host such that packets that are not IPSec-protected will be dropped. The result is a box that is "invisible" on the network—any of the popular port-scanning applications will not report such a device on the network—but, provided SAs are shared with it, will allow the full gamut of services a host or server can provide.

Depending on policy selectors, a single SA pair can secure all traffic between two endpoints—Telnet, SMTP, Web, etc.—or unique SA pairs can protect each stream independently. In either case, the traffic does not exist on the wire in an unsecured state.

Generally, end-to-end security is accomplished by using IPSec in transport mode since the communication endpoints are also the IPSec endpoints. But tunnel mode can be used to provide end-to-end security with the added overhead of an extra IP header. Either mode is perfectly legal.

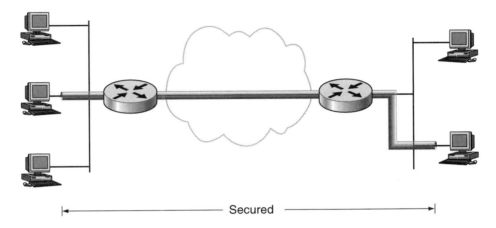

Figure 10.1   End-to-End security through the network.

A possible drawback to end-to-end security is that various applications that require the ability to "inspect" or modify a transient packet will fail when end-to-end confidentiality is employed. Various Quality of Service (QoS) solutions, traffic shaping, firewalling, and traffic monitoring tools will all be unable to determine what sort of packet is being transmitted—it's just an IPSec packet—and will therefore be unable to make the decisions that they're supposed to make. In addition, Network Address Translation (NAT) will fail because it is attempting to modify a packet that has been secured. In fact, NAT can be thought of as just the sort of *attack* that IPSec is designed to prevent. Since NAT is very popular, there is work on-going in the IETF to allow the two to be used simultaneously. Re-addressing entire networks or enabling security is not a choice most network administrators want to make!

Virtual Private Networks

When IPSec is deployed in intermediate networking devices—another way of saying routers—virtual private networks (VPNs) can be established (Figure 10.2). A VPN is *virtual* because it is not a physically distinct network. Tunnels are used to establish connectivity between disparate physical networks. A VPN is *private* because the tunnels are encrypted to provide confidentiality. A VPN is a *network* because, well, this is networking! We're connecting two different networks and establishing what is, in effect, a single, albeit virtual, entity: a new network.

VPNs are becoming important when people realize the cost savings that can be achieved by switching from traditional leased line types of networks to those that utilize public networks. Since these networks are literally public, a company is reluctant to just connect their corporate network to it. Proprietary information could inadvertently leak out and hackers would almost certainly come in. A VPN can give a company the security it needs at a great savings in cost over a leased line.

VPNs are constructed by deploying IPSec on routers that provide the physical network connection to a protected network. On one side of the routers, the *red* side (red because of the image it invokes of danger, caution, and attention) is a protected network to which access must be strictly controlled. On the other side, the *black* side (black because we can't see what's in the packets being emitted), is the unsafe and unsecured network—usually the big I, Internet. When two such routers establish IPSec tunnels through which they send traffic from locally protected subnets to remotely protected subnets, it is called a VPN.

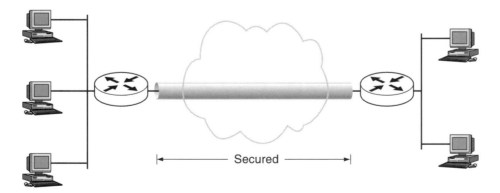

Figure 10.2   A VPN across the Internet.

In a VPN, each IPSec-enabled router is a network aggregation point and attempts at traffic analysis of the VPN will fail. All traffic destined for the VPN goes through tunnels on the router and to a snooper in the network all the traffic looks the same—it's just encrypted packets sourced by one router and destined to another router. Depending on the selectors dictating which traffic is part of the VPN, there may be many pairs of SAs defining the VPN or a single pair of SAs defining the VPN. In either case, the only information a snooper could derive is the SPI being used, but since he has no way to equate SPIs with traffic—this part of the IKE exchange is encrypted, after all—this information is not very useful.

Since VPNs are protecting transient traffic—traffic sourced or destined for hosts on a protected network—they must use IPSec in tunnel mode. The only way for transport mode IPSec to be used is if the transient traffic is being tunneled via some other protocol. L2TP is an example of this and will be discussed in Chapter 12.

Road Warriors

In end-to-end security, packets are encrypted and decrypted by the host that produces and/or consumes the traffic. In a VPN, a router on the network encrypts and decrypts packets on behalf of a host (or hosts) on a protected network. A combination of the two is generally referred to as the *road warrior* configuration (Figure 10.3).

A road warrior is typically an individual who does not reside at a fixed location but still requires access to a protected network. The most common situation is a traveling employee who must securely access corporate resources from a hotel, or airport dial-up, or from any Internet point of presence (POP) available.

In a road warrior scenario, the road warrior's computer supports IPSec either natively or by a bump-in-the-stack shim. He is able to secure outbound packets before they reach the wire and able to verify the security on inbound packets before they reach IP processing. The road warrior's IPSec peer is a router that protects the network the road warrior wishes to access. This router can simultaneously be supporting a VPN—terminating IPSec tunnels with other routers—and allowing secure remote access to other roaming road warriors.

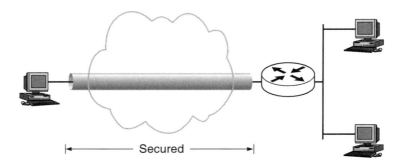

Figure 10.3   The Road Warrior.

One side of this connection will be both the communications and IPSec endpoint but the other side will be providing IPSec as a service to another network entity. Therefore, the road warrior scenario is similar to the VPN in that it either must be IPSec in tunnel mode or the transient traffic—from the road warrior's portable computer to the protected network—must be tunneled by some other protocol.

Nested Tunnels

Sometimes there are multiple levels of network security that need to be supported. The canonical example of this is a corporation that has a security gateway to protect its network from competitors and hackers, and inside the network has another security gateway protecting a sensitive subnet from its own employees. Imagine the human resources, or mergers and acquisitions departments of a major corporation. The information managed by those departments cannot be made available to all employees, just as other proprietary corporate information on its main network cannot be made available to the general public.

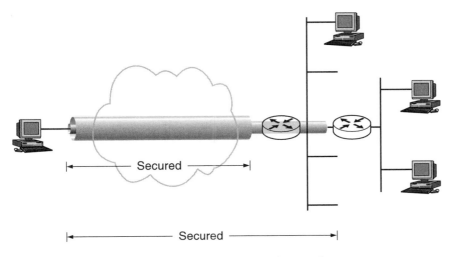

Figure 10.4   Nested Tunnels.

In this situation, when one wishes to access a protected subnet inside a protected network, nested tunnels are necessary (figure 10.4). Alice is in the mergers and acquisitions department of the NetWidgit Corporation and spent the day evaluating a takeover target. She wishes to share the information she gathered with her co-workers, but is in another town and there are no local offices. With IPSec, Alice can establish an encrypted and authenticated tunnel to the security gateway for the NetWidget Corporation, and, once inside the network (via an IPSec-protected tunnel to the security gateway), establish another encrypted and authenticated tunnel with the security gateway of the mergers and acquisitions department. Her packets, from her portable computer to a server inside her department's subnet, are encapsulated with IPSec packets addressed to the security gateway of Mergers and Acquisitions. Those IPSec packets are further encapsulated with IPSec addressed to the security gateway of the NetWidget Corporation itself. These layers are peeled off like layers of an onion as the packet makes its way toward its ultimate destination (Figure 10.5).

A packet from Alice's department server back to her portable computer is straightforward to construct since each of the encapsulations is atomic. The packet Alice sends to her department server is much more difficult to construct. Her original packet destined for her department server will hit an SPD match in her local policy database. That will trigger an IPSec encapsulation and the resulting IPSec packet will be reinserted back into the packet output path for another policy check. This

IPSec packet, destined for her department's security gateway, will hit another SPD match and result in yet another IPSec encapsulation and reinsertion back into the packet output path. This final header, an IPSec packet from Alice's computer to her corporate gateway, will be sent out the wire.

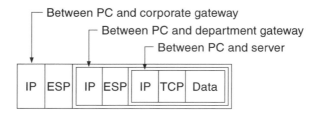

Figure 10.5   The Packet Onion.

Just as complicated is the way this whole thing is established! Alice must have policy in her SPD that specifies traffic to her department's server must be protected by ESP (AH) with the IPSec peer of her department's security gateway. Furthermore, she must have policy that says that all traffic, including ESP (AH) and IKE traffic, to her department's security gateway must be protected with ESP (AH) with the IPSec peer for that traffic being the corporate gateway. The first packet she attempts to send to the server on a network behind two security gateways will trigger an IKE exchange to her department's security gateway. This IKE packet will trigger another IKE exchange, this one to her corporate gateway! Once the second IKE exchange, to the corporate gateway of NetWidget, is complete and SAs exist between Alice's computer and her corporate gateway, the first IKE exchange can be securely tunneled through the gateway to her department's gateway. Only when that IKE exchange is complete and two pairs of SAs exist—both inbound to Alice but outbound to the different security gateways—can the original packet be sent.

Policy for nested tunnels is difficult to set up, but once it is established it can be left in place. Alice has no need to modify the security policy on her mobile PC once it has been defined. Following the packet flow for nested tunnels (two IKE exchanges being kicked off for a single packet, IPSec securing an IKE exchange, etc.) is likewise confusing, but once you've stepped through it, it becomes obvious what is happening and the strength and beauty of IPSec becomes apparent.

Chained Tunnels

A common deployment of network security is a *hub-and-spoke*, as seen in Figure 10.6. The network architect is usually thinking about link encryption when this is designed but there can be other reasons, such as many-to-many encryption.

In such a design, there is usually a router that terminates multiple tunnels. Packets destined from one network to another that traverse a hub-and-spoke network are encrypted by a security gateway, decrypted by the hub, reencrypted (most likely with a different key), and decrypted by the security gateway protecting the remote network. Sometimes there are several hubs and the decryption and reencryption is done several times. Each of the tunnels in the path are chained together.

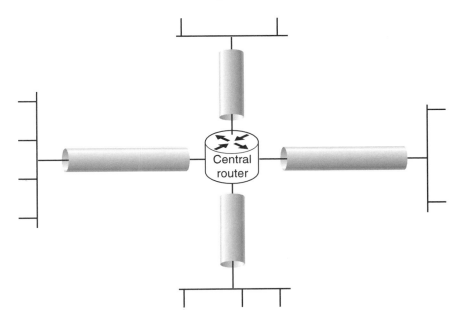

Figure 10.6   Chained Tunnels in a Hub-and-Spoke.

Obviously, the performance of this design is not as good as a traditional VPN, because the same packet will be encrypted many times. The setup latency for the first packet will also be quite poor because the packet will be delayed at each stop while the next tunnel in the chain is established. In spite of these drawbacks, this is a fairly common deployment. The primary reason is one of management. In a network with hundreds, even up to one thousand, stub networks trying to configure a peerwise relationship with every other security gateway, protecting a stub network would be a colossal feat! Adding one new stub network would entail visiting, and configuring, every single stub gateway. It's much easier to have several hubs in the network, each terminating a handful of tunnels, some to other hubs, some to stub gateways.

Unfortunately, there is really no easy solution to this problem. IPSec is a point-to-point protocol and each point has to know the other. Each stub gateway has to know the identity of every possible peer and the network it protects. That way, when the gateway gets a packet it knows to whom it must be encapsulated.

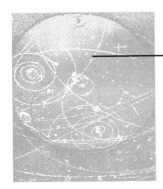

Deployment Scenarios (Using IPsec to Secure the Network)

We have seen how IPsec operates in a stack, how a selector database is constructed, how IPsec is applied to packets matching selectors, and how IKE negotiates security associations for use by IPsec. But how is IPsec actually deployed to help protect a network?

Before we dive into various deployment scenarios, though, it will be helpful to define how IPsec is presented to an administrator. One way it can be represented is as a *virtual interface*. All packets going into and out of this interface have IPsec applied to them. This is a useful representation on a router because routers have the ability to configure virtual interfaces for other encapsulation schemes (for example, GRE). The benefit of this representation is that routing protocols can be run on a interface, just like any other interface. The drawback of this representation is that now routing is playing a role in securing the network.

Another way of representing IPsec is as another step in IP processing. Prior to making a forwarding decision, the policy database is consulted to determine whether a packet should have IPsec applied to it or not. If IPsec is not required for a packet it is merely forwarded as the next step in IP processing. If IPsec is required the packet is encapsulated (the destination address may possibly change) and then it is re-inserted back into IP processing where it may or may not require another IPsec encapsulation (remember the packet *onion* from chapter 10). This method is simpler to represent IPsec to the administrator and will be used when describing various deployment scenarios here. It should not be difficult to imagine each scenario with a *virtual interfa*ce representation—it just requires a bit more configuration.

Each configuration scenario is implemented using a policy which will be described using a simple policy language. Implementations of IPsec will probably use a different grammar to specify configuration. Some will be solely graphical, others solely command-line based, and others will be a mix of the two. Regardless of how a specific device is configured, the information that needs to be configured will remain essentially the same and that will allow the simple pseudo-grammar used here to be translated into actual configurations straightforwardly.

To define a policy we must identify what traffic to protect, with whom it should be protected, how it is to be protected, and how we establish an authenticated connection with our remote peer. If we pare down the number of configuration options our policy language can be simpler without any loss of power. We will therefore limit ourselves to three types of ciphers—AES, 3DES, and CAST, two hash algorithms—HMAC-SHA and HMAC-MD5, two Diffie-Hellman groups—the 1024bit and 1536bit MODP groups, two methods of authentication with IKE—pre-shared keys and RSA signatures, and no PFS used in Phase 2 IKE. In addition we'll use IKE's *Main Mode* for Phase 1. This is mandatory to implement for IPSec compliance and will therefore be present in all IPSec implementations.

The policy language will consist of keywords (in **boldface**) and their options (in *italics*). For example, IPsec *protect* policy is represented as:

- **protect** selector **via** peer **using** ipsec-suite **establish** ike-suite

which specifies what traffic to protect, to whom, how to protect it, and how to speak IKE. IPsec *permit* or *deny* policy is represented as:

- **permit** *selector*
- **deny** *selector*

which specifies the traffic to permit or deny.

Now let's define the configuration options themselves. What to protect consists of a selector which identifies a flow:

selector: address <-- --> address [ULP [port]]

The peer is identified by an IP address or fully qualified user name:

peer: address user-fqdn

How the traffic is protected is defined as a "suite" for IPsec:

ipsec-suite: protocol authenticator [cipher] mode

How IKE is spoken is defined as a "suite" for IKE:

Ike-suite: cipher hash group auth-method

Each component of these constructs can then be further defined as:

- Address: W.X.Y.Z or a CIDR-style network specification
- User-fqdn: email-style name (name@company.com)
- Protocol: AH, ESP
- ULP (Upper Layer Protocol): TCP UDP
- Port: a port number for an upper-layer protocol
- Authenticator: HMAC-SHA, HMAC-MD5
- Cipher: 3DES, AES, CAST
- Mode: tunnel, transport

- Hash: SHA, MD5
- Group: modp-1024, modp-1536
- Auth-method: pre-shared, rsa-sig

Let's view a couple of examples of how to use this language:

protect *165.248/16 <-- --> 10.1.1/24*
via *172.24.56.1*
using *ESP HMAC-SHA CAST tunnel*
establish *AES SHA modp-1536 pre-shared*

This describes a policy to protect all traffic between the 165.248/16 network and the 10.1.1/24 network using ESP with HMAC-SHA and CAST in tunnel mode with a peer gateway at gateway 172.24.56.1, and to speak IKE with AES, SHA, pre-shared keys and the Diffie-Hellman group with the 1536 bit prime modulus.

Policy to allow traffic from 165.248.23.8 to 10.1.1.74 and deny everything else would be:

permit *165.248.23.8 <-- --> 10.1.1.74*
deny *0.0.0.0 <-- --> 0.0.0.0*

Site-to-Site Policies

In a site-to-site deployment, IPSec gateways protect traffic for networks behind them, that is traffic that originates on a protected network behind one IPSec gateway and is destined for the protected network behind another IPSec gateway. Each traffic flow requiring IPSec protection requires a separate policy statement, even if different flows go to the same peer.

The flow to be protected is identified by a selector and that selector is installed in the SPD. Associated with the selector is an IP address of the peer with whom the IPSec connection is to be made to protect the flow.

With site-to-site deployments peers have mirror images of each other's policy—from gateway A's point of view traffic is from A's network to B's network and B is the peer, while from B's point of view traffic is from B's network to A's network and A is the peer.

Remote Access Policies

Remote access policy differs from site-to-site IPsec policy configuration. It is used to specify policy for Road Warriors (Chapter 10) who typically obtain dynamic IP addresses from their hotel, conference, or from an Internet kiosk. Therefore at the time a VPN gateway is configured the IP addresses of Road Warriors cannot be known. This means that the remote portion of the selector must be a wildcard (we will represent this wildcard address as 0.0.0.0) and the address in the **via** specification for the gateway's policy will also quite often be the wildcard. In addition, when using IKE's *Main Mode* for Phase 1 it is not possible to use pre-shared key authentication when the remote peer's IP address is not known a priori. This is due to a peculiarity in the IKE protocol—the pre-shared key must be based on the IP address since an encryption key to protect the peer's identity must be computed, in part, using the pre-shared key prior to knowing that identity! Since we're sticking with *Main Mode*, all remote access policies will therefore use *rsa-sig* as the authentication method.

Because the IP address of a remote access peer is not significant, a gateway will require another way of identifying to whom (in the **via** portion of our grammar) and how it will speak IPSec. If all remote access users—anyone who can be authenticated—have the same policy the identifier can be a wildcarded IP address. To constrain access to certain authenticated users, or to provide different groups of Road Warriors with different access, a user's fully qualified domain name (a user's email address) is used.

Consider the following remote access gateway policy to protect traffic to the 165.248/16 network, from any user who can be authenticated, using ESP with HMAC-MD5 and 3DES for IPsec policy and CAST, SHA, and the 1536bit Diffie-Hellman group for IKE policy. Our simple policy language would describe this as:

> **protect** *165.248/16 <-- --> 0.0.0.0*
>
> **via** *0.0.0.0*
>
> **using** *ESP HMAC-MD5 3DES tunnel*
>
> **establish** *CAST SHA modp-1536 rsa-sig*

Note the wildcard address in the **via** specification. This signifies that this policy is for any user. This rule can be further constrained by indicating a user's fully qualified domain name (*user-fqdn*) with the **via** specification. The policy could be further constrained to only apply to people who can be authenticated from the eng.foo.com domain with the following rule:

> **protect** *165.248/16 <-- --> 0.0.0.0*
> **via** **@eng.foo.com*
> **using** *ESP HMAC-MD5 3DES tunnel*
> **establish** *CAST SHA modp-1536 rsa-sig*

The indication of a user's identity (whether she is alice@eng.foo.com or not) is typically indicated in the user's certificate.

Assuming that the gateway with the above policy is accessible via the Internet with the IP address 172.24.46.83, each Road Warrior that needed to remotely access the 165.248/16 network would need the following policy prior to hitting the road:

> **protect** *0.0.0.0 <-- --> 165.248/16*
> **via** *172.24.46.83*
> **using** *ESP HMAC-MD5 3DES tunnel*
> **establish** *CAST SHA modp-1536 rsa-sig*

Remote access selectors with wildcard addresses are not stored in the SPD to be inspected during IP processing like selectors for site-to-site policy. After all, you would not want to attempt to protect all traffic to an unspecified peer! Remote access selectors are merely retained as policy statements. These policy statements are checked during a Quick Mode IKE exchange to determine whether the identity of the peer (authenticated during a phase one exchange) is allowed to access the protected network indicated. If so, a real, dynamic, selector is created and installed in the SPD. The remote access selector is used as a template to create the dynamic selector and the wildcard information is filled in with the peer's actual address. This dynamic and temporary selector is deleted from the SPD when the IPsec SAs it points to are deleted.

For brevity's sake we will not concern ourselves with establishing a certification authority to handle the public key infrastructure to enable signature-based authentication. We will only assume that a user's identity, which can be applied to a *user-fqdn* regular expression, can be obtained from the user's certificate—either in the Distinguished Name or in one of the extensions—in that public key infrastructure.

Firewall and VPN Gateway Interaction

An IPsec compliant device is required to perform rudimentary firewalling functionality. This consists of checking a selector during IPSec input processing to see whether the packet should be *permitted* or *denied*, or whether it should have IPSec protection in the form of AH or ESP. This can be used to allow or prohibit access to individual hosts, entire networks, or even to specific forms of traffic. If this type of filtering is all that's needed a separate firewall would be extraneous.

In most cases, though, a firewall can be used to provide further protection such as stateful packet filtering, and protection against well-known attacks like fragmentation overflow attacks and TCP SYN denial of service attacks. For packets that would be passed by IPsec (via a *permit* selector) it would be nice to have some assurance on the benevolence of these packets before they reach the network. Because of this, firewalls and VPN gateways are often deployed together.

When a firewall and VPN gateway co-exist at a network egress point there are three different ways in which they can interact: in parallel, firewall in front, or VPN gateway in front (Figure 11.1). When a VPN gateway and firewall are co-resident on the same box the distinct functionality still lies in one of these combinations, usually "VPN gateway in front".

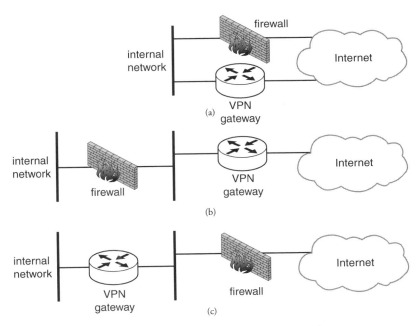

Figure 11.1   VPN and Firewall Interaction.

When the two devices sit in parallel they both represent valid points of egress from the protected network and ingress to the protected network. In this configuration the network connection to the cloud must be configured to route IKE (UDP port 500) and IPsec traffic (protocols 50 and 51) to the VPN gateway and all other traffic to the firewall. Routing inside the protected network is more complicated though. In the protected network the VPN gateway must be a preferred route for traffic which requires IPsec protection and the firewall must be the preferred route for everything else. If both devices speak a routing protocol they can be easily configured to advertise their preferred routes and dynamically establish the necessary routing state in the protected network. If either one does not then routes must be configured manually. Since these routes have critical security implications great care must be used when configuring them. Whether the devices speak a routing protocol or not, there is additional and critically significant (from a security standpoint) configuration necessary. As the protected network grows or changes, extreme care must be taken to ensure that proper routing of traffic is maintained. For this reason a parallel configuration of VPN gateway and firewall is seldom used.

Another configuration is where the two devices are connected in serial with the firewall connected to the protected network and the VPN gateway connected to network cloud. The VPN gateway has policy to protect certain traffic and *permit* everything else. This obviates the need for specific routing configuration. It also is an easy way to deploy IPsec without having to reconfigure your firewall—something firewall administrators are loath to do. The firewall in this configuration inspects all traffic, even that traffic that was IPsec protected. Naively that may be viewed as a positive but what this means is that there is a point on the network— namely the network between the VPN gateway and the firewall—where critically important packets are left unprotected.

The final option is where the two devices sit in serial with the VPN gateway connected to the protected network and the firewall connected to the network cloud. In this case the firewall is configured to allow IKE (UDP port 500) and IPsec (protocols 50 and 51) to the VPN gateway and only the VPN gateway. The VPN gateway is configured to protect certain traffic and *permit* the firewall to handle everything else. The drawback of this configuration is that the firewall now cannot inspect the IPsec protected traffic if it has been encrypted and unless the firewall is intelligent enough to recognize AH it will not know how to inspect any IPsec protected traffic. This is not so serious though when one considers that IPSec is already providing a cryptographic form of protection to these packets which is stronger than anything a firewall can do.

There is no one single best way to have a VPN gateway and firewall interact. Each one has its benefits and drawbacks. Depending on the security policy—and paranoia—of the network administrator one may be better than the other. Each deployment scenario will discuss the trust relationship and recommend a relationship between a firewall and the VPN gateway. In no way is this a hard-and-fast rule. Your mileage may vary.

A Few Words About Addressing

To avoid using IP addresses that have been assigned to a real company, all addresses used in this chapter will be from the private and globally non-routable address space set aside by IANA, the Internet Assigned Numbers Authority. When a gateway is connected to a cloud it is assumed that the IP address that connects it to the cloud is routable in the cloud. Addresses behind the gateway may be private and are not assumed to be routable in the cloud.

Whether addresses behind gateways are routable or not there is no network address translation (NAT) being performed in any of these deployment scenarios. Since tunnel mode encapsulates packets from one protected network to another, these protected networks can use addresses that are not routable in the cloud that connects them. The only requirement is that their own connection to the cloud is routable in the cloud.

Four Office Company Example

Let us now consider a small company, NetWidgit, with four offices, a main office and three remote branch offices (Figure 11.2). Communication between these offices is confidential and needs to be protected. Wisely, NetWidgit has decided to employ IPsec to protect this communication but that brings up some deployment options and issues.

Each remote office has a connection to the Internet through which IPsec-protected packets are routed but access to the Internet need not be granted at the remote branch offices. Each of our deployment scenarios for NetWidgit will deal with cases where the remote offices are and are not permitted to have Internet access. When a device has Internet access it must deal with co-existance with a firewall (see above).

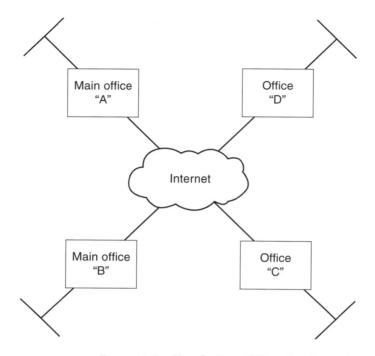

Figure 11.2   Simple Four Office Configuration.

In this example of the Four Office Company, each office (remote and main) represents part of the same company. The trust relationship between all nodes in the VPN is assumed to be extensive (employees have physical access to confidential information) and not suspicious (one node does not trust another any more or less than the rest). Because of this trust relationship, the firewall and VPN gateway will be in a serial configuration with the firewall connected to the Internet and the VPN gateway connected to the protected network. This maximizes the security at the cost of minimal firewall configuration without opening up the protected network to an attack that does not already exist (namely a disgruntled employee on the protected network wrecking havoc).

Fully-Meshed Configuration

In a fully-meshed configuration there are peer-wise relationships between each office and the other three offices. For the small NetWidgit network there would be six separate peer-wise connections for the four offices. As the number of peers grows the number of peer-wise connections grows faster. For instance, if NetWidget had five offices there would be ten peer-wise connections. If there were ten offices there would be forty-five peer-wise connections (see Figure 11.3)! Once we step through the (relatively) simple fully-meshed configuration for NetWidgit it should be straightforward to imagine how to implement fully-meshed configurations for much larger networks.

four offices, six connections

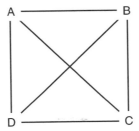

five offices, ten connections

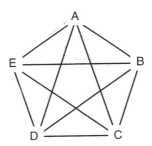

ten offices, forty-five connections

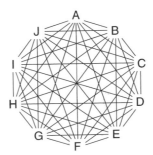

Figure 11.3   Fully Meshed Configuration.

First, let's consider a simple case where access to the global Internet access is permitted only from the main office of NetWidgit, and that all peer-wise connections will use the same IPsec and IKE policy suites to protect the traffic and that all traffic between the sites will be protected—no need to restrict it to a specific upper-layer protocol.

Each remote site will be configured in a similar manner: policy to protect traffic from its own protected network to each of the other three protected networks will be via the gateway for that protected network and policy for everything else will be via the gateway at the main office. Office A will have policy to protect traffic to office B:

> **protect** *10.2/16 <-- --> 10.3/16*
> **via** *172.24.16.3*
> **using** *ESP HMAC-SHA AES tunnel*
> **establish** *CAST SHA modp-1536 pre-shared*

policy to protect traffic to office C:

> **protect** *10.2/16 <-- --> 10.4/16*
> **via** *172.24.16.4*
> **using** *ESP HMAC-SHA AES tunnel*
> **establish** *CAST SHA modp-1536 pre-shared*

and policy to protect all other traffic to the main office:

> **protect** *10.2/16 <-- --> 0.0.0.0*
> **via** *172.24.16.1*
> **using** *ESP HMAC-SHA AES tunnel*
> **establish** *CAST SHA modp-1536 pre-shared*

While it is not strictly necessary some may wish to have an explicit drop rule at the end:

> **drop** 0.0.0.0 <-- --> 0.0.0.0

The other remote offices will have similar configurations with office B having policy to office A, office C and the main office; and office C having policy to office A, office B and the main office. The main office, though, will be different. It has policy to protect traffic to each of the three remote offices:

protect *0.0.0.0 <-- --> 10.2/16*
via *172.24.16.2*
using *ESP HMAC-SHA AES tunnel*
establish *CAST SHA modp-1536 pre-shared*

protect *0.0.0.0 <-- --> 10.3/16*
via *172.24.16.3*
using *ESP HMAC-SHA AES tunnel*
establish *CAST SHA modp-1536 pre-shared*

protect *0.0.0.0 <-- --> 10.4/16*
via *172.24.16.4*
using *ESP HMAC-SHA AES tunnel*
establish *CAST SHA modp-1536 pre-shared*

remote access policy to allow Road Warriors to access the each protected network:

protect *10.1/16 <-- --> 0.0.0.0*
via *0.0.0.0*
using *ESP HMAC-SHA AES tunnel*
establish *CAST SHA modp-1536 rsa-sig*

protect *10.2/16 <-- --> 0.0.0.0*
via *0.0.0.0*
using *ESP HMAC-SHA AES tunnel*
establish *CAST SHA modp-1536 rsa-sig*

protect *10.3/16 <-- --> 0.0.0.0*
via *0.0.0.0*
using *ESP HMAC-SHA AES tunnel*
establish *CAST SHA modp-1536 rsa-sig*

> **protect** *10.4/16 <-- --> 0.0.0.0*
> **via** *0.0.0.0*
> **using** *ESP HMAC-SHA AES tunnel*
> **establish** *CAST SHA modp-1536 rsa-sig*

and an explicit *permit* rule to allow other traffic to be protected by a firewall:

> **permit** *0.0.0.0 <-- --> 0.0.0.0*

Road warriors would need policy to protect traffic to each of the four protected networks via the main office's gateway:

> **protect** *0.0.0.0 <-- --> 10.1/16*
> **via** *172.24.16.1*
> **using** *ESP HMAC-SHA AES tunnel*
> **establish** *CAST SHA modp-1536 rsa-sig*

> **protect** *0.0.0.0 <-- --> 10.2/16*
> **via** *172.24.16.1*
> **using** *ESP HMAC-SHA AES tunnel*
> **establish** *CAST SHA modp-1536 rsa-sig*

> **protect** *0.0.0.0 <-- --> 10.3/16*
> **via** *172.24.16.1*
> **using** *ESP HMAC-SHA AES tunnel*
> **establish** *CAST SHA modp-1536 rsa-sig*

> **protect** *0.0.0.0 <-- --> 10.4/16*
> **via** *172.24.16.1*
> **using** *ESP HMAC-SHA AES tunnel*
> **establish** *CAST SHA modp-1536 rsa-sig*

Now let's consider the case where each of the remote branch offices, in addition to the main office, are permitted to have access to the global Internet. This will also allow the remote access policies for each protected network to go directly to that protected network.

There is now no difference between the remote branch office policy and the main office policy. Each gateway defines protection from its protected network to the three other protected networks and defines remote access policy for its protected network. Office A will have policy to protect traffic to the main office:

> **protect** *10.2/16 <-- --> 10.1/16*
> **via** *172.24.16.1*
> **using** *ESP HMAC-SHA AES tunnel*
> **establish** *CAST SHA modp-1536 pre-shared*

policy to protect traffic to office B:

> **protect** *10.2/16 <-- --> 10.3/16*
> **via** *172.24.16.3*
> **using** *ESP HMAC-SHA AES tunnel*
> **establish** *CAST SHA modp-1536 pre-shared*

policy to protect traffic to office C:

> **protect** *10.2/16 <-- --> 10.4/16*
> **via** *172.24.16.4*
> **using** *ESP HMAC-SHA AES tunnel*
> **establish** *CAST SHA modp-1536 pre-shared*

policy for remote access users:

> **protect** *10.2/16 <-- --> 0.0.0.0*
> **via** *0.0.0.0*
> **using** *ESP HMAC-SHA AES tunnel*
> **establish** *CAST SHA modp-1536 rsa-sig*

and an explicit permit rule at the end to allow other traffic to be protected by a firewall:

> **permit** *0.0.0.0 <-- --> 0.0.0.0*

The other remote offices and the main office would all have similar policy protecting traffic from their local protected network to each other's protected network and an explicit *permit* rule at the end.

Since each protected network is permitted to access the Internet directly, Road Warriors would have gateway-specific policy and no longer need to go through the main office to access remote office networks:

protect *0.0.0.0 <-- --> 10.1/16*
via *172.24.16.1*
using *ESP HMAC-SHA AES tunnel*
establish *CAST SHA modp-1536 rsa-sig*

protect *0.0.0.0 <-- --> 10.2/16*
via *172.24.16.2*
using *ESP HMAC-SHA AES tunnel*
establish *CAST SHA modp-1536 rsa-sig*

protect *0.0.0.0 <-- --> 10.3/16*
via *172.24.16.3*
using *ESP HMAC-SHA AES tunnel*
establish *CAST SHA modp-1536 rsa-sig*

protect *0.0.0.0 <-- --> 10.4/16*
via *172.24.16.4*
using *ESP HMAC-SHA AES tunnel*
establish *CAST SHA modp-1536 rsa-sig*

Fully meshed deployments are nice because there are no extra hops for a packet to go through to get from one protected network to another. Each protected network has a peering relationship with each other protected network. On the downside they are complicated to set-up and they don't scale well. To add a new node to an *N-node* fully meshed VPN requires *N* separate policy statements on the new node and one new policy statement on the *N* other nodes. When *N* grows large, that's a lot of configuration!

Hub-And-Spoke Configuration

A way to minimize configuration of large VPNs is to utilize a hub-and-spoke configuration. In this configuration each "spoke" has a peer-wise configuration with the "hub" but not with all other "spokes". This makes growth of the VPN more manageable as the size of the VPN grows because adding a new node to an *N-node* hub-and-spoke VPN requires a policy statement on the new "spoke" (to connect it to the "hub") and a policy statement on the hub (to connect it to the new "spoke"). The downside is that traffic between "spokes" must be routed through the "hub". That means double the encapsulation and double the cryptographic operations to protect the traffic. Network throughput will, most likely, be affected.

A hub-and-spoke deployment at NetWidgit will entail a simple and essentially identical configuration on the three remote branch offices (the "spokes") and a more complicated configuration on the main office (the "hub"), see Figure 11.4.

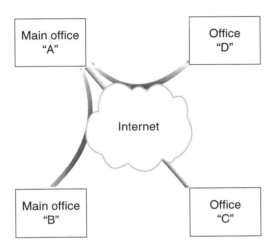

Figure 11.4   Hub-and-Spoke Network.

This topology lends itself nicely to the simple configuration—namely, that the only Internet access is via the main office. This way all the remote offices merely specify that all traffic is sent to the main office. For example, office A specifies traffic from its protected network is sent to the main office:

> **protect** *10.2/16 <-- --> 0.0.0.0*
> **via** *172.24.16.1*
> **using** *ESP HMAC-SHA AES tunnel*
> **establish** *CAST SHA modp-1536 pre-shared*

Each remote office would be similarly configured. Office B would specify traffic from its protected network, 10.3/16, etc.

The main office would then have policy statements to protect traffic to all the remote office's networks and remote access policies to allow Road Warriors to access those networks via the main office. In fact, the hub-and-spoke configuration on the main office's gateway (and the Road Warrior's remote access policy) is identical to that of the fully-meshed configuration when the only Internet access was via the main office (see above). The difference between the two is with protected traffic between remote offices, in the fully-meshed case it was sent directly, in the hub-and-spoke case it must go through the hub.

Now, to add a new remote office all that needs to happen is to update the main office gateway's policy to include a statement to the new office. Retaining our convention, let's assume the new network is 10.5/16 and the gateway is *172.24*.16.5. The new policy added to the main office gateway would therefore be:

> **protect** *0.0.0.0 <-- --> 10.5/16*
> **via** *172.24.16.5*
> **using** *ESP HMAC-SHA AES tunnel*
> **establish** *CAST SHA modp-1536 pre-shared*

and the new office would require the following policy statement:

> **protect** *10.5/16 <-- --> 0.0.0.0*
> **via** *172.24.16.1*
> **using** *ESP HMAC-SHA AES tunnel*
> **establish** *CAST SHA modp-1536 pre-shared*

In addition, remote access Road Warriors would need to obtain updated policy to obtain access to this new protected network:

> **protect** *0.0.0.0 <-- -->10.5/16*
> **via** *172.24.16.1*
> **using** *ESP HMAC-SHA AES tunnel*
> **establish** *CAST SHA modp-1536 rsa-sig*

But no configuration of the other remote offices—offices A–C—is needed. When the number of remote offices is large it is easy to see the benefit to using a hub-and-spoke set-up instead of a fully-meshed set-up.

If we wish to allow each remote office to access the Internet directly but retain our hub-and-spoke configuration for ease of growth each remote office would need policy for each protected network, including the new one, via the main office gateway and an explicit *permit* policy statement to pass non-VPN traffic to a firewall. It should not be hard to see what is happening. We have just lost the benefit of the hub-and-spoke configuration—addition of a new office now requires all other offices to be reconfigured!

Multiple Company Extranet Example

Now let's consider a different deployment case. That of an Extranet that is built to enable multiple companies—let's say four to retain consistency with our example above—to collaborate and/or cooperate in some new business development.

All companies in this case are independent companies. They all have their own access to the Internet and all maintain their own independent security policy. In fact, one of these companies could be NetWidgit from the Four Office Company example above with a fully meshed or hub-and-spoke VPN tying all its offices together in addition to the collaborative Extranet built between it and its partners. IPsec is powerful and flexible enough to allow a company to build a corporate and a collaborative Extranet together.

The trust relationship between these companies will be one of mutual suspicion. They may be partnering together for one aspect of their business but they may compete in another. For this reason it may not be acceptable to have the same firewall/VPN gateway relationship we had above. IPSec input processing requires checking a packet against a selector after the packet has been processed. This ensures that merely establishing a security association will not open up a network to all traffic that a peer wants to put in the tunnel. For example, if a security association was created to protect TCP traffic to a particular host then only TCP traffic to that particular host will be allowed, all other traffic sent under that security association, even if it was properly authenticated and decrypted, will be dropped. In some cases though this may not be enough. The suspicious nature of this Extranet relationship may force companies to place the firewall between the VPN gateway and the protected network. Such an arrangement will provide additional firewalling protection to packets which had been IPsec protected. Let's assume this is the case for this example.

Now you may be saying to yourself, if the firewall is protecting the network, it is effectively treating traffic from the VPN gateway as if it was from the Internet, so why not just get rid of the VPN gateway? Firewalls, even the smart kind, are kind of dumb. They blindly enforce rules on packets but they assume that the packet has not been forged, replayed, inspected, or modified en route by a bad guy. An Extranet protected only by a firewall would not only lose the ability to remain confidential, it would also open the Extranet up to attack. The IPSec-enabled VPN gateway will ensure that packets are not modified or replayed and also establish a cryptographic binding to the source to ensure they are not forged.

Single Site Hosts Extranet

In this situation the physical equipment that supports the collaborative work of the Extranet is hosted at a single site. This site could be a member of the collaborative group or it could be third party hosting. Let's assume it is the former because it makes the security implications more interesting.

The company hosting the Extranet is concerned about restricting the Extranet partners to the Extranet only. The actual machines a partner may use to access the Extranet (from where the partner is coming) are not necessarily important, as long as access (to where the partner is going) is restricted. This can be accomplished by opening up the Extranet to the partners' entire networks. Another way could be to establish a trusted Certification Authority to issue certificates only to trusted Extranet partners and then having remote access policy to restrict Extranet access. Either way accomplishes the same thing—from the point of view of the hosting company, it doesn't matter where they're coming from, it matters where they're going!

The security of the equipment that is not part of the multi-party Extranet must also be maintained since these parties are still mutually suspicious. The company hosting this Extranet does not want to give access to its other resources to its Extranet partners. This can be accomplished ensuring that traffic to and from the Extranet is not routed through the corporate network or by using IPsec policy and firewalls to enforce corporate security and ensure that no Extranet partners *sneak* off to other confidential parts of the company that is hosting the Extranet. Let's assume the latter, again because it makes the security implications more interesting. The Extranet equipment will be on a subnet—the 10.1.89.128/23 network—of hosting party's secure network.

There are also security implications among the other parties of the Extranet that are not hosting the equipment. They want to allow their company to access the equipment used for collaboration but not the other way around. That is, they don't want to give access to their resources to Extranet partners, all they want to do is ensure their own access to the Extranet. This is best accomplished with a stateful inspection firewall which will allow traffic *in* only if it is part of a stream that initiated the connection *out*. An especially paranoid partner may wish to be even more protective though, and allow Extranet access only from a few select machines in his network.

Note that these threats are not symmetric. The hosting company wants to allow anyone from a partner's network into the Extranet and only the Extranet. The non-hosting partners want access to the Extranet but still want to prohibit any access to their networks.

Similar to our previous example in which there was a central office and several remote branch offices, here there is a hosting company and several collaborative partners that comprise the Extranet, Figure 11.5. Note that the network being used for the collaborative Extranet is on the company's protected network. In addition, note that Company D (from the 10.4/16 network) wishes to restrict Extranet access from one small subnet on its network (the 10.4.24.113/28 network). This will provide it with added security assurance in addition to its IPSec and firewall policy at the cost of requiring workers who wish to take part in the collaborative work to physically move to the 10.4.24.113/28 subnet.

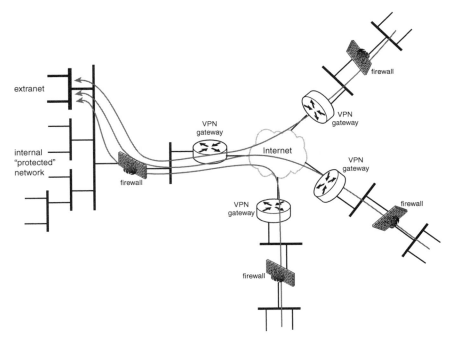

Figure 11.5   Single Site Extranet.

First let's consider the situation where there is no Extranet Certification Authority and no remote access policies. The hosting company wants to allow traffic that is only for machines used in the collaborative Extranet and exclude everything else. IPsec policy to express this is:

> **protect** *10.1.89.128/23 <-- --> 10.2/16*
> **via** *172.24.16.2*
> **using** *ESP HMAC-MD5 3DES tunnel*
> **establish** *AES SHA modp-1536 pre-shared*

> **protect** *10.1.89.128/23 <-- --> 10.3/16*
> **via** *172.24.16.3*
> **using** *ESP HMAC-MD5 3DES tunnel*
> **establish** *AES SHA modp-1536 pre-shared*

> **protect** *10.1.89.128/23 <-- --> 10.4.24.113/28*
> **via** *172.24.16.4*
> **using** *ESP HMAC-MD5 3DES tunnel*
> **establish** *AES SHA modp-1536 pre-shared*

and an explicit *permit* rule to allow other traffic to be protected by a firewall:

> **permit** *0.0.0.0 <-- --> 0.0.0.0*

The firewall would need to be able to restrict access to non-Extranet resources in the hosting company's network, in addition to whatever policy it already has. In addition, the network connecting the VPN gateway and the firewall is now unprotected and other techniques—physical security perhaps—will have to be employed to ensure there is no breach of security there.

Policy for the Extranet partners will be similar, each one protecting traffic from their network to the Extranet network inside the host's network going through the host's gateway. Policy for Company B to the Extranet:

> **protect** *10.2/16 <-- --> 10.1.89.128/23*
> **via** *172.24.16.1*
> **using** *ESP HMAC-MD5 3DES tunnel*
> **establish** *AES SHA modp-1536 pre-shared*

policy for Company C to the Extranet:

> **protect** *10.3/16 <-- --> 10.1.89.128/23*
> **via** *172.24.16.1*
> **using** *ESP HMAC-MD5 3DES tunnel*
> **establish** *AES SHA modp-1536 pre-shared*

policy for Company D's small subnet to the Extranet:

> **protect** 10.4.24.113/28 *<-- --> 10.1.89.128/23*
> **via** *172.24.16.1*
> **using** *ESP HMAC-MD5 3DES tunnel*
> **establish** *AES SHA modp-1536 pre-shared*

and each an explicit *permit* rule to allow other traffic to be protected by a firewall:

> **permit** *0.0.0.0 <-- --> 0.0.0.0*

The firewall between each partner's VPN gateway and his protected network must then have stateful packet filtering rules to only allow connections between 10.1.89.128/23 and the local network if they have been initiated from the local network. This will prevent a partner from accessing the Extranet machines and then reversing course and going out of the Extranet and into another partner's protected network.

If there is a Certification Authority, IPsec configuration is easier (but that is more than exceeded by the work required to get a Certification Authority up and running). The CA could even be one already established and in use at the host company. All that is required is that it issue certificates to partners with some identifying information. Let's assume that is the user's email address @ *extranet.foo.com.*

Remote access policy to limit access only to Extranet partners could be added to the above configuration. This would allow road warriors of the various Extranet partners to acquire access to the Extranet while on the road.

The entire configuration above could even be scrapped in place of remote access rules. Site-to-site rules are not strictly necessary. In this case the VPN gateway of the company hosting the Extranet would then need the following IPSec policy:

> **protect** *10.1.89.128/23 <-- -->0.0.0.0*
> **via** **@extranet.foo.com*
> **using** *ESP HMAC-MD5 3DES tunnel*
> **establish** *AES SHA modp-1536 rsa-sig*

and an explicit *permit* rule to allow other traffic to be protected by a firewall:

> **permit** *0.0.0.0 <-- --> 0.0.0.0*

Remote access clients of the Extranet partners would then need:

> **protect** *0.0.0.0 <-- --> 10.1.89.128/23*
> **via** *172.24.16.1*
> **using** *ESP HMAC-MD5 3DES tunnel*
> **establish** *AES SHA modp-1536 rsa-sig*

This simplifies configuration quite a bit. The only caveat is that you must ensure that the Certification Authority will only issue certificates with the *extranet.foo.com* fully-qualified domain name to valid Extranet partners. Control over access to the Extranet is now in the hands of the Certification Authority.

Each Site Hosts Extranet

When each site hosts some part of the Extranet—computers, printers, audio-visual equipment, etc.—the security needs of each partner now mirror that of Company A when it hosted the entire Extranet. Each partner now must allow access in to some part of its network and ensure that no one *sneeks* off.

First, let's consider the case where there is no certification authority. In this situation it is extremely difficult to set-up policies which are not strictly based on IP source and destination addresses. Partners used to have asymmetric policies which allowed access *from* anywhere in their network but prohibited access *to* their network. Now they have to allow their partners in. Each partner will have to establish which part of its network will be part of the Extranet and when employees wish to collaborate in the Extranet they will have to physically move onto the local subnetwork which houses the local part of the Extranet (Figure 11.6). This makes for a simple policy configuration—each site has policy to protect Extranet traffic to the other three sites. In fact, this will look very much like the fully-meshed example above. Company A protects Extranet traffic to Companies B, C, and D:

protect *10.1.89.128/23 <-- --> 10.2.42.1/24*
via *172.24.16.2*
using *ESP HMAC-MD5 3DES tunnel*
establish *AES SHA modp-1536 pre-shared*

protect *10.1.89.128/23 <-- --> 10.3.11.89/28*
via *172.24.16.3*
using *ESP HMAC-MD5 3DES tunnel*
establish *AES SHA modp-1536 pre-shared*

protect *10.1.89.128/23 <-- --> 10.4.24.113/28*
via *172.24.16.4*
using *ESP HMAC-MD5 3DES tunnel*
establish *AES SHA modp-1536 pre-shared*

and an explicit *permit* rule to allow other traffic to be protected by a firewall:

permit *0.0.0.0 <-- --> 0.0.0.0*

Company B protects Extranet traffic to Companies, A, C, and D.

protect *10.2.42.1/24 <-- --> 10.1.89.128/23*
via *172.24.16.1*
using *ESP HMAC-MD5 3DES tunnel*
establish *AES SHA modp-1536 pre-shared*

protect *10.2.42.1/24 <-- --> 10.3.11.89/28*
via *172.24.16.3*
using *ESP HMAC-MD5 3DES tunnel*
establish *AES SHA modp-1536 pre-shared*

protect *10.2.42.1/24 <-- --> 10.4.24.113/28*
via *172.24.16.4*
using *ESP HMAC-MD5 3DES tunnel*
establish *AES SHA modp-1536 pre-shared*

and an explicit *permit* rule to allow other traffic to be protected by a firewall:

permit *0.0.0.0 <-- --> 0.0.0.0*

The configuration for Company C and Company D would be straightforward then where policy protects traffic from the local portion of the Extranet to the other three partner's remote portions of the Extranet.

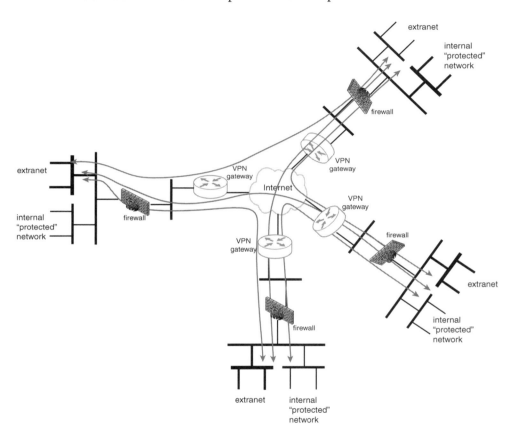

Figure 11.6   Multi-Site Extranet.

The presence of an Extranet Certification Authority makes things a bit different. Wildcard policy statements are realistic now and it is no longer necessary to force workers onto a certain subnet just to take part in the collaborative Extranet. But the benefit of allowing local employees to not have to physically move to work in the Extranet comes with a cost: it is necessary to treat local employees the same way that a partner's employees are treated. An employee of Company C who is not physically on the local portion of the Extranet will have to authenticate herself to Company C's VPN gateway in the same way an employee of Company D must.

From the point of view of each company's VPN gateway the configuration is now much simpler. There need only be a single wildcarded policy. Company A will have:

> **protect** *10.1.89.128/23 <-- --> 0.0.0.0*
>
> **via** **@extranet.foo.com*
>
> **using** *ESP HMAC-MD5 3DES tunnel*
>
> **establish** *AES SHA modp-1536 rsa-sig*

and an explicit *permit* rule to allow other traffic to be protected by a firewall:

> **permit** *0.0.0.0 <-- --> 0.0.0.0*

Company B will have:

> **protect** *10.2.42.1/24 <-- --> 0.0.0.0*
>
> **via** **@extranet.foo.com*
>
> **using** *ESP HMAC-MD5 3DES tunnel*
>
> **establish** *AES SHA modp-1536 rsa-sig*

and an explicit *permit* rule to allow other traffic to be protected by a firewall:

> **permit** *0.0.0.0 <-- --> 0.0.0.0*

Companies C and D will similarly have a single wildcarded statement protecting its portion of the Extranet and an explicit *permit* statement.

The configuration of each user who wishes to have access to the Extranet will be a bit more complicated though due to the fact that the Extranet is disparate. Each company's employee who wishes to do collaborative Extranet work will need the following:

> **protect** *0.0.0.0 <-- --> 10.1.89.128/23*
>
> **via** *172.24.16.1*
>
> **using** *ESP HMAC-SHA AES tunnel*
>
> **establish** *CAST SHA modp-1536 rsa-sig*

protect *0.0.0.0 <-- --> 10.2.42.1/24*
via *172.24.16.2*
using *ESP HMAC-SHA AES tunnel*
establish *CAST SHA modp-1536 rsa-sig*

protect *0.0.0.0 <-- --> 10.3.11.89/28*
via *172.24.16.3*
using *ESP HMAC-SHA AES tunnel*
establish *CAST SHA modp-1536 rsa-sig*

protect *0.0.0.0 <-- --> 10.4.24.113/28*
via *172.24.16.4*
using *ESP HMAC-SHA AES tunnel*
establish *CAST SHA modp-1536 rsa-sig*

Again, notice the similarity to the remote access case of the fully-meshed corporate VPN above. Since all employees are treated equally, an employee of Company D wishing to access the Company D Extranet resources would be treated in the same fashion as an employee of Company A wishing to access the Company D Extranet resources.

Outsourcing Networks

For organizations that want to outsource the deployment of their networks, it is possible for ISPs (Internet Service Providers) to design, deploy and maintain the network. An organization may decide to outsource the deployment of its network because of the following issues:

- Reduce management overhead
- Better performance as the ISP can potentially have faster machines particularly in CO based solution

The ISP has two design choices: either deploy the gateways that are implementing IPSec in the edge of the organization or deploy the gateways that are implementing IPsec at the edge of the ISP network. The former option is called CE (Customer Edge) and the latter is called Provider Edge (PE) based solution.

The biggest issue with this solution is "trust". The following are some questions to be addressed:

- Who controls the policy for security?
- The mechanism to create secure Intranets and Extranets
- How often one gets to update policies or create Intranets and Extranets
- The time it takes to service a request
- Most importantly, guaranteeing security of packets, e.g. no one is snooping on the packets, or modifying data or injecting traffic

In this section, we will examine the issues, limitations and advantages of outsourcing networks. In addition, we will also consider cases and the policy required to design and implement outsourced Intranets and Extranets.

PE versus CE based solution

As mentioned in previous sections, there are two methods in which an ISP can design an outsourced secure network. The devices (firewalls and gateways) that implement security can be located either at the edge of the ISP's network (PE based) or at the customer edge (CE based). These deployment scenarios are shown in Figure 11.7.

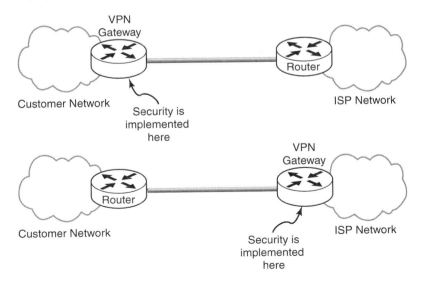

Figure 11.7   CE- and PE-Based Deployment Scenarios.

Both these solutions pose different challenges. In the CE based solution, the ISP is probably carrying only the organization's traffic on the gateway that is sitting at the edge of the organization. Hence, they can give more control to the organization to manage this gateway. However, there is a price associated with this. It requires someone in the organization to be able to configure policies to build secure Intranets and Extranets. However, this undercuts one of the goals of going to an outsourced network in the first place. There may be issues with liabilities as the ISP may have to guarantee a certain level of security.

PE-based solutions has greater emphasis on trust as the ISP may be carrying traffic from multiple companies on the gateway. If the security on the gateway is compromised it has wide ranging implications as it may affect multiple organizations. This may force the ISP to limit the exposure it gives to organizations on setting or changing their policies. For example, the policy change capability may just be limited to changing the algorithms or restrict access to remote users but not allow creation of Intranets or Extranets.

There is no one rule that fits all for the issues discussed above. It is driven by contractual obligations, the requirements imposed by the organization, and the limitations of the ISP.

Deployment Scenarios

In this section, we will consider the three different scenarios

- Building Intranets
- Building Extranets
- Build third party based Extranet solution

Intranets

In previous sections, we considered the deployment scenario for building Intranets. The policy configuration for an outsourced Intranet is identical to those discussed in non- outsourced solutions. The only difference is in the case of a PE-based solution. In this case, the policy is configured on the ISP's edge gateway instead of the gateway located in the customer's network.

The only other deployment issue is in the case of global organization where the geographically distributed locations may have different ISPs. In this scenario, the ISPs need to coordinate among themselves to set up the policies, which is an involved process.

Extranets

Deploying an outsourced Extranet where the machines participating in the Extranets are located in the customer's network is simple if the following conditions are met:

- All the machines in each organization participating in the Extranet are in physically separate network.
- The organization has a direct connectivity to the ISP's network and there are no other connections to the Internet, e.g., via a dialup modem.
- Once on a machine that is part of an Extranet, employees cannot initiate connections to other machines in the organization that do not belong to the Extranet.

The Extranets can be implemented in both PE- and CE-based solutions. The main difference between the two solutions is the placement of firewall. In case of PE-based solution, the firewall is placed in the front on the gateway implementing security in the ISP network as shown in Figure 11.8. This solution also requires that all the traffic originating from within the Extranet network is always forwarded to the PE firewall for the firewall to perform stateful filtering. This enables denying access to the machines that do not belong to the Extranet from within the Extranet.

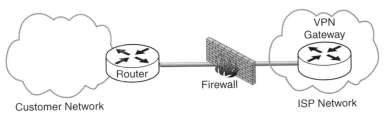

Figure 11.8   PE-Based Security Solution.

In case of a CE-based solution, the firewall is placed in front of the gateway in the customer's environment as shown in Figure 11.9. This firewall performs stateful filtering of packets to deny access to the machines not part of the Extranet.

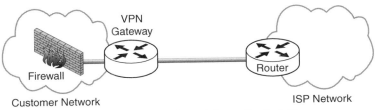

Figure 11.9   CE-Based Security Solution.

Continuing with our four Extranet partner example, let us consider the case where each partner has put the machines participating in the Extranet in a separate network as shown in Figure 11.10.

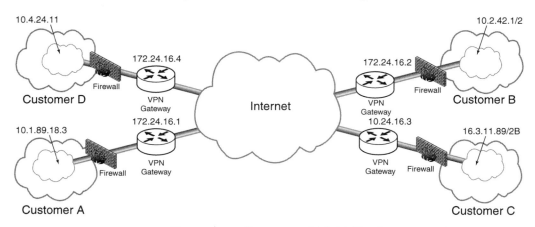

Figure 11.10 Outsourced Multi-Site Extranet Solution.

The policy on the gateway IRA is:

> **protect** *10.1.89.128/23 <-- --> 10.2.42.1/24*
> **via** *172.24.16.2*
> **using** *ESP HMAC-MD5 3DES tunnel*
> **establish** *AES SHA modp-1536 pre-shared*

> **protect** *10.1.89.128/23 <-- --> 10.3.11.89/28*
> **via** *172.24.16.3*
> **using** *ESP HMAC-MD5 3DES tunnel*
> **establish** *AES SHA modp-1536 pre-shared*

> **protect** *10.1.89.128/23 <-- --> 10.4.24.113/28*
> **via** *172.24.16.4*
> **using** *ESP HMAC-MD5 3DES tunnel*
> **establish** *AES SHA modp-1536 pre-shared*

and an explicit *permit* rule to allow other traffic to be protected by a firewall:

> **permit** *0.0.0.0 <-- --> 0.0.0.0*

The policies for IRB, IRC, and IRD mirror that of IRA.

If CA-based policy is used, then it is possible to allow access from the Extranet into the corporate network as it is possible to identify the person trying to access the corporate network from the Extranet network. In this case, the policy to access the corporate network is based on certificates.

The policy on IRA is as follows:

> **protect** *10.1.89.128/23 <-- --> 0.0.0.0*
> **via** **@extranet.foo.com*
> **using** *ESP HMAC-MD5 3DES tunnel*
> **establish** *AES SHA modp-1536 rsa-sig*

> **protect** *10.1/16 <-- --> 0.0.0.0*
> **via** **@.foo.com*
> **using** *ESP HMAC-MD5 3DES tunnel*
> **establish** *AES SHA modp-1536 rsa-sig*

The first policy is to access the Extranet network and the second policy is to access the corporate network. However, the configuration for each Road Warrior gets more complicated as they have to have a policy to access the Extranet hosted in each company.

Third Party Extranet

Many of the complications seen in the previous section can be avoided by a third party Extranet solution. This is because the organizations do not have to worry about someone accessing the corporate network from the Extranet network as the Extranets will be in physically separate network. The policy configuration reduces considerably compared with multiple companies hosting the Extranets. The policy does not have to change every time a new company becomes an Extranet partner.

The main issue with this is that data storage and the security is outsourced. This again comes back to the trust issue. Many companies already offer outsourced data storage solutions. Third party Extranets can be considered as the next step. However, certain guidelines have to be followed in deploying the Extranets. The machines in the hosting company's network should participate in only one Extranet or else the data may be compromised.

Let us go back to the four company Extranet example except in this case, the Extranet is hosted by a third party. The deployment of this Extranet is shown in Figure 11.11.

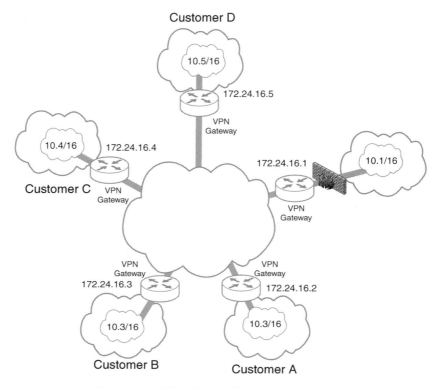

Figure 11.11 Third-Party Extranet

The following rule still applies: The access to the Extranet is asymmetric, i.e., valid machines or users from the participating companies can access the Extranet. However, users cannot access any of the systems by originating traffic in the Extranet. Hence, the firewall that connects to the Extranet cloud should perform stateful filtering of packets.

The policy configuration on the gateway connected to the Extranet is as follows:

> **protect** *10.1/16 <-- --> 10.2/16*
> **via** *172.24.16.2*
> **using** *ESP HMAC-SHA AES tunnel*
> **establish** *CAST SHA modp-1536 pre-shared*

> **protect** *10.1/16 <-- --> 10.3/16*
> **via** *172.24.16.3*
> **using** *ESP HMAC-SHA AES tunnel*
> **establish** *CAST SHA modp-1536 pre-shared*

> **protect** *10.1/16 <-- --> 10.4/16*
> **via** *172.24.16.4*
> **using** *ESP HMAC-SHA AES tunnel*
> **establish** *CAST SHA modp-1536 pre-share*

> **protect** *10.1/16 <-- --> 10.5/16*
> **via** *172.24.16.5*
> **using** *ESP HMAC-SHA AES tunnel*
> **establish** *CAST SHA modp-1536 pre-share*

and a policy for the remote access users wanting to access the Extranet:

> **protect** *10.1/16 <-- --> 0.0.0.0*
> **via** *0.0.0.0*
> **using** *ESP HMAC-SHA AES tunnel*
> **establish** *CAST SHA modp-1536 rsa-sig*

and an explicit rule to drop all other traffic:

> **drop** *0.0.0.0 <-- --> 0.0.0.0*

The policy configuration on Company A to access the Extranet is:

> **protect** *10.2/16 <-- --> 10.1/16*
> **via** *172.24.16.1*
> **using** *ESP HMAC-SHA AES tunnel*
> **establish** *CAST SHA modp-1536 pre-shared*

Companies B, C, and D will have similar policies, except that the source subnets will be their subnets.

The main advantages of the third party Extranets are:

- It is more scalable compared to each site hosting the Extranet. The policy of each user accessing the Extranet does not need any modifications when another company joins the Extranet partnership.

- In terms of scalability, this solution has the same advantages as that of a single company hosting the Extranet. However, the outsourced solution has the potential to provide better infrastructure than what a company can provide, particularly if the Extranet needs to be built for relatively short period of time. The time for deployment can be considerably reduced this case.

Issues in Outsourced Networks

There are numerous issues that have to be addressed in outsourcing secure networks. Security is a very sensitive issue. The reason one would want to secure a network is to stop others from snooping or modifying the packets. The fact that there is a dependence on a third party to provide the security may make some people nervous. However, this should not be a deterring factor in outsourcing most of the secure networks. These issues can be resolved by proper contractual obligations between the ISPs and the organization outsourcing the networks and the ISPs taking proper measures to provide the level of security required by the organizations.

Policy

It is evident that policy plays a key role in the deployment of secure networks. If the policy is compromised, then security of the network is compromised. For example, the attacker can just change the policy to use DES instead of 3DES or even worse, do NULL encryption. In this case, even though the packets are being secured, they are being secured with either a less powerful encryption algorithm, or even worse, sent out in clear text.

The issue of how to create the policy and maintain it is key in outsourced secure networks. It is possible that the customers may demand that they have complete control on the policy. However, this has implications to the ISP because they have to:

- Validate that nothing the customer does violates the contractual obligations.
- It is possible that the ISPs are servicing multiple clients and the policy is maintained in the same database. In this case, they have to restrict the access the customer has to the policy so that they cannot access the policy that belongs to other customers.

The fact that there are no standards that determine how policy is deployed and stored raises a good question: How should a policy be implemented? On one extreme, the ISP can say that the customer cannot have any access to the database, or on the other extreme they can give full access. There may be intermediate solutions such as the customer having the ability to specify denial of access for a remote access client; this is particularly important when the employee is terminated and they should no longer be accessing the network. The solution that the ISP can provide is dependent on how they have deployed their policy and what capabilities the schema provides.

If the policy uses certificates, there is the whole issue of establishing the Certificate Authority so that the ISP can properly authenticate the users. The two issues that stand out in the management of these certificates is the root certificate the ISPs should use to authenticate who can access the protected networks and how one would revoke the certificates. Both of these are extremely critical issues that should be addressed. Issuing and maintenance of certificates and the Certification Authorities is a whole subject by itself.

Security In ISP Network

The main customer issues the ISP has to address are:

- Gateway and Firewall Security: The ISPs have to guarantee the security of the devices that perform security and where policy is maintained. They will have to do this by making sure that these systems are physically secure and the access to this system is restricted. If the security of these systems is compromised, then the security of the entire network is compromised.

- The connection between the customer edge gateway and the ISP edge gateway that is securing all the customers traffic should be a direct link. There should not be any intermediate devices, as the more devices the packet passes through in clear text, the greater the probability of the security being compromised.

- Packet snooping: The ISPs also have to make sure that they prevent snooping in their network. Their network should be architected to prevent the placement of snooping devices on the link between the customer's edge and the ISP edge. Snooping opens up a whole lot of issues. As these packets are captured before the packets are encrypted, it is possible for the rogue person to capture the contents in clear text or modify clear text, or inject packets in either direction.

Multiple ISP's Issues

In case of global organizations, two or more ISP's may have to collaborate to provide the secured outsourced solutions. Although from the deployment perspective the policies and configuration remain the same, the issue of trust and responsibility becomes tricky. From a customer's perspective, they would like to have one ISP provide the guarantee of securing their network. It is then up to ISP's to define the domain of control and guarantee the security for their clients.

Summary

Deploying IPSec on a network requires care. One must always keep in mind the threat that IPSec is being deployed to counter against. That can influence how VPN gateways and firewalls interact and can also dictate what sort of access is allowed. When supporting remote access it is important to keep in mind that policies are no longer symmetric, and that quite often a certification authority will be needed to bind user's identities to public keys.

Some of the configurations for the various deployment scenarios we discussed are very similar, even though the network to be protected and the threats to be protected against were all quite different. It is important, though, to keep in mind that when planning and designing a secure network one must look at the needs and the threat to develop the model and produce the configuration, not the other way around. It is possible (and less work) to take an existing configuration and shoehorn in the network design, but that would most likely result in unforeseen scaling problems at best and security flaws at worst.

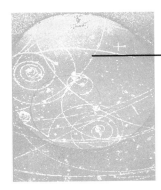

12

IPSec Futures

While IPSec is a versatile and functional protocol for securing IP, it is not a complete solution for all deployments, and there are still other issues that may need to be addressed. Many protocols desire to use IPSec to satisfy their security concerns and these have different problems that IPSec addresses incompletely. Indeed, while IPSec is a solution to a large problem, it is a problem to other protocols—for instance, network address translation (NAT).

Compression

Compression algorithms work by detecting patterns in data and eliminating duplicates. Encryption renders plaintext into seemingly random ciphertext. The better the encryption algorithm, the more random the ciphertext will appear. Regardless of the algorithm, the effective randomness of the cipher text means that it cannot be compressed. Compressing encrypted data can even result in expansion!

As more people start using encryption at the network layer, they will soon realize that their link-layer compression (e.g., in PPP) is not only failing, but is actually a detriment to their bandwidth because it will most likely increase the amount of data being sent over PPP. Turning off link-layer compression will help make things better, in the sense that the encrypted data will not be expanded by the compression algorithm, but the user will still notice that his effective bandwidth is not what it was before he decided to encrypt his data.

When security becomes enough of a nuisance that its benefits are weighed against the benefits of not having security, some people will opt for no security, the path of least resistance. And that is A Bad Thing. Ideally, one should not have to notice security.

The IP Payload Compression Protocol (PCP) was designed to address this problem. PCP is a stateless protocol that provides network layer compression. The idea is to compress, then encrypt. That way, the benefits of both compression and encryption can be realized.

Histories are used by compression algorithms to keep track of past patterns—by learning from the past history of the data, they are not condemned to repeat it, and in fact they eliminate it. But, PCP cannot take advantage of a compression algorithm's history because it must be stateless. This is because there is no guarantee that IP packets will even be delivered, much less delivered in order, and it is therefore impossible to maintain a proper compression history. The overhead of trying to maintain a history, and having to repeatedly flush it and start over when a packet is dropped or received out of order, is not worth the effort. Therefore, when a compression algorithm that utilizes histories is employed by PCP, it must flush its history buffer after each compression and decompression.

PCP, like AH and ESP, is an IP protocol. It has been assigned the number 108. An IP packet whose protocol field is 108, or an IPSec header whose *next header* field is 108, indicates that following is a PCP header and compressed data. Figure 12.1 shows an PCP header.

Figure 12.1   The PCP Header.

The *next header* field should be obvious at this point. It indicates what type of data was compressed. The PCP header contains a field much like the SPI field of an IPSec header—a compression parameters index (CPI). This field, along with the destination address of the outer IP header, identifies a compression security association.

It was decided to make the CPI two bytes (instead of four like an SPI) for two reasons: alignment and a desire to keep the header as small as possible to not override the savings obtained by compressing. By making a two-byte CPI, the compressed data will begin on a 32-bit aligned boundary (keeping with IPSec) and the header is only 4 bytes long. This leaves a single byte, which is not used, and is therefore marked in the standard fashion as reserved.

The PCP security association is very minimal. Since there is really no state to retain (no key, no antireplay protection, and no history for instance), all that is needed is an algorithm identifier. In that way, a single entity can support multiple compressed sessions with various peers with different algorithms, if desired.

Like AH and ESP, PCP can be negotiated by IKE. The IPSec DOI contains a DOI-specific protocol value (which differs from its IP protocol) for PCP and also algorithm identifiers for the two-compression algorithms defined for use with PCP: LZS and Deflate. In theory, IKE could negotiate PCP in the absence of any accompanying IPSec protocol, but what's the point? The whole reason PCP was defined was to enable compression when encrypting at the IP layer or below. If encryption is not being negotiated there is no point in having IKE go through its two phases and public key operations, only to negotiate compression parameters. Also, since the performance of PCP is lessened because of its stateless requirement, if someone wanted to compress and not encrypt, they could realize much better results by compressing at a higher layer where a history can be utilized—for instance, the session layer.

Processing of PCP differs from the IPSec protocols because compression is not always successful. Sometimes a PCP header will not be added to outbound packets and therefore a PCP header cannot be expected in each inbound packet, unlike IPSec processing where the header is always added and always expected.

Output Processing

In output processing, PCP is always done prior to either AH or ESP. If the compression algorithm defined in the PCP SA utilizes a compression history, that history must be flushed before the algorithm is used to compress data for PCP. The protected payload—either an upper-layer protocol in the case of transport mode, or an entire IP datagram in the case of tunnel mode—is then compressed by the algorithm defined in the PCP SA. If compression was successful, a PCP header is prepended to the compressed data and the resulting package is passed to IPSec for further processing and encapsulation. If compression is not successful, if the data did not actually get smaller, then the original uncompressed data is passed to IPSec processing without a PCP header. An outbound packet will only have a PCP header if the data was successfully compressed, which makes sense. This makes input processing a bit easier.

Input Processing

In input processing, the IPSec- and (possibly) PCP-protected packet is going to be sent to IPSec input processing because the protocol field of the IP header will be either AH or ESP. As the packet is decapsulated and the various IPSec headers are peeled off, the next header field of the IPSec headers must be checked. When that field indicates that a PCP header follows, we know that following that header will be compressed data. If the algorithm in the PCP SA—identified by the CPI in the header, the protocol (PCP), and the destination address in the outer IP header—utilizes a compression history, that history must be flushed prior to decompression. If the data cannot be successfully decompressed, the packet must be dropped, because it would be impossible to reconstruct the original data. If successful, the decompressed packet will be either an IP datagram—if PCP was performed in tunnel mode—or upper-layer protocol data—if PCP was performed in transport mode. In the latter case, a new IP datagram must be constructed. The next header field in the PCP header becomes the protocol in the new IP datagram, the payload length is adjusted, and a new checksum is computed.

Since a PCP header will not always exist in an inbound packet, the lack of one must not be construed as an error condition in the way it is when an expected IPSec header is missing. If IKE negotiates ESP and

PCP together, the packet may or may not have a PCP header, but it must always have an ESP header. Similarly, if IKE negotiates AH and ESP and PCP all together, the packet must always have an AH header and an ESP header but, depending on the data, may or may not contain a PCP header.

Taking the time and processing power to compress data only not to use the result can be a severe drag on performance. This can negate any benefit that compression would have. Some heuristics can be employed in PCP processing to maximize compression and minimize the number of times that compression is unsuccessful. Depending on the algorithm a lower-bound of data length can be fixed. Data less than, say 128 bytes, should not even be attempted to be compressed. The data is so small anyway, and any compression benefit would probably not be worth the effort; we'd be adding four bytes for the PCP header anyway. Also, by noting that successive packets will most likely not compress if the packet before did not, a good heuristic to employ is not to attempt compression on the next n packets upon unsuccessful compression of a packet. (Depending on the algorithm and the traffic, n can be 5 or 10 or maybe more.) A good example of this is when the traffic being protected is Web traffic. Any GIF image in a Web page would not compress because it's already compressed, but the text in the page would compress quite successfully. The packets that comprise the GIF will be successive, and when the first fails compression, the rest will too. By not attempting compression on the next n packets, this segment can be skipped over and processing power saved by not wasting time attempting to compress packets that will most likely not compress.

Just as there are different layers in the OSI networking model where encryption is possible, compression can be implemented at various layers as well. Compressing at a layer higher than IP will have the benefit of the resulting traffic being represented by fewer packets instead of the same number of smaller packets. Routing fewer packets is preferable to routing smaller packets. Also, when compression is done at a protocol layer higher than the network layer, a history may be utilized. Compression works much better with histories, so data will usually compress better at the session layer for example than at the network layer.

In spite of its drawbacks, PCP has been implemented by a number of vendors. It's not clear whether they all support PCP by itself or only in conjunction with an IPSec protocol, but PCP does exist and it is being used.

Multicast

IPSec is a point-to-point protocol. One side encrypts, the other decrypts, and both sides share a key or keys. There is a single recipient and single sender for each IPSec packet. In multicast, there are many recipients of a single packet, and quite often, many senders to a particular (single) multicast address. This is a completely different paradigm for IPSec. Antireplay protection cannot work if there are many senders. Data source authentication cannot work if all people in a group share a key. In addition, IKE won't work because it is designed to establish a shared key between two parties, but in multicast there must be a shared group key (or perhaps a tree of shared keys) that each recipient must have. Obviously, applying IPSec to multicast is tricky.

An IPSec SA is identified by the triple of protocol, SPI, and destination address. This address can be a multicast address. The only issue there is allocation of the SPI. In regular IPSec, it is the destination that chooses the SPI. In multicast, there is no single "destination" for a given address. Instead, the SPI is allocated by a group controller who is also, most likely, responsible for key generation and access control (more on this later when we discuss multicast key management).

So by just flipping the responsibility for SPI generation we can use IPSec to secure multicast traffic, right? Not quite. Remember that IPSec provides not only confidentiality and data integrity, it also provides source authentication and antireplay services. The latter two will fail in a multicast environment where many entities share a key and can all send packets to the same address. If everyone shares a key, all you can say about the sender of a "secured" multicast packet is that it was sent by someone in the group, not necessarily by the claimed sender. Similarly, if many people are sending packets to the same multicast address with the same SPI, there is no way to synchronize the antireplay counters so that no single counter value is used more than once and that the window could properly advance.

Source Authentication

Antireplay is something many users of multicast can live without, but source authentication of multicast traffic is not. It is critical for many multicast applications, and is a nontrivial problem that has yet to be adequately solved. Imagine a company that sells news or information. The company's reputation is based on the reliability of the information it sells. If it decided secure multicast was a way to save money and still deliver its information only to select recipients (which is similar to the motivation in setting up a VPN instead of paying for an expensive leased line), it would quickly lose its reputation and its customers, because any subscriber could forge "news" items or inject bogus information into the otherwise legitimate feed. Obviously, this problem has to be solved.

One way is to have each sender digitally sign each packet sent. This would provide nonreputable source authentication, but at a great cost. Current digital signature technologies (RSA, DSA) are too slow for bulk data protection. The bit rate of delivery would drop so drastically as to be largely unusable for most multicast applications. A speed-up can be realized by using a small exponent for an RSA key pair. This might be acceptable to certain applications for which forgery of the entire stream is a problem, but one or two packets is not. For others, though, this is still unacceptable.

Another technique described by Gennaro and Rohatgi in the proceedings of Crypto '97 uses a single public key (asymmetric) signature and a symmetrically-keyed hashing technique that takes advantage of the fact that the sender can know what the next packet it is going to send will be (Figure 12.2). This idea uses a strong digital signature on a keyed hash of the second packet appended to the first packet sent. The signed digest in the first packet is a keyed hash of the second packet and it can be checked when the second packet is received. Accompanying the second packet is a digest from a keyed hash of the third packet. If a keyed hash of the second packet (including the digest for the third packet) can validate the signature obtained in the first packet, the sender of the first packet can be unambiguously identified. Then, when the third packet is received, which carries a keyed hash digest of the fourth packet, it can be authenticated by computing a keyed hash digest and checking that against the value in the second packet, and so on.

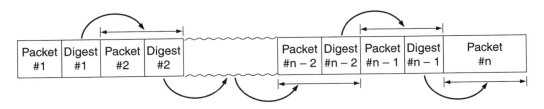

Figure 12.2   Source Authentication of Multicast a la Gennaro and Rohatgi.

Notice that each keyed hash is over the entire next packet, *including the digest of the subsequent packet*. This is to prevent someone from hijacking the stream in the middle and injecting bogus packets into the stream. Of course, the requirement this places on the sender is that the sender must know all of the input prior to sending the first packet. For many situations this is unacceptable, but for some, like the multicasting of movies or software distributions, it is entirely acceptable. The sender can generate the entire stream and sends out the first packet only after the entire data set has been processed.

The only requirement on the receiver is that he or she maintain a small buffer to hold the authenticating information for the next packet.

This is a very clever idea that is extended to multisender groups in the paper by using one-time signatures. Of course, this technique has problems if a packet is lost or received out of order since the chaining technique would collapse. Chung Kei Wong and Simon Lam in the paper "Digital Signatures for Flows and Multicasts," extended this technique to adapt to unreliable communications.

Another technique for source authentication of multicast traffic (by G. Itkis, in a presentation made to the Crypto '96 conference) uses the authentication digest technique of AH, but extends it to use many digests. The idea is that for any particular sender of a group, there are n keys. Each member of the group, and therefore recipient of the traffic, is granted k of the n keys, where $k < n$ (Figure 12.3). Each packet is sent with n digests representing a keyed hash with each of the n keys, and each recipient validates those digests that correspond to the keys he or she holds. If any of the digests for which he or she holds a key is incorrect, the packet is dropped. If they are all correct he or she must then assume the rest of the digests that were not checked are correct. Obviously, one member could forge packets to other members who shared the same keys, but given a suitably large n and a relatively small k the number of members that share the same set of keys will be small. It is possible to forge packets if a coalition of i members were to form, such that the union of all keys shared by all i members is equal to n. The probability of such a coalition forming is remote, though, because members do not have a way of learning who other members are (or of learning which members are unscrupulous enough to enter into such an illegitimate coalition) or what keys other members are holding. The drawback of this technique is the added computation on the sender of n keyed hashes and also the difficulty in determining the distribution of keys such that it will be difficult, if not impossible, for members of the group to form a forgery coalition.

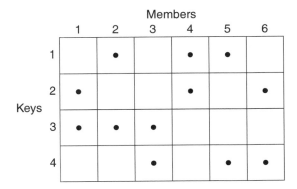

Figure 12.3   Source Authentication of Multicast a la Itkis.

This idea has been subsequently incorporated into a paper "Multicast Security: A Taxonomy of Secure Multicast Protocols and Efficient Authentication Schemes" by Canetti, Garay, Itkis, Micciancio, Naor, and Pinkas, which was presented at the INFOCOM '99 conference. This paper also includes several complexity measures between this scheme and a scheme using digital signatures.

Obviously, no single method of providing source authentication of multicast is acceptable for all, or even most, applications. Much work continues to be done in this field.

Key Management

Key management is also a difficult problem in multicast security. As mentioned, IKE is designed to establish a shared key (or keys) between two peers. It does so by performing an authenticated Diffie-Hellman exchange. While it is possible to extend a Diffie-Hellman to more than two members, it becomes a computational nightmare. Also, the addition or deletion of a single member would require another n-way exchange (where n is the current number of members of the group) at great computational cost. Some new key management technique is necessary. Most multicast key management protocols use a centralized key distribution center, or centers, that provide the key to qualified entities.

Other issues affecting multicast key management are join latency—it should not take prohibitively long to obtain the key(s) and receive secured multicast traffic; rekeying—it should be easy to retire an old key and distribute a new one to all key members; and, forced member removal—if a member of the group must be removed, the group must be rekeyed in such a way such that this member is not able to obtain the new key.

There are quite a few multicast key-management protocols. Some are specific to a multicast routing protocol while others are protocol-independent. Some construct a key distribution tree, which is congruent to a multicast (data) delivery tree, while others require no such structures.

All of the most popular methods of multicast key management share a common method of using unicast technology for initial key acquisition. A new or candidate member of a secure group uses a unicast protocol to obtain the key from a key holder or key manager. Almost all differ in who that key holder or key manager is, and where in the network that entity resides, though. They also differ in how rekeying is done; many of the key-management proposals try to optimize the time it takes to forcibly remove a member from the group.

Key Management for Multicast

Three members of the United States National Security Agency, Debby Wallner, Eric Harder, and Ryan Agee, wrote an influential paper on multicast key management and submitted it to the IETF. This document describes a wide variety of applications and explores the various architectural requirements they place on a secure multicast solution.

While the analysis of the various scenarios is quite complete (and the reader is encouraged to obtain a copy of this work), it is the architecture analysis and, most important, the recommended architecture that makes this paper important. Four possible architectures are discussed, each of which performs basically the same function, albeit in slightly differing manners.

The first is the most obvious: manual key distribution. The group key is distributed to members in some out-of-band manner without any sort of on-line key exchange. It is possible to take advantage of this single step to distribute multiple keys, each with a limited lifetime. The drawback of this approach is that it scales poorly to large or dynamic groups. It is also inadequate if forced member removal is necessary.

The next technique described is where a shared secret is established between each group member and the key holder. This shared secret can be, for instance, the result of an authenticated Diffie-Hellman exchange. This secret can be used as a key encrypting key (KEK), which can be used to distribute the shared group key to individual members. Each member would retain the secret it shares with the key distributor, but the key distributor would have to retain the secrets of all the group members to whom it has distributed the key. This is attractive due to its simplicity and the ability to implement such a system in a straightforward way. The drawback is, again, scaling. As the number of members in the group rises, so does the work required by the key distributor. It must establish a shared secret with each party, and for large groups, the key distributor could easily be overwhelmed. At the least, the key acquisition latency would be too great. Another drawback is what happens when a single member is forcibly removed. The new key would have to be individually distributed to each remaining group member. Again, the latency to rekey would be too much for large groups.

The rekey latency can be addressed by adding a "complimentary variable" to the shared KEK scheme described above. In this technique, a set of these variables is sent to each member, along with the group key (all encrypted by the KEK, of course). Each member is assigned a complimentary variable but is given the complimentary variable of every other member of the group. So for a group of n members, there will be n complimentary variables and each member j receives all variables i where $i = 1,2,..., n$, but $i\,! = j$. In other words, each member knows the complimentary variable of every other member but does not know her own. To forcibly remove a member from the secure group, say "member 20," the group owner sends a message saying "remove member 20 and all members generate a new key using the existing key and the complimentary variable for member 20 (this can be done, for instance, by hashing the two together). Since member 20 did not have her own complimentary variable, she is unable to compute the new key and is, effectively, out of the group. The main drawback to this is that each time a member joins the group a new complimentary variable must be sent out to all established group members. Another drawback is that each member must store the complimentary variable of every other member of the group, and for large groups, this storage requirement can become unbearable.

In light of the deficiencies of these approaches, the technique recommended by the authors is that of a hierarchical tree. In this technique there is no one single key, there are many. The keys are maintained by the group owner by constructing and maintaining the hierarchical tree (Figure 12.4). Each node in the tree represents another key. At the root of the tree is the main group key. Each group member is a leaf of the tree and each member is given the set of keys from the root, through all intermediate nodes, to the leaf that represents itself.

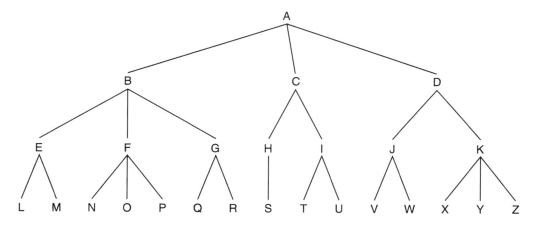

Figure 12.4   The Hierarchical Tree.

To construct such a tree, the key server (who may or may not be the root of the tree) establishes a shared secret (a KEK) with each leaf node, each user. The root key and the key of the leaf's parent nodes are transmitted to it encrypted in its KEK. The tree nodes (all parts that are not leaves) are merely logical and do not represent any actual group entity. Addition of a new user entails only establishment of a KEK and then a single message containing all the keys of its parent nodes encrypted in that KEK.

Forced member removal is interesting. Imagine that the tree in Figure 12.4 should be rekeyed in such a manner that member N is unable to obtain the new key—that member N is forcibly removed from the group. To do this, all keys held by user N must be renewed and distributed to all the people that need them, in this case, those that hold keys F, B, or A.

The rekey is performed bottom up. Therefore, the first key to change is key F. Before that key can be used, it must be transmitted to all those that use it, in this case O and P (remember N is being removed). Therefore, the new key F is sent to leaf O in O's key and to leaf P in P's keys. Next, B is replaced by sending it encrypted in E, the new F, and G. A is then rekeyed by sending it to all members encrypted in the new C, D, and the new B.

Rekeying is much less labor-intensive and impacts a smaller amount of members than the previous techniques. For a group of *n* members, the group owner must do *2 * log n* key encryptions to rekey the group. In addition, the storage requirements to implement this technique are not onerous. For a tree of depth d, each user must store $d+1$ keys while the group owner must keep all keys.

Secure Multicast Key Distribution

A multicast key distribution protocol specific to core-based trees (CBT) is described by Tony Ballardie in RFC1949. CBT is a multicast architecture that uses central routers, called *cores*, to build a multicast delivery tree.

RFC1949 ties multicast key distribution to the actual joining of the secure group. Access control is applied to the multicast join and the key is distributed along with a join acknowledgment. The utility of this approach is open to debate since there is no way to insure that only group members receive multicast traffic. It is generally placed on a shared medium, after all. Given that the data is encrypted, this is generally not viewed as a problem. On the other hand, by tying key acquisition to the group join, two birds are effectively being killed with a single stone.

In RFC1949, a *group access package* comprised of the group key, a key encrypting key (for rekeying the group key), and security association information, is distributed by authorized routers of the distribution tree to joining nodes. Each router that is part of the CBT tree will eventually become a group key distribution center (GKDC) and has the authority to distribute a group access package to a host wishing to join the secure group.

IPSec is assumed to protect the multicast data traffic using an SA created from the group access package.

When a node wishes to join a secure CBT tree, it sends an IGMP report to the group. In this report is a token, similar to the cookies that IKE uses, which is generated by, and is unique to, the host. This token is signed by the host wishing to join the group, and therefore to acquire the group key.

The local designated router (DR) authenticates the report by checking the signature on the token. If valid and the local designated router is already a GKDC, it can perform an access control check on the host and directly distribute a group access package if the host passes. If the DR is not a GKDC, and is therefore not part of the CBT, it must form a join request and target the tree's core. The join request contains the host's token, the DR's token, and is digitally signed by the DR. The entire message is sent to the core via the next-hop router on path back to the core.

The next-hop router must then authenticate the join request and, if successful, construct a new join request with the original host's token, its own token. This new join request is digitally signed by the next-hop router and sent toward the core. This is repeated until the core, or a DR that is already a GKDC, receives the join message.

When the core (or a GKDC on the CBT) receives the join, it must authenticate the host that started this whole chain of messaging. If the host passes the access control check, it constructs a join acknowledgment message and sends it back along the path that the original join took. Just as the join was reconstructed and resigned at each hop, so must the join acknowledgment be authenticated, decrypted, reconstructed, re-encrypted, signed, and forwarded on toward the host. At each hop, the group access package, including access control information, will be retained, since each router, now part of the tree, becomes a GKDC.

This group access package is actually the access control list for the group, plus two sets of group key, plus key encrypting key, plus SA parameters. One of the sets is encrypted in the public key of the host that is the ultimate destination of the join acknowledgment and the other is encrypted in the public key of the next-hop router. The final hop is at the host, who can decrypt the access control package (since it was encrypted by the core with his public key) and recover all information necessary to create an SA to receive the multicast data.

The hop-by-hop processing required by RFC1949 will impose considerable join latency on members. As the tree is built, the need for a join request to be sent all the way to the core is mitigated, but there will, most likely, still be cases where a single request for the key (and also for membership in the group) will require several hops, and therefore several public key operations. There is also an issue with this technique necessitating storage of the group key (and the key encrypting key) in all routers that comprise the CBT. The more people, or in this case routers, that know a key, the less likely that key will remain a secret. RFC1949 is a secure and scalable method of distributing group keys, but its costs are considerable.

MKMP

A protocol called the multicast key management protocol (MKMP) has been proposed by Dan Harkins and Naganand Doraswamy (yes, the authors of this book) as a way to quickly distribute keys to members of a multicast group in a manner that can scale from small groups to large, and from dense groups to sparse. It is not bound to any key-management protocol or secure multicast framework. In this manner, it is appropriate for use in most any secure multicast deployment.

In MKMP there is a single entity, called the group key manager (or GKM) who is responsible for generating the keys used to protect the multicast data and also for generating all access control information. The GKM also decides whether to delegate key distribution authority to other entities, called group key distributors (GKDs). It is this delegation that allows MKMP to scale.

If the GKM elects not to delegate authority to distribute keys, it would resemble the second technique described by Wallner, et al, where each group member shares a secret with the key manager. In this case, the GKM must be prepared to satisfy all requests for the key. For a group that is anticipated to have not very many members, this isn't a problem. (Note that the GKM will know how large the group can become because he is constructing the access control information. He or she alone can determine who obtains the key.) For a large group, this may be a problem, because a protocol that provides mutual authentication, like MKMP, requires public key operations to do the authentication.

When key distribution delegation is desired, the GKM solicits key distributors by sending a special message to the multicast data group. This message contains the identities of the entities that the GKM desires to become key distributors, or GKDs, and is sent with the Router Alert (RFC 2113) option set (Figure 12.5). This identity can be an explicit IP address, a subnetwork, a distinguished name from a certificate, the distinguished name of an acceptable certification authority (CA), or any combination of the same. For instance, the GKM can solicit GKDs that reside in a particular subnet and have certificates that are signed by a particular CA.

Of course, initially, the multicast data distribution tree will be either nonexistent or quite small, and the solicitation message will not travel far and will most likely not be received by any of the targeted key distributors. As hosts join the group and obtain the key from the only available source—the GKM—the multicast tree will be constructed and the solicitation message will be able to be received by more designated key distributors.

By setting the Router Alert option on the solicitation message, all routers on the multicast distribution tree will inspect this packet. A non-MKMP-aware router will not know how to parse it and will merely forward the packet on, albeit on its slow switched path. An MKMP-aware router will be able to parse the packet and determine whether it is on the list of potential GKDs. If it is, and it desires to become a GKD, it can obtain the group key from the GKM using the MKMP's key distribution protocol. Along with the key, the GKD also obtains group access control information so it can know who is allowed to obtain the key and who is not allowed to obtain the key, and something called the group information tuple, or GIT. The GIT is a token that can be used to prove key distribution authority to host. The GIT contains the multicast data group address and the identity of the GKD, thus binding the router to the group. The GIT is signed by the GKM to prove that the router identified in the GIT as a GKD is authorized to distribute the key. Otherwise, why would a host believe a router that claims the authority to distribute keys for a specific multicast data group?

As the multicast data distribution tree is built, the solicitation messages will be received by more and more routers and therefore have a higher chance of reaching potential GKDs. For any given area, the first host that joins the group will have to obtain the key from the GKM because there will be no branch of the multicast data distribution tree for it to attach to and therefore no neighborhood GKD. This branch must be built using the underlying multicast routing protocol (PIM, CBT, etc.). But after that initial key acquisition from the GKM, the key solicitation messages will be received by routers on the multicast data distribution tree and any potential GKD in that area would receive the message and acquire the key, thereby becoming a full-fledged GKD. Subsequent requests to obtain the group key by candidate group members in that area can be made to the GKD.

Note that GKDs will therefore arise only in areas that already have multicast data group members. This is A Good Thing. There will be no unnecessary distribution of the key to entities that would not have an opportunity to distribute the key. The fewer places this group key resides, the higher the chance of it remaining secret.

A host that wishes to obtain the key must first decide from where to obtain it. From the GKM or from a neighborhood GKD? This determination is made by probing for a GKD in its immediate area. This probe takes the form of a message sent to a special multicast address, the ALL_MKMP_DEVICES group, in a flood-and-prune-style with administrative scoping to prevent it from being sent to too wide an area. This flood-and-prune method of probing will result in a temporal state being retained in routers that must flood this packet out of its other interfaces. For routers that run multicast routing protocols like PIM this won't be a problem, but for other protocols, like DVMPR, this could be a problem because the state will be retained for upward of two hours.

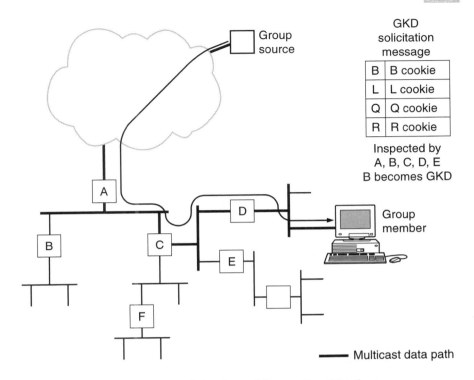

Figure 12.5 Solicitation of Group Key Distributors.

If a router receives a probe for a group for which it is a GKD, it must respond to the sending host with a probe response indicating that it is a duly authorized GKD for the particular multicast data group. This response must therefore contain the GIT that the GKD received from the GKM at the time it obtained the group key.

A host that receives a response to its probe can obtain the key from the router that responded, provided, of course, that the GIT is authentic and has been signed by the GKM. A host that receives no response to its probe must obtain the key from the GKM itself.

In this manner key distribution scales with the group for which the key is being distributed.

MKMP also defines a key distribution protocol[5] that allows for the key to be distributed in a mutually authenticated manner. It contains a liveness proof to prevent replay attacks against the key holder. It also distributes the key with a minimum of expensive public key operations. Key

---

5. The key distribution protocol itself has been patented by Cisco Systems, Inc. but will be licensed for use in MKMP in a standard, nondiscriminatory manner. The fee, if any, for its use in MKMP will be nominal.

distribution takes place between a key acquirer and key holder (either the GKM or a GKD to which this responsibility has been delegated). The protocol uses public key cryptography to encrypt a random number of the key acquirer's choosing. This random number is encrypted in the public key of the key holder and transmitted to the key holder. The key holder can then decrypt the random number and generate another, seemingly random, number by taking the exclusive-or (XOR) of the secret key and the key acquirer's random number. This new number, the result of the XOR operation, is encrypted in the public key of the key acquirer and transmitted back. The key acquirer, upon receipt, can decrypt this number and take the XOR of it with his or her original random number and construct the secret key. Each side must also compute an authenticating hash that contains cookies (when the group key is requested both the GKM and GKDs generate a cookie, similar to an IKE cookie, unique to the requestor) and state from the exchange that binds the parties to the exchange and proves that they are active participants in the exchange.

MKMP assumes that IPSec will be used to secure the actual transmission of the multicast data. It therefore also provides a mechanism for the key holder to distribute security association information to the key requestor along with the key.

MKMP can scale, but its ability to scale depends on proper delegation of distribution authority. If the GKM makes a poor choice of routers to whom it solicits key distribution authority, it can end up servicing most, if not all, requests for the key. On the plus side, MKMP distributes the key with only two public key operations on each side. Contrast this with the technique of using an authenticated Diffie-Hellman exchange to establish the shared key between the member and key holder, which would require two exponentiations for the Diffie-Hellman and probably two public key operations for the authentication. On the downside, the flood-and-prune technique MKMP employs to probe for GKDs may be inappropriate for certain multicast data routing protocols.

There are quite a few protocols to distribute a group key, many more than are described here. Each has its benefits and costs that must be weighed when choosing a protocol to use. Because no one protocol is satisfactory, work continues on new protocols and also on improving existing protocols by lessening the impact of, or eliminating, their weaknesses. The descriptions of these protocols may change in the future.

Multicast security is being addressed in the IRTF (a sister of the IETF that does the *R*esearch prior to the *E*ngineering, it's the Internet Research Task Force) because the issues with it are so large that it is necessary to do some *research* prior to beginning the *engineering* of a solution. The IRTF working group is called SMuG, for Secure Multicast Group. This group is chartered to deal with all aspects of multicast security and introduces techniques and protocols back into the Multicast Security (MSEC) Working Group of the IETF where solutions based on IRTF research are engineered to become standard protocols.

Key Recovery

Encryption poses certain questions and concerns. By using encryption, a company can keep confidential information secret while utilizing a public network. It can be used in e-commerce situations—in fact, e-commerce must use encryption because otherwise credit card and personal information would be transmitted from customer to store insecurely. Encryption can also be used by unscrupulous individuals to hide their nefarious acts. For instance, a child pornographer could encrypt all evidence of his illegal activity or terrorists could use IPSec to securely plan and carry out acts of terrorism.

Because of the latter, many governments in the world severely restrict when, where, and by whom encryption can be used. This makes it easier to keep tabs on certain groups or individuals, but also prevents the Internet from being used to its full advantage.

In an attempt to balance the competing concerns of law enforcement, business, and individuals, a concept of *key recovery* has been proposed. The idea is that the key(s) used for encryption will be stored in a repository maintained by a bonded company that will only give up the keys when presented with a lawful warrant. It sounds nice in theory, but in practice has many problems that are not properly addressed. A thorough evaluation of key recovery was compiled by several noted cryptographers (Abelson, Anderson, Bellovin, Benaloh, Blaze, Diffie, Gilmore, Neumann, Rivest, Schiller, and Schneier) in the paper "The Risks of Key Recovery, Key Escrow, and Trusted Third-Party Encryption" and readers are encouraged to find a copy of this paper.

It should also be noted that, ignoring all the technological problems of implementing a key recovery infrastructure, there are also very serious civil liberty concerns. Few people have an implicit trust of their government and there is ample evidence of government agencies, from almost *every* country in the world, engaging in illegal collection of evidence and illegal spying. Making technological allowances for what is for all intents and purposes spying outrages many people. It may also be in violation of law in certain countries. The Fourth Amendment to the United States Constitution provides for search and seizure by lawfully authorized government agents, but nothing states that the targets of the search must make affirmative efforts to guarantee the success of the search. In fact, the Fifth Amendment states that a man cannot be forced to be a witness against himself, which is basically what forced key recovery is doing. This is an emotional issue that probably cannot be resolved. There are just too many strongly held beliefs on each side.

Cryptography is no longer a science reserved to governments or their militaries. The genie is out of the bottle, so to speak, when cryptographic tools are readily available at local computer stores or on the Internet. The notion of key recovery may be too late.

IPSec and Key Recovery

IKE uses an ephemeral Diffie-Hellman exchange to derive the shared secret used for IPSec key generation. Through the beauty of Diffie-Hellman, only the active participants in the exchange know the secret. Also, each flow (protected by a single SA or SA bundle) has unique session keys. There is no long-term secret (as in months or years) that could be stored with the key recovery center to enable key recovery of IPSec-protected sessions. The long-term keys IKE uses are for authentication only and there is no reason why these keys should be escrowed at a key recovery center. This makes key recovery in IPSec very problematic.

A proposal has been made on how to extend IKE to do key recovery. This proposal takes advantage of the fact that additional, optional payloads can be chained on to any IKE message. It also makes use of ISAKMP options for the commit bit flag and the authentication-only flag.

Remember, when the commit bit is used in an IKE quick mode exchange, the exchange is extended on a single message. This message is not very interesting and only consists of the authenticating hash and a message saying "I'm connected." There is nothing particularly secret there, and passing that final message in the clear would not be a serious detriment to the security of the overall quick mode exchange.

The key recovery extension to IKE passes this last message in the clear by setting the authentication-only (i.e., no encryption) flag. (The message remains authenticated because the hash is included, but none of the payloads are encrypted.) It also adds a new payload, a key recovery payload, to the message. This payload contains the SA information, including the keys, and is encrypted in the public key of the key recovery center.

To "recover" the keys, the agents send a copy of the key recovery payload to the key recovery center (along with their warrant, of course!). The payload is decrypted by the center and the resulting information—SPI, algorithms, keys—is given back to the agents who use it to decrypt the targeted traffic.

Interestingly, an IKE implementation that implements this proposal could interoperate with another implementation that doesn't. Of course, this has problems because it works only if the responder is the party that wishes to do key recovery. If the initiator of the quick mode desires to do key recovery (for whatever reason) and the responder does not, the key recovery payload will not be sent. The initiator has no way of forcing the responder to send this information. Should the initiator terminate the session because the key was not leaked? That's not really clear.

This proposal to add key recovery capability to IKE was not introduced in the IETF, where all the other documents that define IKE and IPSec were, because the IETF has made a public statement against key recovery. RFC1984 (the number selection was probably intentional) is the statement of the Internet Architecture Board (IAB) and the Internet Engineering Steering Group (IESG) which formally declares the IETF's opposition to key recovery. Even without the formal statement represented by RFC1984 it is doubtful that the IPSec working group of the IETF would embrace this proposal. There are just too many technical, legal, and political issues that surround key recovery.

L2TP

A protocol called the Layer 2 Tunneling Protocol (L2TP) has been defined by the PPP Extensions working group of the IETF as a way to, you guessed it, tunnel layer 2 data. Remember the OSI model of networking from Chapter 2. The link layer is layer 2, the layer at which data is sent directly from one entity to another over the physical connection (which is at layer 1).

The link layer can be either packet-switched or circuit-switched but regardless, the data being transferred is addressed from one physical entity to another. There is no concept of a route across the network at layer 2. One can say that layer 2 transmissions are point to point.

In fact, the main use of L2TP is to tunnel data that is already in the point-to-point protocol (PPP). Usually, when one uses a modem the data is sent from the local computer's modem to a remote modem encapsulated in PPP. The physical connection is the phone circuit and data is transferred directly from one physical endpoint to another. The information being sent across this point-to-point link is PPP-encapsulated data, usually IP datagrams. Upon receipt of PPP data, the PPP header is stripped off to reveal the IP data inside. This data is then routed normally as if it had been encapsulated in an Ethernet frame and taken off a directly connected network.

Quite often the modem that a local computer dials into is not on the network to which the PPP-encapsulated data is destined. For instance, a traveling businessman in a hotel room can dial a local Internet Service Provider (ISP) who will terminate his PPP packets and forward the resulting IP datagrams onto the Internet toward his ultimate destination. Using a local service provider would most likely be cheaper due to long distance phone charges or the maintenance of an 800 number by the businessman's company. The problem then is that the businessman's computer has an ISP-assigned address (which is foreign to the network that he is trying to reach) and will most likely fail any sort of access control or security check that the network will apply to his packets.

If the PPP data, which is layer 2 data, could be transmitted across the network and be terminated by a server on the network to which he is trying to reach, he could take advantage of all the services of his network (local IP address, resource sharing, security, and access control) and save on the cost by still placing a local call to a local ISP. This is where L2TP comes into play.

L2TP tunnels begin and terminate at the network layer. An L2TP Access Concentrator (LAC) is the client end of the connection while an L2TP Network Server (LNS) is the server side. The PPP packets are encapsulated in an L2TP header that are, themselves, encapsulated in IP. These IP packets can traverse the network just like ordinary IP datagrams. When such a packet is received, the LNS demultiplexes the session using information in the L2TP header. It can then decapsulate the PPP data in a session-specific manner and forward the internal IP datagrams onto the local network.

There are two types of L2TP configurations: *compulsory*, where the client connects to an ISP acting as a LAC which tunnels PPP packets to the LNS (Figure 12.6a); and *voluntary*, where the client acts as the LAC and brings up an L2TP tunnel directly with the LNS after first bringing up a connection to the ISP (Figure 12.6b). In the former, L2TP runs in the ISP-controlled LAC. In the latter, L2TP runs on the client itself.

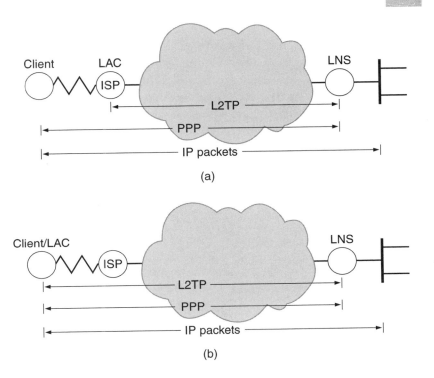

Figure 12.6   Network Access with L2TP.

When using L2TP, the businessman can obtain an IP address from the enterprise network he is trying to access. This will allow his local computer to appear as if it is on the enterprise network. The addressing could even be non-routable in the ISP's domain! From a logical point of view, it will be the same as his computer being directly connected to the enterprise network via an Ethernet Network Interface Card (NIC). All resource sharing functionality that he can take advantage of at work is available on the road. In addition, the network administrator can monitor the session because the point-to-point connection is actually being terminated at his LNS.

L2TP can be implemented as a UDP-based IP protocol (Figure 12.7). To envision how the various encapsulations work, start with the packet generated by the businessman's computer in our example. It is an IP packet sourced by his computer and destined for his company's remote network (note that the source IP addresses of this packet may be on the same network). This packet is then encapsulated in PPP that terminates on his company's LNS. These PPP packets are encapsulated in L2TP also terminated on the LNS. The L2TP packets are UDP packets encapsulated in an IP datagram that is addressed from an IP address assigned by the local ISP to which the businessman is dialing into and destined to the ISP's network access server (NAS). This IP packet will again be encapsulated in PPP, this time terminated by the ISP's NAS. This final, heavily encapsulated packet will be sent over the circuit-switched layer 2 phone line. Note that the local businessman's computer has two IP addresses. One, assigned by the ISP is the IP address of the physical connection—most likely a modem—while the other, assigned by the remote network with which he is connecting, is a logical IP address of his computer. The computer "thinks" its IP address is the logical one.

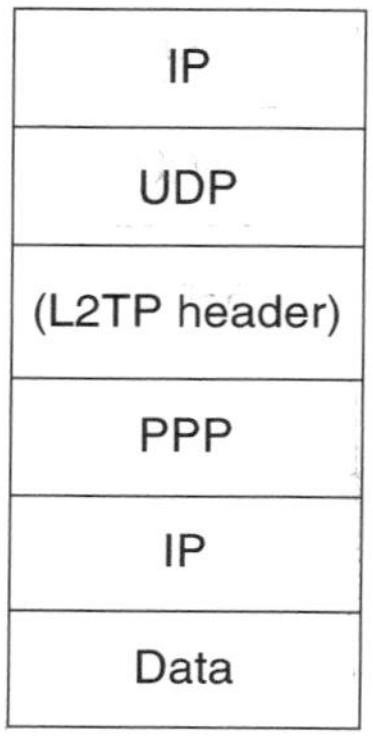

IP
UDP
(L2TP header)
PPP
IP
Data

Figure 12.7   An L2TP Packet.

L2TP does not provide any security. Since L2TP runs over IP, it is possible to use IPSec to secure the tunnel. The data to protect are IP packets from the businessman's computer, either acting as an LAC or using the ISP's NAS as the LAC, to his company's LNS and back. IPSec can therefore be used in transport mode; the data is already being tunneled and therefore the extra overhead of another IP header is unnecessary. (Given the amount of overhead already, any savings will help.)

By using L2TP with IPSec it is also possible to protect non-IP data. Since L2TP tunnels layer 2 packets, any layer 2 protocol, for example IPX or AppleTalk, can be tunneled. When used in this fashion the L2TP tunnel will most likely not terminate on the box that is natively speaking IPX or AppleTalk. Instead, the LAC and LNS interconnect an IPX or AppleTalk network to an IP network. The L2TP tunnel between them is across the IP cloud. In effect, a layer 2 VPN has been set up because these two disparate networks are now virtually connected across a foreign (speaking) network. IPSec can then be used to protect this layer 2 VPN and provide the security necessary. This is very important because there is no IPX or AppleTalk analogy to IPSec; that is, there is no layer 3 security service that operates on native IPX or AppleTalk. The only way to get confidentiality and data integrity on an IPX or AppleTalk network is by tunneling it through L2TP and protecting that tunnel with transport mode IPSec. There is no requirement that L2TP be run over IP (its transport specification is so generic that it has been claimed that L2TP could be implemented over "running shoes"—i.e., couriers could run back and forth with messages between tunnel endpoints), but to use IPSec for protection there is.

Public Key Infrastructure

Public keys can be used to verify digital signatures, but what does that tell us about the individual or entity performing the signature? Only that he, she, or it holds the corresponding private key. What is needed is a way to bind an identity to a public key in such a way that we will know with certainty that the holder of the corresponding private key is a particular identity. Certificates can be used to accomplish this task.

Certificates are documents that bind an identity to a public key. This binding is enforced by a digital signature of a Certification Authority (CA). A CA is a trusted entity, trusted to provide certificates bearing its signature only to individuals or entities that can prove their identity in a satisfactory manner to the CA. In effect, CAs are digital notary publics; they are trusted third parties. Being digital documents, certificates must be constructed in a well-defined format to enable their contents to be properly read. The ITU X.509 format is the most popular.

When all members of a group place trust in a common CA and are all issued certificates by that CA, they form a Public Key Infrastructure (PKI). Each member of the group will be able to present its certificate to every other member of the group and, provided it can demonstrate proof of possession of the corresponding private key, identify itself as the individual or entity described in the certificate. This allows for scalable authentication because each member need only enter into a single trust relationship with the CA. Without a PKI, every member of the group would have to enter into a pairwise trust relationship with every other member. That scales poorly as the group enters any reasonable size.

To join a PKI, an entity must enter into a trust relationship with the CA. The entity must obtain the CA's certificate (which, being the "authority" can be a self-signed certificate), prove its identity to the CA's satisfaction, and then present a public key for which it holds the corresponding private key. The CA then constructs a certificate that bears the identity the entity was able to prove, the public key the entity presented, and identification information of the CA itself, all signed by the CA's private key. A certificate can also contain additional information, such as alternate identities and usage restrictions.

For two members of a PKI to authenticate each other they must perform three steps: They must obtain each other's certificate; verify the authenticity of that certificate; and, then, use the public key from the certificate to verify the digital signature of the other member. This last step is crucial and is quite often forgotten when people say, "we're authenticating using a certificate." Merely obtaining a certificate from someone doesn't authenticate him or her. You must also make the peer prove possession of the corresponding private key.

Certificates can be obtained any number of ways. They can be passed in line as part of any authentication protocol—such as IKE. They can be obtained from a common directory via a protocol such as LDAP (the Lightweight Directory Access Protocol). They could even be published in a newspaper. The very nature of certificates—that they are necessary to authenticate the identity contained in the certificate, and that they are secured by the CA's signature and therefore require no additional security regimen—means that the method that can put certificates in the most hands with the least problems will be the best. There is practically no reason to limit the distribution of a certificate. The more people that have the certificate, or have a way of obtaining it, the more useful it is.

Authentication of a certificate is a complex task that may require a recursive authentication of other certificates. At its heart, though, it involves checking the CA's signature on the certificate itself and making sure that the certificate is still current and has not been revoked. Since the CA is already trusted to not issue bogus certificates, any certificate that bears its authentic signature can be verified and the public key embedded in the certificate can be authoritatively bound to the identity in the certificate. A certificate can be treated as any other document that is signed (recall the description of digital signatures from Chapter 1). The entire certificate is hashed to form a digest and this digest is signed by the certification authority. The signature becomes part of the certificate itself. Part of the format of the certificate is the hash algorithm used to form the digest and the signature algorithm of the certification authority.

Once a certificate has been obtained and verified, the public key contained in the certificate can be removed and used to verify any other digital signature. IKE authentication using digital signatures or any of the encrypted nonce authentication methods requires the public key of the peer to either verify the signed hash or encrypt the nonce. Using certificates allows IKE to trust the public key and equate an identity to the peer upon completion of the authentication phase of the exchange. Once we authenticate a peer using a certificate that has been signed by a trusted CA, we know to whom we're speaking—the identity in the certificate—and can use that information to restrict or allow access to resources and to constrain any further negotiation.

The type of PKI described above is a simple, single-level type of PKI. Only members of the PKI can authenticate other members of a PKI. If Alice is a member of one PKI and Bob is a member of a different PKI, they cannot authenticate each other. For Alice and Bob to authenticate each other, their separate PKIs must enter into a mutual trust arrangement; they must form a trust model. This arrangement can be a joint exchange of certification authority. The CA of Alice's PKI can sign the certificate of the CA of Bob's PKI and vice versa. Such an arrangement is referred to as cross certification (Figure 12.8). Alice trusts her CA to not use its signature improperly and it signed a certificate bearing the public key and identity of another CA—it certified another CA. The other CA further certified the identity of Bob and issued him a certificate. Alice now has a clear path to verify Bob's certificate and each step on the path represents a trust relationship.

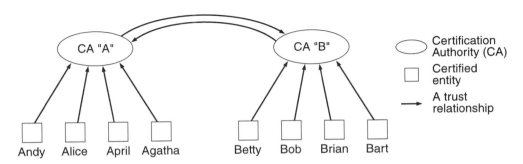

Figure 12.8   Cross Certification.

Another trust model that can be used in building a PKI is a hierarchical one. In this model there exists a "root" CA that all entities implicitly trust. But instead of having a flat PKI where this CA issues all certificates, it instead signs the certificates of other certification authorities. These other CAs can, in turn, sign the certificates of still more CAs. In this way a hierarchical tree of trust is built (Figure 12.9).

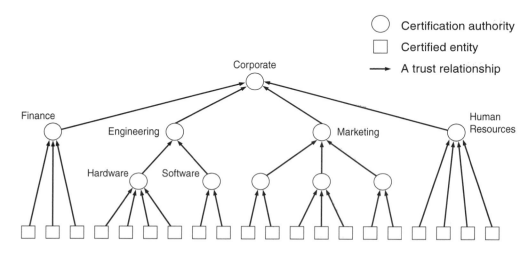

Figure 12.9   Hierarchical Trust Model.

Hierarchical relationships exist naturally, so this model is well suited to adapting a PKI to an organization and not the other way around. For instance, have different departments and those departments can have groups. In this way an engineer working in the security group of the network protocols division of a corporation can have a certificate that is signed by the CA of the security group. The certificate of that CA is signed by the network protocols division CA which can, in turn, be signed by the engineering department CA that is then signed by the corporate CA. Validation of a certificate entails "walking" a chain of certificates until a common trust point—a node on the tree—is reached. To validate the employee's certificate, a member of the human resources department may have to walk the chain all the way back to the corporate CA, while a member of the integrated circuit design team (who is also in the engineering department) may only need to walk as far as the engineering CA.

Certificates cannot last forever. If an employee left a company her certificate should not allow her to authenticate herself as an employee anymore. Therefore, each CA maintains a list of revoked certificates—a Certificate Revocation List, or CRL. This CRL is, ideally, published in an easily available repository or directory. As part of certificate validation (signature checking, chain walking, etc.) the CRL must be checked to determine whether this certificate is current or has been revoked. Obviously, any certificate on the CRL should not be accepted.

An important issue in building a PKI is the problem of the name space. The identity information contained in a certificate could be a name, address, city, and country of residence. Or it could be a name, division, and employee number. Or, if the entity is not even a human being, an IP address. Each CA describes the identity of an entity using information it deems important. What one CA thinks important another may think trivial, perhaps so trivial as to not even mention it. There could even be conflicts in name spaces between CAs.

For any security scheme involving authentication to scale to a reasonable size, some form of PKI must be built. Using preshared keys with IKE works, but the burden of preshared key distribution rapidly becomes onerous as the group grows. Similarly the bureaucracy for securely distributing public keys for use with IKE's other authentication methods would also collapse under its own weight. Clearly, IKE and IPSec need a PKI, but the issues of certificate format, certificate acquisition, trust models, certificate expiry, and revocation, etc., are not part of the IKE and IPSec specifications. That problem was (and still is being) solved by another working group in the IETF, the public key infrastructure (PKIX) working group. The PKIX group has defined an architectural model of a PKI and has developed a series of standards-track RFCs to describe it. The PKIX working group uses the work from other standards bodies (ITU, ANSI) but defines its use for the Internet. For instance, the definition of certain extensions to the X.509 standard are very broad and the PKIX working group has developed a profile for their use in the Internet. This is an on- going task, and as more and more PKIs are deployed, knowledge learned from the experience is translated back into the process as new documents or refinements of existing documents.

A PKI is not a technology solution in and of itself. It is an enabling technology. It is also an investment, and the benefits of it do not immediately outweigh the cost of deployment. Because of this, PKI deployment is a slow task and the number of fully functioning PKIs in existence today is quite small. While the early bird may catch the worm, it's usually not the first person through a mine field that survives, and that sentiment is seen in PKI development. PKIs are complex, and many thorny issues arise when they are built. It's not as easy as just saying, "We're going to use certificates for authentication" (although the amount of times that phrase is used as a complete answer is staggeringly large). As lessons are learned, though, PKIs will become more and more prevalent, thereby enabling the deployment of IKE and IPSec and satisfying the promise of ubiquitous network security on a global scale.

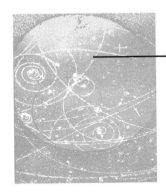

Bibliography

P. Albitz & C. Liu, *DNS and BIND, 3rd edition*, O'Reilly Associates, 1998.

D. Comer, D. Stevens, *Internetworking with TCP/IP,* volumes 1-3, Prentice Hall, 1991.

W. R. Cheswick & S. M. Bellovin, *Firewalls & Internet Security: Repelling the Wily Hacker,* Addison-Wesley, 1994.

D. Denning, *Cryptography and Data Security,* Addison-Wesley, 1982.

Electronic Frontier Foundation, *Cracking DES: Secrets of Encryption Research, Wiretap Politics and Chip Design,* O'Reilly & Associates, 1998.

S. Garfinkel, *Pretty Good Privacy,* O'Reilly Associates, 1994.

A. Hodges, *Alan Turing: The Enigma of Intelligence,* Simon and Schuster, 1983.

T. Howes, M. Smith, *LDAP: Programming Directory-Enabled Applications with Lightweight Directory Access Protocol*, Macmillan Technical Publishing, 1997.

C. Huitema, *Routing in the Internet*, Prentice-Hall, Inc., 1995.

C. Kaufman, R. Perlman, M. Speciner, *Network Security: PRIVATE Communication in a PUBLIC World*, Prentice-Hall, Inc., 1995.

D. Kosiur, *IP Multicasting*, Wiley, 1998

X. Lai, *On the Design and Security of Block Ciphers*, ETH Series in Information Processing, Vol. 1, Konstanz: Hartung-Gorre Verlag, 1992.

R. McEliece, *Finite Fields for Computer Scientists and Engineers*, Kluwer Academic Publishers, 1987.

B. Schneier, *Applied Cryptography, 2nd edition*, Wiley, 1996

W.R. Stevens, *TCP/IP Illustrated, Volume 1: The Protocols*, Addison-Wesley, 1994.

W.R. Stevens, *UNIX Network Programming*, Prentice-Hall, Inc., 1990.

Gary R. Wright, W. Richard Stevens, *TCP/IP Illustrated, Volume 2: The Implementation*, Addison-Wesley, 1995.

Journals and Technical Reports

H. Abelson, R. Anderson, S.M. Bellovin, J. Benaloh, M. Blaze, W. Diffie, J. Gilmore, P.G. Neumann, R.L. Rivest, J.I. Schiller, and B. Schneier, "The Risks of Key Recovery, Key Escrow, and Trusted Third-Party Encryption," *World Wide Web Journal*, Vol. 2, No. 3, 1997, pp. 241-257.

BBN, "A History of the ARPANET: The First Decade," Technical Report of Bolt, Beranek, and Newman, Inc., 1981.

M. Bellare, R. Canetti, and H. Krawczyk, "Keying Hash Functions for Message Authentication," Advances in Cryptology—Crypto'96 Proceedings, Lecture Notes in Computer Science Vol. 1109, Springer-Verlag, 1996.

M. Bellare and D. Micciancio, "A New Paradigm for Collision-free Hashing: Incrementality at Reduced Cost," Advances in Cryptology—Eurocrypt'97 Proceedings, Lecture Notes in Computer Science Vol. 1233, Springer-Verlag, 1997.

S. Bellovin, M. Merritt, "Encrypted Key Exchange: Password-Based Protocols Secure Against Dictionary Attacks," Proceedings of the 1992 IEEE Computer Society Conference on Research in Security and Privacy, pp. 72-84, 1992.

S. Bellovin, "Problem Areas of the IP Security Protocols," Proceedings of the Sixth Usenix Unix Security Symposium, 1996.

R. Canetti, J. Garay, D. Micciancio, M. Naor, B. Pinkas, "Multicast Security: A Taxonomy of Secure Multicast Protocols and Efficient Authentication Schemes," Proceedings of INFOCOM'99, 1999.

D. Davies, W. Price, "The Application of Digital Signatures Based on Public-Key Cryptosystems," Proceedings of the Fifth International Computer Communications Conference, 1980.

S. Deering, "Multicast Routing in a Datagram Internetwork," STAN-CS-92, Stanford University, 1991

W. Diffie, M. Hellman, "New Directions in Cryptography," IEEE Transactions on Information Theory, Vol. IT-22, No. 6, pp. 644-654, 1976.

T. ElGamal, "A Public-Key Cryptosystem and a Signature Scheme Based on Discrete Logarithms," Advances in Cryptology—Proceedings of Crypto'84, Springer-Verlag, 1985.

J. Ellis, "The Possibility of Secure Non-Secret Digital Encryption," United Kingdom Communications-Electronics Security Group, 1970.

R. Gennaro and P. Rohatgi, "How to Sign Digital Streams," Proceedings of CRYPTO'97.

Hans Dobbertin, "The Status of MD5 after a Recent Attack," RSA Laboratories' CryptoBytes, Vol. 2, No. 2, Summer 1996.

National Institute of Standards and Technology, FIPS186, "Digital SignatureStandard," U.S. Department of Commerce, 1994.

National Institute of Standards and Technology, FIPS46-2, "Data Encryption Standard (DES)," U.S. Department of Commerce, 1977.

National Institute of Standards and Technology, FIPS81, "DES Modes of Operation," U.S. Department of Commerce, 1980.

National Institute of Standards and Technology, FIPS180-1, "Secure Hash Standard," U.S. Department of Commerce, 1995.

Research and Development in Advanced Communications Technologies in Europe, "RIPE Integrity Primitives: Final Report of RACE Integrity Primitives Evaluation," 1992.

R. Rivest, A. Shamir, and L. Adleman, "A Method for Obtaining Digital Signatures and Public-Key Cryptosystems," Communications of the ACM, Vol. 21, No. 2, 1978.

RSA Laboratories, "PKCS#1: RSA Encryption Standard," version 1.5, 1993.

A. Scherbius, "Ciphering Machine," U.S. Patent #1657411.

B. Schneier, "The Blowfish Encryption Algorithm," *Dr. Dobb's Journal*, Vol. 19, No. 4, 1994

J. G. Steiner, B. C. Neuman, and J. I. Schiller, "Kerberos: An Authentication Service for Open Network Systems," Usenix Conference Proceedings, pages 183-190, February 1988.

J. T. Touch, "Performance Analysis of MD5," *Computer Communication Review*, Proceedings of ACM SIGCOMM'95.

C.K. Wong, M. Gouda, S. Lam, "Secure Group Communications Using Key Graphs," Technical Report of Department of Computer Sciences, University of Texas at Austin.

D. Wallner, E. Harder, R.C. Agee, "Key Management for Multicast: Issues and Architectures," National Security Agency technical document.

IETF Documents-RFC's

C. Adams, "The CAST-128 Encryption Algorithm," RFC2144, 1997

A. Ballardie, "Scalable Multicast Key Distribution," RFC1949, 1996

S. Bellovin, "Defending Against Sequence Number Attacks," RFC1948, 1996

S. Deering, "Host Extensions for IP Multicasting," RFC1112, 1989

S. Deering, R. Hinden, "Internet Protocol, Version 6 (IPv6) Specification," RFC2460, 1998

K. Egevang, P. Francis, "The IP Network Address Translator (NAT)," RFC1631, 1994

R. Friend, R. Monsour, "IP Payload Compression Using LZS," RFC2395, 1998

R. Glenn, S. Kent, "The NULL Encryption Algorithm and Its Use With IPSec," RFC2410, 1998

S. Hanks, T. Li, D. Farinacci, P. Traina, "Generic Routing Encapsulation (GRE)," RFC1701, 1994

D. Harkins, D. Carrel, "The Internet Key Exchange (IKE)," RFC2409, 1998

H. Harney, and C. Muckenhirn, "Group Key Management Protocol (GKMP) Architecture," RFC2094

H. Harney, and C. Muckenhirn, "Group Key Management Protocol (GKMP) Specification," RFC2093

Internet Architecture Board, Internet Engineering Steering Group, "IAB and IESG Statement on Cryptographic Technology and the Internet," RFC1984, 1996

P. Karn, W. Simpson, "Photuris: Session-Key Management Protocol," RFC2522

S. Kent, R. Atkinson, "IP Authentication Header," RFC2402, 1998

_____, "IP Encapsulating Security Payload," RFC2406, 1998

_____, "Security Architecture for the Internet Protocol," RFC2401, 1998

D. Katz, "IP Router Alert Option," RFC2113, 1997

H. Krawczyk, "SKEME: A Versatile Secure Key Exchange Mechanism for Internet," IEEE Proceedings of the 1996 Symposium on Network and Distributed Systems Security, 1996

H. Krawczyk, M. Bellare, R. Canetti, "HMAC: Keyed-Hashing for Message Authentication," RFC2104, 1997

C. Madson, N. Doraswamy, "The ESP DES-CBC Cipher Algorithm with Explicit IV," RFC2405, 1998

C. Madson, R. Glenn, "The Use of HMAC-MD5-96 within ESP and AH," RFC2403, 1998

_____, "The Use of HMAC-SHA-1-96 within ESP and AH," RFC2404, 1998

G. Malkin, "RIP Version 2," RFC2453, 1998

D. Maughan, M. Schertler, M. Schneider, J. Turner, "Internet Security Association and Key Management Protocol (ISAKMP)," RFC2408, 1998

D. McDonald, C. Metz, B. Phan, "PF_KEY Key Management API, Version 2," RFC2367, 1998

J. Mogul, S. Deering, "Path MTU Discovery," RFC1191, 1990

J. Moy, "OSPF Version 2," RFC2328, 1998

H. Orman, "The OAKLEY Key Determination Protocol," RFC2412, 1998

R. Pereira, R. Adams, "The ESP CBC-Mode Cipher Algorithm," RFC2451, 1998

R. Pereira, "IP Payload Compression Using DEFLATE," RFC2394, 1998

C. Perkins, "IP Encapsulation within IP," RFC2003, 1996

D. Piper, "The Internet IP Security Domain of Interpretation for ISAKMP," RFC2407, 1998

J. Postel, "Internet Protocol," DARPA Internet Program Protocol Specification, RFC791, 1981

_____, "Internet Control Message Protocol," DARPA Internet Program Protocol Specification, RFC792, 1981

_____, "Transmission Control Protocol," DARPA Internet Program Protocol Specification, RFC793, 1981

_____, "User Datagram Protocol," RFC768, 1980

J. Reynolds, J. Postel, "Assigned Numbers," RFC1700, 1994

R. Rivest, "The MD5 Message-Digest Algorithm," RFC1321, 1992

A. Shacham, A. Monsour, R. Pereira, M. Thomas, "IP Payload Compression Protocol," RFC2393, 1998

W. Simpson, "The Point-to-Point Protocol (PPP)," RFC1661, 1994

W. Townsley, et al, "Layer Two Tunneling Protocol 'L2TP'," RFC2661

IETF Documents-Internet Drafts

M. Condell, C. Lynn, J. Zao, "Security Policy Specification Language," draft-ietf-ipsec-spsl-00.txt, 1999.

D. Harkins and N. Doraswamy, "A Secure, Scalable Multicast Key Management Protocol (MKMP)," draft-irtf-smug-mkmp-00.txt

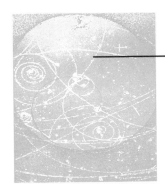

Index